Barcode in Back

MW01121292

The Criminology of White-Collar Crime

The Criminology
of White-Collar Crime

Sally S. Simpson
Editor

University of Maryland, College Park, MD

David Weisburd
Editor

Hebrew University, Jerusalem, Israel; George Mason University,
Manassas, VA

 Springer

Editors

Sally S. Simpson
University of Maryland
College Park, MD
ssimpson@crim.umd.edu

David Weisburd
Hebrew University
Jerusalem, Israel
George Mason University
Manassas, VA
msefrat@mscc.huji.ac.il

ISBN 978-0-387-09501-1   e-ISBN 978-0-387-09502-8
DOI 10.1007/978-0-387-09502-8

Library of Congress Control Number: 2008942519

Printed on acid-free paper

springer.com

Contents

Part III   Crime Prevention and Control

Contributors

Robert Agnew Department of Sociology, 1555 Dickey Drive, Emory University, Atlanta, GA 30322, USA

Robert Apel School of Criminal Justice, University at Albany, SUNY 135 Western Avenue, Albany, NY, USA

Michael L. Benson University of Cincinnati, Cincinnati, OH, USA

Francis T. Cullen University of Cincinnati, Cincinnati, OH, USA

Laura Dugan Department of Criminology and Criminal Justice, The University of Maryland, College Park, MD, USA

John E. Eck University of Cincinnati, Cincinnati, OH, USA

Carole Gibbs School of Criminal Justice and Department of Fisheries and Wildlife, Michigan State University, East Lansing, MI 488, USA

Peter Grabosky ARC Centre of Excellence in Policing and Security, Regulatory Institutions Network, Research School of Pacific and Asian Studies, Australian National University, Australia

Michael Levi Cardiff University, Wales, UK

Tamara D. Madensen University of Nevada-Las Vegas, Las Vegas, Nevada, USA

Raymond Paternoster Department of Criminology and Criminal Justice, University of Maryland, 2220 LeFrak Hall, College Park, MD, USA

Nicole Leeper Piquero Virginia Commonwealth University, Richmond, VA, USA

Natalie Schell Department of Criminology and Criminal Justice at the University of Maryland/College Park, MD, USA

Sally S. Simpson Department of Criminology and Criminal Justice at the University of Maryland/College Park, MD, USA

Tom R. Tyler Department of Psychology, New York University, New York, NY, USA

David Weisburd The Hebrew University, Jerusalem, Israel; George Mason University, Manassas, VA, USA

About the Authors

Robert Agnew is Samuel Candler Dobbs Professor of Sociology and Chair of the Sociology Department at Emory University. He has published four books and approximately 70 articles on the causes of crime and delinquency, with his most recent books being *Juvenile Delinquency: Causes and Control* (Oxford University Press, 2009), *Why Do They Do It? A General Theory of Crime and Delinquency* (Oxford University Press, 2005), and *Pressured Into Crime: An Overview of General Strain Theory* (Oxford University Press, 2006). He is best known for his development of general strain theory, one of the leading theories of crime and delinquency. He has served as Associate Editor of Theoretical Criminology and on the editorial boards of Criminology, Social Forces, and other journals. He has been active in many professional organizations and groups dealing with crime and delinquency. And he is a Fellow of the American Society of Criminology.

Robert Apel received his Ph.D. from the University of Maryland in 2004 and is currently Assistant Professor in the School of Criminal Justice at the University at Albany, State University of New York. His research interests include employment and labor markets, incarceration and reentry, violence and injury, and applied econometrics. He is the Principal Investigator of a grant from the National Institute of Justice to study the causal impact of first-time incarceration on life outcomes in late adolescence and early adulthood. His recent publications appear in *Criminology*, *Crime and Delinquency*, *Journal of Quantitative Criminology*, and *Justice Quarterly*.

Michael L. Benson is Professor of Criminal Justice at the University of Cincinnati. Writing mainly in the areas of white-collar and corporate crime, he has published in numerous journals, including *Criminology, Justice Quarterly, Journal of Research and Delinquency, American Sociological Review, American Journal of Sociology,* and *Social Problems.* He received the Outstanding Scholarship Award of the Society for the Study of Social Problems Division on Crime and Juvenile Delinquency for his coauthored book, *Combating Corporate Crime: Local Prosecutors at Work.* His most recent book is *Corporate Crime Under Attack: The Fight to Criminalize Business Violence.* With Sally Simpson, he is currently completing a book on white-collar crime from an opportunity perspective for Routledge.

Francis T. Cullen is Distinguished Research Professor of Criminal Justice and Sociology at the University of Cincinnati. His works include *Reaffirming Rehabilitation, Combating Corporate Crime, Corporate Crime Under Attack, Rethinking Crime and Deviance Theory, Taking Stock: The Status of Criminological Theory, Criminological Theory: Context and Consequences,* and *Criminological Theory: Past to Present—Essential Readings.* His current research focuses on the impact of social support on crime, the measurement of sexual victimization, public opinion about crime control, and rehabilitation as a correctional policy. He is a Past President of both the American Society of Criminology and the Academy of Criminal Justice Sciences.

Laura Dugan is an Associate Professor in the Department of Criminology and Criminal Justice at the University of Maryland. She is an active member of the National Center for the Study of Terrorism and the Response to Terrorism, the National Consortium on Violence Research, and the Maryland Population Research Center. Her research examines the consequences of violence and the efficacy of violence prevention/intervention policy and practice. She also designs methodological strategies to overcome data limitations inherent in the social sciences. She has written several articles on terrorism, victimization, policy, and methods that have appeared in journals such as *Criminology, Terrorism and Political Violence, Urban Studies, Journal of Quantitative Criminology, Criminology & Public Policy,* and *Law & Society Review.* Professor Dugan received her Ph.D. in Public Policy and Management from Carnegie Mellon University in 1999, a Masters in Statistics from Carnegie Mellon in 1998, and a Masters in Management and Public Policy in 1995.

John E. Eck is a crime scientist at the University of Cincinnati, where he is a professor in the Division of Criminal Justice. With Lin Liu he coedited *Artificial Crime Analysis Systems: Using Computer Simulations and Geographic Information System,* the first book on the simulation of crime patterns. And with Ronald V. Clarke, he is the coauthor of *Crime Analysis for Problem Solvers,* a manual for police officials on how to prevent crime. Eck received his doctorate from the University of Maryland in 1994, and a master's degree in public policy from the University of Michigan in 1977. From 1977 to 1994, he directed research at the Police Executive Research Forum, in Washington, D.C. Eck has written extensively on problem-oriented policing, crime mapping, drug markets, computer simulation of crime patterns, and crime prevention. He was a member of the National Academy of Sciences Committee on Police Policy and Research and is a judge for the British Home Office's Tilley Award for Problem-Solving Excellence. He is the author of numerous articles on policing, crime mapping and analysis, evaluation methods, and crime simulation.

Carole Gibbs is an Assistant Professor at Michigan State University with a joint appointment in the School of Criminal Justice and the Department of Fisheries and Wildlife. She received her Masters and Ph.D. in Criminology and Criminal Justice from the University of Maryland, College Park and her bachelors in Criminal Justice from the University of Alabama at Birmingham. She is part of an interdisciplinary team developing a series of courses on Conservation Criminology. Her most recent research involves examining the relationship between corporate citizenship, sanctions, and environmental performance. She is also currently conducting research on the global movement of electronic waste and the relationship between structural disadvantage, lead, and crime.

Peter Grabosky is a Professor in the Regulatory Institutions Network, Research School of Pacific and Asian Studies, Australian National University, and a Fellow of the Academy of the Social Sciences in Australia. He holds a Ph.D. in Political Science from Northwestern University, and has written extensively on criminal justice and public policy. His general interests are in harnessing resources outside the public sector in furtherance of public administration. He was previously Deputy Director of the Australian Institute of Criminology, and has held a number of visiting appointments, including Russell Sage Fellow in Law and Social Science at Yale Law School, and visiting professorships at Chuo University; the United Nations Asia and Far East Institute for the Prevention of Crime and the Treatment of Offenders (UNAFEI); and the Chinese People's Public Security University. He is currently Deputy Director of the Australian Research Council Centre of Excellence in Policing and Security, and Co-Chair of the Campbell Collaboration Crime and Justice Advisory Group. Recent books include: *Lengthening the Arm of the Law* (with Ayling and Shearing) (Cambridge University Press 2009), *Electronic Crime* (Pearson Prentice Hall 2007), and *Cyber Criminals on Trial* (with Smith and Urbas) (Cambridge University Press 2005).

Dr. Michael Levi has degrees from Oxford, Cambridge, Southampton, and Cardiff Universities and has been Professor of Criminology at Cardiff University School of Social Sciences since 1991. He is editor-in-chief of *Criminology and Criminal Justice* and an editor for other major journals. He was granted a D.Sc. (Econ.) from Cardiff University (2007) and elected to the Academy of Social Sciences (2006). In 2007, he was awarded a 3-year Professorial Fellowship by the UK Economic and Social Research Council to develop research on transnational economic and organized crime and on responses to it. His books include *The Phantom Capitalists: the Organisation and Control of Long-Firm Fraud*, 2nd edition (Ashgate, 2008), *Drugs and Money* (with Petrus van Duyne, Routledge, 2005), *The Investigation, Prosecution and Trial of Serious Fraud* (TSO, 1993), and *Regulating Fraud* (Routledge, 1987). In 2008, he wrote for and edited a special Issue of *Criminology and Criminal Justice* on The Organisation of Serious Crimes: Developments in Research and Theory and has also published widely in the *British Journal of Criminology*, *Crime and Justice*, and in *Crime, Law and Social Change*. He is the author of "Organised Crime and Terrorism" and "Violent crime" in *The Oxford Handbook of Criminology*.

Raymond Paternoster is Professor in the Department of Criminology & Criminal Justice at the University of Maryland and Faculty Research Affiliate at the Maryland Population Research Center. He has published articles in the area of rational choice and offender decision making, capital punishment, school dropout and delinquency, and the relationship between adolescent employment and life outcomes in addition to crime. He currently is doing research on adolescent work stability and crime and competent decision making, cultural and personal capital, and crime.

Nicole Leeper Piquero is an assistant professor of criminal justice in the Wilder School of Government and Public Affairs at Virginia Commonwealth University. Professor Piquero earned her Ph.D. in criminology and criminal justice from the University of Maryland in 2001. Her current research focuses on the etiology of white-collar crime, personality dimensions and traits associated with white-collar and corporate crime decision making, and white-collar crime victimization.

Natalie Schell is a Ph.D. student in Criminology and Criminal Justice at the University of Maryland. Her research interests include white-collar crime, gender and crime, and criminological theory. Her master's thesis, which she completed at the University of Maryland, was titled, "Exploring the Relationship between Profit-Squeeze and Occupational Safety and Health Violations." She is currently working on her dissertation, a meta-analysis regarding the effectiveness of ethical codes in preventing unethical and illegal behavior in corporations.

Sally S. Simpson (Ph.D. University of Massachusetts/Amherst) is Professor and Chair of the Department of Criminology and Criminal Justice at the University of Maryland/College Park. Ongoing research projects include a factorial survey of environmental professionals to assess regulatory attitudes toward and strategies for business, a meta-analysis of corporate crime intervention and control strategies for the Campbell Consortium Crime and Justice Group (CCJG), and the WEV study (a multicity retrospective study of incarcerated women's experience of violence). Professor Simpson is past President of the White-Collar Crime Research Consortium and current Chair of the Crime, Law, and Deviance Section of the American Sociological Association. She is a board member of the Maryland Police Training Commission, the Children's Justice Act Committee, and the Maryland Criminal Justice Information Advisory Board.

Tom R. Tyler is a University Professor at New York University. He teaches in the psychology department and the law school. His research explores the dynamics of authority in groups, organizations, and societies. In particular, he examines the role of judgments about the justice or injustice of group procedures in shaping legitimacy, compliance, and cooperation. He is the author of several books, including *The social psychology of procedural justice* (1988); *Trust in organizations* (1996); *Social justice in a diverse society* (1997); *Cooperation in groups* (2000); *Trust in the law* (2002); and *Why people obey the law* (2006).

David Weisburd is Walter E. Meyer Professor of Law and Criminal Justice and Director of the Institute of Criminology at the Hebrew University and Distinguished Professor of Administration of Justice at George Mason University. He is an elected fellow of the American Society of Criminology and of the Academy of Experimental Criminology. He is also editor of the *Journal of Experimental Criminology*. Professor Weisburd was part of the Yale White Collar Crime project, from which his book *Crimes of the Middle Classes* (Yale University Press) was developed. Professor Weisburd has also coauthored *White Collar Crime and Criminal Careers* (Cambridge University Press) and *White Collar Crime Reconsidered* (Northeastern University Press).

Part I
Theoretical Perspectives on Crime

Introduction

Sally S. Simpson and David Weisburd

Abstract Seventy years after Edwin Sutherland introduced the term "white col-lar crime" in his Presidential Address to the American Sociological Association, criminologists and sociologists have failed to develop a comprehensive understand-ing of crime, criminal behavior, and criminal justice. This failure can be traced to disciplinary and epistemological shifts in sociology and criminology that occurred post-1970. The chapters in this volume bring white-collar crime back into the main-stream of criminological inquiry by using recent criminological insights in theory and methods to advance the study of white collar crime.

For Edwin Sutherland, the study of crime and justice was conceptually incomplete because of its narrow focus on traditional crimes and common offenders. Any con-clusions about how law was made, why it was broken, and how (and by whom) it was enforced were "inadequate and invalid . . . because the theories do not consis-tently fit the data of criminal behavior; and . . . because the cases on which these theories are based are a biased sample of all criminal acts" (Sutherland, 1949; 1983: p. 6). To be specific, research had not confronted the problem of white-collar crime. How could crime be caused by poverty when the wealthy also offended? How could criminals be biologically and psychologically deficient when some of the top leaders of industry and pillars of the community were also criminals? Sutherland argued that those who sought to explain variability in crime, criminality, or the criminal justice system began with seriously biased data. And that such data led to theories that incorrectly located the causes of crime in the circumstances of the poor and disadvantaged.

Sutherland's concern with what scholars today would call "sample selection bias" (Berk and Ray, 1982) presented a clear challenge to the criminologists of his day. His argument was that analysis and review of crime without the white-collar crime category would lead to serious mistakes in how we described crime, how we understood its causes, and how we evaluated its treatment in the criminal justice

S.S. Simpson (✉)
Department of Criminology and Criminal Justice at the University of Maryland/College Park, MD, USA
e-mail: ssimpson@crim.umd.edu

S.S. Simpson, D. Weisburd (eds.), *The Criminology of White-Collar Crime*, DOI 10.1007/978-0-387-09502-8_1, © Springer Science+Business Media, LLC 2009 system. How could it not, if we ignored a large category of crime committed by offenders who were so different from the typical street criminals that formed the main focus of inquiry into crime at the time? Criminologists in Sutherland's day certainly were aware of the crimes of "robber barons" and the less serious frauds committed by people in white-collar occupations (Weisburd et al., 1991). That they chose to ignore them represented a type of myopia in their vision that Sutherland's ground-breaking work exposed.

Although many were optimistic that Sutherland's ground-breaking observations would stimulate a paradigmatic shift in the study of crime and justice (see, e.g., Hartung, 1953), the actual impact of Sutherland's critique of the interests of those who studied crime was minor. Criminologists continued to focus their interests on street crime and common criminals, and the white-collar crimes that Sutherland identified were seldom studied. By 1961, Cressey could write that Sutherland's "book has had very little effect on the thinking, theory, and research of psychiatrically and psychologically oriented criminologists" (1961; 1983: p. iv). Instead, Sutherland's initial work ignited challenges from legal scholars (Tappan, 1947) and a few limited studies conducted mostly by his students (described in some detail by Coleman, 1992 and Geis, 1992), but not much more interest in the fledgling field of criminology.

One reason for the failure of Sutherland's critique to influence mainstream criminology was that it was intertwined with a specific theory that Sutherland sought to advance in criminology. Sutherland's empirical studies led to his conclusion that all types of crime (including corporate and white-collar) emerged from the same etiological processes, "namely, differential association" (1949; 1983: p. 234). Accordingly, Sutherland added to his critique of selection bias in traditional criminology— the failure to include the white-collar crime category—a specific position on the etiology of criminal behavior. Sutherland argued for a "general theory of crime" and he presented a specific theory which he argued was free of the biases that had hindered earlier explanations. In this sense, Sutherland's contribution of identifying the white-collar crime category, and in so doing correcting a flaw in earlier inquiries, was inextricably linked for many scholars with his specific theoretical perspective. The failure in some sense of differential association theory in criminological circles appeared to have contributed to the lack of interest in white-collar crime among those who studied crime.

The late 1970s, however, ushered in a new era for white-collar crime research. American sociology, newly energized by numerous challenges to the social order posed by civil rights, the women's movement, antiwar and other student protests, adopted and refined new theories and epistemological approaches. The discipline became radicalized, challenging the status quo and the positivistic traditions that dominated a number of subfields within it (including criminology). This was also a period of renewed concern with the law breaking of the rich and powerful. Americans were confronted with a series of scandals involving large companies and important political figures that once again challenged the assumption that the label of crime should only be applied to the poor and disadvantaged. Perhaps most important of these scandals was Watergate, which brought the specter of white-collar crime to the offices of the president of the United States. These scandals also led to a concern with white-collar crime among law enforcement officials, and the creation of white-collar crime units in federal and local prosecutorial agencies (Edelhertz et al., 1977), and to the first large-scale funding of white-collar crime research by the federal government (see Auchter, 1978).

The challenges of Watergate, federal funding for white-collar crime, and the concern with white-collar crime more generally in this period prompted a number of excellent studies and theoretical insights that have left a lasting mark on what we know and how we think about white collar and corporate crime today. At Yale Law School, a group of scholars led by Stanton Wheeler and supported by the newly established Law Enforcement Assistance Administration began to collect empirical data on white-collar crime that had eluded earlier generations. The Yale studies focused on federal white-collar crimes (see Johnson and Leo, 1993 for a review of the Yale project) and suggested that white-collar crime included not just the rich and powerful but many middle-class Americans (see Weisburd et al., 1991). The pyramid of crime in this case was brought to include not just the poor, who had continued to be the focus of criminology, and the wealthy that had come to concern many white-collar crime scholars, but average Americans. At the University of California at Irvine, another set of interests began to emerge during this period. Here the reinvigoration of white-collar crime research led by Gilbert Geis was to be found in the rekindling of focus on "power" and how it leads not only to abuse, but also to the management of criminal justice and the definitions of crime. Finally, a National Institute of Justice funded project to study corporate crime was awarded to Marshall B. Clinard at the University of Wisconsin (Clinard et al., 1979). Clinard and his research associates compiled the single "largest database ever constructed on major American corporations' violations of federal laws" (Yeager, 2008: p. 10). Their work contextualized offending by firms within economic and political environments, demonstrating (as Sutherland had found decades earlier) that corporate offending showed clear patterns. Many firms were recidivists. Large companies tended to be the worst offenders and violations were concentrated in certain industries. However, the authors were quick to point out that these "predictive" variables were only modest in size, putting future researchers on notice that more work was needed to unravel such a complex phenomenon (Clinard and Yeager, 1980: p. 126–132). A myriad of scholars began to look at white-collar crime in this period, and it seemed as if the white-collar crime category would become as Sutherland had hoped a major concern of criminology (see, e.g., Box, 1983; Pearce, 1976; Shover et al., 1986; Szasz, 1986a,b,c).

But the reemergence of white-collar crime as a focus of interest among criminologists was accompanied by another trend which was to strongly influence its study. The growing public interest in white-collar crime in the late 1970s was preceded by a series of critiques of criminal justice in America beginning with the report of the President's Commission on Law Enforcement and the Administration of Justice which wrote in 1965:

In sum, America's system of criminal justice is overcrowded and over-worked, undermanned, underfinanced, and very often misunderstood. It needs more information and more knowledge. It needs more technical resources. It needs more coordination among its many parts. It needs more public support. It needs the help of community programs and institutions in dealing with offenders and potential offenders. It needs, above all, the willingness to reexamine old ways of doing things, to reform itself, to experiment, to run risks, to date. It needs vision.

More generally, and throughout the 1960s and 1970s the public and scholars began to see criminal justice agencies as "part of the problem" that led to social unrest during that period and not necessarily working to help in producing a solution to difficult social issues (Weisburd and Braga, 2006).

As a result, the federal government initiated the development of academic programs to advance police science and criminal justice. Supported by the Law Enforcement Assistance Administration, these programs signaled the emergence of a fledgling discipline of criminology and criminal justice. Though the first US School of Criminology was founded in the early 1960s in Berkley California, the emergence of criminology as a discipline separate from sociology in the United States developed during this period.[1]

And at this point there began to develop a tension between sociology and criminology. Many of the new police science programs were atheoretical and conservative in orientation, serving the needs of law enforcement and other criminal justice agencies. Some sociology programs responded to the new development of separate criminology and criminal justice programs by raising the question of whether criminology was a legitimate subfield within the discipline and questioned whether having criminologists on the faculty was necessary. This debate has not receded and may have intensified in recent years. For instance, several years ago, in a public statement of editorial policy, a prominent sociological journal (*Social Forces*) declined to publish articles with criminological or criminal justice content. More recently, John Sutton ended his *American Sociological Review* article on imprisonment with the following comment, "Crime and Punishment are too important to be left to the criminologists" (2004: p. 185)

This tension was felt most acutely by faculty and students within doctoral programs. Not surprisingly, the field of criminology began to carve out its own (often multi) disciplinary space, drawing from fields as diverse as biology, psychology, law, economics, political science, and public policy. New doctoral programs in criminology and criminal justice splintered out of sociology or emerged independently—some out of the LEAA-backed police training programs (reinforcing charges of conservatism and a lack of academic rigor). Many of these new programs developed strong academic credentials that challenged the dominance of sociology in the

---

[1] It is important to note that Criminology programs in Europe and Israel found their initial homes in Law Schools rather than Sociology, and this trend continues till today.

field of criminology. Today, there are more than 30 doctoral programs in Criminology and Criminal Justice, and most of the major scholars who study criminology and criminal justice are found in independent programs and not in sociology departments.

Criminology as an independent field of study seems to have "made it." Whether the indicator is graduate students, doctoral programs, highly regarded journals, or the establishment of prestigious prizes for academic work, criminology today stands solidly as an independent field of study. Indeed, the challenge has now come full circle. Many sociologists are likely regretting the sociological reaction against criminology, as the number of students with interests in criminology and criminal justice grows and those in other areas of sociology declined. A recent task force put together by the American Sociological Association to investigate "Sociology's Crime Problem" discovered that the majority of students now enrolled in sociology are taking classes in the subfield of criminal justice (Jaschik, 2008). The overall trend is that criminal justice has overtaken sociology as a discipline, generating more majors and more degrees in the aggregate. While sociology increased the number of bachelor's degrees completed by 14.5% (to 31,406) between 2001 and 2006, criminology increased its baccalaureate degrees by 35.7% (to 34,209). Master's degrees awarded in sociology decreased by 15% at the same time that MA degrees increased by 135.5% and 56.5% in criminology and criminal justice, respectively (Jaschik, 2008).

Our point here is not to trace the emergence of a new field of social science, but to highlight what we believe caused distinct lines of scholarship to develop in the white-collar crime area. Instead of Sutherland's vision that the study of crime and justice would necessarily be one that simultaneously considered all types of crimes and offenders to enrich and broaden our understanding of these issues more generally, two distinct disciplinary approaches to white-collar crime developed.

The more dominant approach (sociological) tended to retain its link to critical perspectives and more qualitative (sometimes antipositivist) types of analysis. Sutherland's original critique of who committed crime and how society responded to violations was broadened to add behaviors by the socially powerful (e.g., elites, corporations, government officials, and the military) that are not criminal or necessarily illegal (see, e.g., Simon and Eitzen, 1982). The sociology of deviance subfield further blurred the boundaries between illegal acts and other kinds of behaviors that were stigmatized by society (drug and alcohol abuse, gambling, homosexuality, mental illness, and eating disorders, among others) but here too was the familiar criticism of conservatism, i.e., studies of deviance failed to consider deviant behavior by the powerful (Liazos, 1972). In this sense, the study of white-collar crime in sociology became divorced from the emerging new home of criminology in criminology and criminal justice programs.

In criminology and criminal justice programs themselves, there was little emphasis on or frankly much interest in white-collar crime. The intellectual boundaries of the nascent discipline were framed by a changing social and cultural context and the influence of fields other than sociology. Its emergence coincided with the War on Crime and later, a War on Drugs and the purported failures of "treatment" (Martinson, 1974). It is not surprising then that the field focused primarily on street crime with an emphasis on law, law breaking, and responses to crime (prevention and control). Although little attention was given to white-collar crime, there were many theoretical and methodological advances that pushed scholarship well beyond its traditional sociological roots. This meant that the study of white-collar crime "missed the boat" or at least was put aside with little interaction with the emerging themes and concerns of criminology, while sociological interest in the problem of crime waned more generally. Study of white-collar crime in this context was not strongly influenced by a host of new insights and concerns brought by criminologists. Nor was the field influenced much by the intellectual debates and methodological insights that characterized the emerging and independent discipline of criminology.

We do not want to overstate this point. Early on and more recently, criminological scholarship on white-collar crime (a good deal of it conducted by sociologists or those trained originally in sociology) has adopted more of an applied, quantitative, and policy-relevant approach.[2] The roots of this approach can be found in the work of the Yale program in white-collar crime and other research efforts advanced by sociologists in the 1970s suggesting to us that the disciplinary fractures in study of white-collar crime are to some degree artificial. But more generally we think that the disciplinary bifurcation is intellectually unhealthy and short sighted.[3] It may have contributed to a lack of governmental funding for research projects in the white-collar crime area, too few data sets for primary and secondary analysis, little regard and attention for high-quality and important research, and ennui among graduate students in both fields who dismiss white-collar crime research as stagnant and mired in the 1960s (Simpson, 2003).

In this book, we have brought together a group of well-regarded scholars who are experts in the study of crime and justice. Some of these researchers specialize in white-collar and corporate crime but others do not. Many are crime and justice generalists. Contributors were given the task of bridging the knowledge gap, to fulfill Sutherland's vision that white-collar crime can and should influence the study of crime more generally. Therefore, each scholar was asked to select a specific topic (typically within their field of expertise) and apply the ideas, knowledge, and problem to white-collar crime or, if the research emerged out of a more traditional white-collar crime area, to discuss the implications of the work for the study of crime and justice more generally.

This exercise produced a group of papers that we believe bring white-collar crime back into the mainstream of criminological inquiry. But importantly, they also use recent criminological insights in theory and methods to advance the study

---

[2] See, for instance, fear of crime research (Rossi et al., 1974; Cullen et al., 1982), studies of white-collar sentencing (Wheeler et al., 1989; Hagan et al., 1980; Benson and Walker, 1988), studies of white-collar offenders (Weisburd et al., 1991; Weisburd and Warning, 2001), and empirical studies of corporate crime etiology (Simpson, 1986; 1987; 2002).

[3] Some of our sociological colleagues believe that criminology should return to its roots in sociology (Sampson, 2000). We respectfully disagree. The interdisciplinary development of criminology and criminal justice is, to our mind, a positive development.

of white-collar crime. We have organized them into several themes that we think enhance and build on the strengths of both bodies of research: theory, emergent themes and methodological issues, and crime prevention and control. In the theory section, we feature two papers. The first, by Robert Apel and Raymond Paternoster, draws lessons from their research on adolescent employment and crime. Noting that a common theme in white-collar crime research (going back to Sutherland's idea of differential association) is that corporate culture is a key causal mechanism for crime, Apel and Patnernoster question this assertion. Instead, they wonder whether some companies have higher rates of crime due to "assortive mating" processes, that is, Are certain types of people attracted to companies that have particular characteristics? This argument adds a different dimension to Sutherland's original concern with selection bias. Criminologists recognize that individual differences between people can affect such things as who one picks as a mate, juvenile work experiences, and where one chooses to live. These processes, in turn, affect criminal behavior and crime rates in particular places (such as organizations and neighborhoods). Apel and Paternoster suggest that selection bias is "a serious issue for white-collar crime scholars who wish to make a causal inference about the effect of particular features of corporations, such as their moral or ethical climate."

In the chapter by Robert Agnew, Nicole Leeper Piquero, and Francis Cullen, general strain theory (GST) is offered to account for white-collar offending. Like Sutherland's differential association, the authors recognize the need for a general theory of crime to explain and predict the occurrence of white-collar crime as well as more traditional forms of crime. GST was developed to account for participation in a variety of street crimes by different populations (juveniles and adults, males and females, across social classes and races). Yet, until this application, the theory had not been expanded to white-collar crime and offenders. Drawing from the senior author's earlier work (Agnew, 2001), the authors postulate that white-collar crime is more likely to occur as a consequence of individual (or corporate) level "status" strain and strain in the economic and work-related spheres (compared to other kinds of strain). The relationship between strain and crime, however, is conditioned by conventional coping skills, resources, opportunity, and individual characteristics (such as personality traits and characteristics). Access to and utilization of coping strategies, resources, and opportunities will vary by social position. Thus, while access to a supportive network of family and friends may protect a traditional offender from stealing, the authors point out that embezzlers often steal when they are under financial strain *and* cannot share their financial problems with significant others. The modifications and adjustments of the theory to fit white-collar crime have broadened the scope of the original theory and have led to refinements that would not have occurred without this application.

The section on emergent themes and methodological issues is led off with a paper by one of the coeditors (Simpson) and Natalie Schell. For the past 20 years, criminologists have attempted to reconcile two contradictory but consistent empirical findings. Specifically, although the best predictor of future delinquency and criminality is past involvement in illegal activity, most antisocial children do not grow up to be delinquent or criminal adults. These empirical regularities have produced two lines of thinking. One argument suggests that the people who engage in criminal behavior do so because they have a stable trait or characteristic (persistent heterogeneity) that makes them susceptible to crime, hence increasing the likelihood that offenders will engage in crime over the life course. Alternatively, a state dependence argument suggests that criminality is not a life sentence. Although there are many reasons why criminal involvement increases the risk of future crime (such as stigmatization and isolation of offenders from conforming others), an early life of crime can be reversed because people are capable of change. Noting that corporations have similar crime patterns to individuals (e.g., chronic offenders and a strong link between past and future crime), Simpson and Schell ask whether corporate actors have certain persistent traits that increase the likelihood of recidivism over the life course. Or, do companies with extensive criminal histories change to law-abiding behavior? To examine these questions, the authors adopt a powerful methodological and statistical tool (random effects design) developed from longitudinal and cohort studies of individuals over the life course—one rarely utilized in corporate crime studies. Following the health and safety violations of a group of 55 firms over a ten-year period (1990–2000), they discover a positive dynamic process at work. Companies are able to change course as a consequence of occupational safety and health administration (OSHA) interventions (discovery, intervention, and sanctioning). Simpson and Schell are unable to unravel whether the change is due to regulatory persuasion or punishment, but their results offer stronger support for a state dependence argument than persistent heterogeneity. Their research also demonstrates the strength and utility of adopting new methods and analytic tools from criminology for the study of corporate crime.

In the chapter by Michael Levi, "fear of crime" is deconstructed from its origins in traditional street crime. Levi shows how white-collar crimes generate less fear because of the nature of the crimes themselves. White-collar crimes rely on trust between perpetrator and victim. "Fraudsters flourish where either we are not fearful of being deceived or the fraudsters have social engineering techniques that deceptively allay our fears." Robbers, on the other hand, rely on victim fear to insure compliance. Beyond these basic comparisons, however, we know very little about fear of white-collar crime. Levi provides a broad conceptual overview of victimization risk, media influence, and fear of white-collar crime from the perspective of individuals and businesses. He suggests that business as usual would likely be disrupted if fears were high because "there are no practical steps that one can take other than to withdraw from the market." The implications of this for individuals and businesses, rich and poor consumers, and different kinds of places (cities, nations, and global environments) are recurrent themes throughout the essay.

Terrorism, especially post-9/11, has become a dominant theme in criminology. Generally, criminologists who study terrorism compare and contrast the ways in which terrorists, their groups, and activities parallel those of traditional street offenders and criminal organizations (e.g., gangs). In the next chapter, Laura Dugan and Carole Gibbs do the same thing but instead of street gangs and organized crime, they focus on corporate crime. The object of this exercise is to improve the detection and prosecution of both kinds of illegal activities. Observing that corporations and terrorist groups have many similarities (e.g., survival pressures, organizational complexity, decentralization) that hamper law enforcement efforts, Dugan and Gibbs suggest the need for nontraditional forms of crime detection and control including interorganizational task forces, encouraging whistle-blowers, and an emphasis on prevention. Although the authors identify as many differences as similarities in these offense types, by emphasizing the commonalities between them and showing how prevention and control strategies derived from one type of crime can potentially inform knowledge of and response to the other, law enforcement efforts benefit more generally.

In the technology and global era, the opportunities for white-collar crime are ubiquitous. Using Cohen and Felson's (1979) routine activity theory (criminal victimization occurs as a consequence of the confluence of motivated offenders, vulnerable targets, and absence of capable guardians) and a number of case studies to illustrate his points, Peter Grabosky shows that a world shrunken by technology yet highly interdependent has widened both the opportunities for white-collar crime and the scope of victimization. Global power inequities mean that some populations are more vulnerable to white-collar crimes than others. Similarly, because crime control tends to be highly nationalized, some nation states are simply unable to be effective (or capable) legal guardians. Therefore, it is necessary to think beyond the law for crime prevention and control. Grabosky offers several recommendations to affect the three elements of crime (motivated offenders, capable guardians, and vulnerable targets): (1) raising the consciousness of potential offenders and capable guardians, (2) developing new institutions for crime control, and (3) increased reliance on informal sources of control.

The last paper in this section by Nicole Leeper Piquero and coeditor David Weisburd builds on the criminal career framework (an approach that empirically examined the specific dimensions of a criminal career, including onset age, crime persistence, specialization, frequency, and desistence from crime). The empirical observations derived from this approach (and its theoretical cousin, life course criminology) were built from biased samples. With a few exceptions (Weisburd and Warning, 2001; Piquero and Benson, 2004), criminal career and life course research suffer from exactly the same problem of sample selection bias that Sutherland identified 60 years ago. Using recently developed dynamic modeling techniques (trajectory models), Piquero and Weisburd set out to test whether the new techniques would confirm findings from earlier research on white-collar criminal careers conducted by Weisburd and Warning (2001). Trajectory analysis revealed several distinct groups of offenders with quite different developmental trends: low-rate offenders, high-rate offenders, and an intermittent criminality group. Although these groups are generally consistent with the patterns identified in the earlier study, the trajectory models identified group membership with greater precision than before. Piquero and Weisburd suggest that there were fewer stereotypical criminals (i.e., similar to street offenders) than originally identified and more "opportunity seekers." The dynamic modeling of white-collar criminal careers appears to confirm developmental theorists' assertions that there are multiple pathways into crime.

The final section of the book is devoted to crime prevention and control. The first chapter in this section by Benson, Madensen, and Eck uses three criminological theories (routine activity theory, crime pattern theory, and situational crime prevention theory) to identify the features or characteristics of places that allow crimes to occur. Once these features are identified (especially as they relate to "how" crimes occur in particular places), the authors then link a number of theoretically informed strategies to prevent and control white-collar crime. We have already seen how routine activity theory predicts the occurrence of white-collar crime (Grabosky, Chapter 7). Crime pattern theory suggests that crimes are dependent on the "nodes" and "paths" commonly used by the offender. White-collar offending is more likely to occur along paths used most often and by more individuals (organizational networks with a large number of participants, for instance, will have more white-collar crimes than those with fewer users). Routine activity theory and crime pattern theory explain how criminals gain access to illegal opportunities; situational crime prevent theory tells us why some criminal opportunities are more attractive than others (costs and benefits). Thus, prevention efforts must disrupt crime opportunities and control efforts need to increase the cost of crime relative to its benefits. The authors provide several suggestions for how this can be accomplished, including the use of case studies.

In the final chapter, Tom Tyler brings his keen theoretical and empirical observations about procedural justice to the administration of justice for corporate offenders. The regulatory arena continues to be a contested terrain. Sutherland observed that white-collar offenders were not subjected to punitive and harsh sanctions, partly because their acts were adjudicated by administrative agencies and not by criminal justice agents. Debates continue as to the "proper" goals of regulation (punishment or persuasion) and whether regulatory regimes are effective. Tyler dives into this debate when he compares the utility of two regulatory strategies: command and control versus the self-regulatory model. Specifically, Tyler asks whether organizational rules and authorities are perceived to be legitimate and whether (or the degree to which) organizational rules correspond to individual employee's moral values. Using the empirical literature as a guide, he concludes that the most successful strategies for white-collar crime prevention and control will motivate employees to act on their own feelings of personal responsibility and ties to the organization (loyalty) along with their own sense of morality and ethics.

Sutherland's goal to have a fuller and more comprehensive understanding of crime, criminal behavior, and criminal justice is one to which we aspire as well. The chapters in this volume fulfill that goal and we hope to set the tone for similar research in the future. It is indeed time to develop a criminology of white-collar crime. This is important for criminology, as well as the study of white-collar crimes and criminals.

References

Agnew, R. 2001 "Building on the Foundations of General Strain Theory: Specifying the types of strain most likely to lead to crime and delinquency." *Journal of Research in Crime and Delinquency* 38: 319–361.

Auchter, B. 1978 Federal Level Research and Demonstration in White Collar Crime Control—Efforts of the Law Enforcement Assistance Administration. Washington, D.C.: U.S. Government Printing Office.

Berk, R. A. and Ray, S. C. 1982 "Selection Bias in Sociological Data." *Social Science Research*, Volume 11: 352–398.

Benson, M. L. and Esteban W. 1988 Sentencing the White-Collar Offender. *American Sociological Review* 33: 301–309.

Box, S. 1983 *Power, crime, and mystification*. New York: Routledge

Clinard, M. B., Yeager, P.C., Brissette, J.M., Petrashek, D. and Harries, E. 1979 *Illegal Corporate Behavior*. Washington, D.C.: U.S. Government Printing Office.

Cohen, L. E. and Felson, M. 1979 Social Change and Crime Rate Trends: A Routine Activity Approach. *American Sociological Review* 44: 588–608.

Clinard, M. B. and Peter C. Y. 1980 *Corporate Crime*. New York: The Free Press

Coleman, J. W. 1992 "The Theory of White-Collar Crime." PP. 58–77 in Kip Schlegel and David Weisburd (Eds.), *White-Collar Crime Reconsidered*. Boston: Northwestern University Press.

Cressey, D. R. 1961 "Forward" to Edwin R. Sutherland, *White Collar Crime (pp iii-xii)*. New York: Holt, Rinehart and Winston.

Cullen, F. T., Bruce G. L., and Craig W. P. 1982 "The Seriousness of Crime Revisited: Are Attitudes Toward White-Collar Crime Changing?" *Criminology* 20 (May):83–102.

Edelhertz, H., Stotland, E., Walsh, M., and Weinberg, M. 1977 Investigation of White Collar Crime—A Manuel for Law Enforcement Agencies. Washington, D.C.: U.S. Government Printing Office.

Geis, G. 1992 "White-Collar Crime: What is It?" PP. 31–52 in Kip Schlegel and David Weisburd (Eds.), *White-Collar Crime Reconsidered*. Boston: Northwestern University Press.

Hagan, J., Nagel, I. (Bernstein), and Albonetti, C. 1980 "The Differential Sentences of White Collar Offenders in Ten Federal District Courts." *American Sociological Review*, 45:802–820.

Hartung, F. E. 1953. "White Collar Crime: Its Significance for Theory and Practice." *Federal Probation*, 17:31–36.

Jaschik, S. 2008 "Sociology's Crime Problem." *Inside Higher Ed*, Insidehighered.com, August, 4th.

Johnson, D. T. and Leo, R. A. 1993 "The Yale White Collar Crime Project: A Review and Critique. Law of Social Inquiry 1 (1 Winter): 63–99

Liazos, A. 1972 "On the Poverty of the Sociology of Deviance: Nuts, Sluts, and Perverts." *Social Problems* 20: 103–120

Martinson, R. 1974 "What Works? Questions and Answers About Prison Reform." *The Public Interest*, 35: 22–34.

Pearce, F. *1976 Crimes of the Powerful*. London: Pluto Press.

Piquero, N. L. and Benson, M. L. 2004 "White-Collar Crime and Criminal Careers." *Journal of Contemporary Criminal Justice* 20: 148–165.

Rossi, P. H., Waite, E., Bose, C. E., and Berk, R. E. 1974 "The Seriousness of Crimes: Normative Structure and Individual Differences," *American Sociological Review* 39:224–237.

Sampson, R. J. 2000 Whither the Sociological Study of Crime? Annual Review of Sociology, Vol. 26: 711–714

Simon, D. R., and Eitzen, D.S., 1982 *Elite Deviance*. Boston: Allyn & Bacon.

Simpson, S. S. 1986 "The Decomposition of Antitrust: Testing a Multilevel, Longitudinal Model of Profit-Squeeze," *American Sociological Review* 51: 859–975, 1986.

Simpson, S. S.1987 "Cycles of Illegality: Antitrust in Corporate America," *Social Forces* 65: 943–963.

Simpson, S. S. 2002 "Corporate Crime, Law, and Social Control. New York: Cambridge University Press.

Simpson, S. S. 2003 "The Criminological Enterprise and Corporate Crime" *The Criminologist* 28 (4, July/August): 1–5.

Shover, N., Clelland, Donald.A., and Lynxwiler, John. *1986 Enforcement or negotiation: Constructing a regulatory bureaucracy*. Albany: SUNY Press.

Sutherland, G. H. 1949. *White-Collar Crime*. New York: The Dryden Press.

Sutherland, G. H. 1983. *White-Collar Crime: The Uncut Version*. New Haven, CT: Yale University Press.

Sutton, J. R. 2004. "The Political Economy of Imprisonment in Affluent Western Democracies, 1960–1990." *American Sociological Review* 69: 170–189.

Szasz, A. 1986a. "Corporations, Organized Crime and the Disposal of Hazardous Waste: An Examination of the Making of a Criminogenic Regulatory Structure." *Criminology*, 24(1):1–27.

Szasz, A. 1986b. "The Process and Significance of Political Scandals: A Comparison of Watergate and the 'Sewergate' Episode at the Environmental Protection Agency." *Social Problems*, 33(3):202–217.

Szasz, A. 1986c. "The Reversal of Federal Policy toward Worker Safety and Health: A Critical Examination of Alternative Explanations." *Science and Society*, 50(1): 25–51.

Tappan, P. *1947* "Who is the Criminal?"*American Sociological Review*, 12:96–102.

Weisburd, D., Wheeler, S., Waring, E., and Bode, N. 1991. *Crimes of the Middle Classes*. New Haaven, CT: Yale University Press.

Weisburd, D. and Elin, W. (with Ellen Chayet). 2001. *White Collar Crime and Criminal Careers*. Cambridge: Cambridge University Press.

Weisburd, D.. and Braga, A. A. 2006. Introduction, *Police Innovation: Contrasting Perspectives*. Cambridge: Cambridge University Press.

Yeager, P. C. 2008 "Science, Values, and Politics: An Insider's Reflections on Corporate Crime." Forthcoming in Mary Dodge and Gilbert Geis (Eds), Special Issue, *Crime, Law and Social Change*.

Understanding "Criminogenic" Corporate Culture: What White-Collar Crime Researchers Can Learn from Studies of the Adolescent Employment–Crime Relationship

Robert Apel and Raymond Paternoster

Abstract A prominent theory of white-collar crime holds that organizations have distinctive cultures which are more or less tolerant of law violation for the benefit of the firm. This explanation purports to account for why college-educated, relatively affluent, and seemingly conventional persons can commit crime when they are employed in white-collar occupations. The vexing paradox of "why good people do dirty work" can be resolved by positing that some organizations turn a blind eye to ethical and legal infractions if it benefits the firm, thereby creating a culture of rule breaking which is learned just as any other business practice is learned. Another theoretical view posits that firms with a tolerant view toward business ethics may attract people with "loose" ethics, which itself leads to corporate and white-collar offending. The second view harmonizes with the notion of "assortative mating"—that people are attracted to those environments with which they are more compatible by disposition. The difference between these two views is not trivial. One posits that the ethical climate of an industry or firm has a causal impact on the occurrence of white-collar crime; the other is compatible with the view that the relationship between culture and crime is spurious. Using as a case study research within another criminological tradition—the relationship between youth employment and delinquency—we argue that disentangling causation from selection should be a research priority for the study of white-collar crime.

Introduction

Real interest in the scientific study of white-collar crime can reasonably be traced back to the work of sociologist Edwin Sutherland. On December 27, 1939, at a joint meeting of the American Economic Association and the American Sociological Society (which, due in no small measure to its unfortunate acronym, later became the American Sociological Association), Sutherland presented a presidential address

R. Apel (✉)
School of Criminal Justice, University at Albany, SUNY 135 Western Avenue,
Albany, NY, USA
e-mail: rapel@albany.edu

S.S. Simpson, D. Weisburd (eds.), *The Criminology of White-Collar Crime*,
DOI 10.1007/978-0-387-09502-8_2, © Springer Science+Business Media, LLC 2009

entitled "The White Collar Criminal." In this address and his subsequently published paper, Sutherland (1940) made several important observations: (1) "respectable" middle- and upper-class persons commit acts which are costly both financially and in terms of loss of life and limb and should thus be considered "crime"; (2) these acts of white-collar crime are committed as a result of one's involvement in a business or occupation; (3) white-collar crime is more prevalent in some industries than others; (4) within branches of the same industry or business, some firms are more involved in white-collar offenses than others; (5) neither conventional street crime nor white-collar crime can be attributed to factors such as poverty or economic deprivation, or to the socio- or psychopathic attributes of involved individuals; (6) the factors that explain lower- or working-class crime are the same as those that account for white-collar offending; and (7) all crime must be learned and this learning takes place though contact with others and their "definitions" of the law.

In his presidential address, Sutherland also noted why then-existing theorists of criminal conduct (which proffered explanations based on notions of poverty and individual psychological or personality deficiencies) were led astray in their own theoretical work. The problem, he explained, was that the samples upon which empirical criminology was based were biased—they included only certain types of criminal offenders (crime "in the street") while excluding others (crime "in the suite"), and hence any theoretical deductions based upon such observed empirical data were invalid. With respect to the causes of both types of offending ("regular" street crime and white-collar/corporate crime), Sutherland alluded to what a truly general theory of crime would consist of—the concepts of differential association and social disorganization (or what he later termed "differential social organization")—but he did not spell out such a theory either in his 1939 presidential address or his paper that was published the next year. Rather, he spent nearly the next 10 years working on his general theory of crime—a theory that would encompass both conventional street crime and white-collar offending—which appeared in his seminal book *White Collar Crime* (Sutherland 1949).[1]

There were two empirical regularities about white-collar crime that Sutherland had to account for: (1) some types of industries seemed to be more fertile ground for crime than others, and (2) within certain industries, some firms or organizations were more involved in illegal actions than others. In other words, just as at the individual level, there were "acute" offenders at the corporate level—a small number of companies that accounted for an unusually large proportion of the total number of white-collar crimes committed. Moreover, he had to account for these empirical regularities without resorting to characteristics of the individuals involved (e.g., their personal wealth or any deficient mental/attitudinal trait).[2] To explain the

---

[1] Geis and Goff (Sutherland 1983: p. x), in an introduction to a later edition of Sutherland's book, wrote that Sutherland only added the last chapter on the theory of white-collar crime because he believed the book to be too statistical.

[2] Sutherland's antipathy toward personality or "type of person" theories of crime is well documented in the literature (Laub and Sampson 1991).

pattern of offending both across and within types of businesses, Sutherland argued that responsibility lay within the practice of business itself. That is, some industries (and some firms within industries) possess a set of norms or cultural proscriptions that are "favorable to the violation of law," and crime flourishes within these industries and firms regardless of the individual attributes of those holding positions within them. Put differently, white-collar crime is produced because there is a culture within an industry or within a firm/business that provides both the normative approval of illegal acts and a structure of incentives to reward compliance with these norms as well as punishments for noncompliance. In Sutherland's (1983: 245) own words:

> White collar criminals, like professional thieves, are seldom recruited from juvenile delinquents. As part of the process of learning practical business, a young man with idealism and thoughtfulness for others is inducted into white collar crime. In many cases he is ordered by managers to do things which he regards as unethical or illegal, while in other cases he learns from those who have the same rank as his own how they make a success. He learns specific techniques of violating the law, together with definitions and situations in which those techniques may be used. Also, he develops a general ideology. This ideology grows in part out of the specific practices and is in the nature of generalization from concrete experiences, but in part it is transmitted as a generalization by phrases such as "We are not in business for our health", "Business is business", and "No business was ever built on the beatitudes." These generalizations, whether transmitted as such or constructed from concrete practices, assist the neophyte in business to accept illegal practices and provide rationalizations for them.

This culture of favorable attitudes toward law violation, as well as the associated incentive and penalty structure, would then be learned by those employed within the organization like any other set of norms or business practices.

Now the question may be raised as to why corporate culture or the various neutralizations and rationalizations for misconduct that are learned as part of one's business position were considered as causes of white-collar crime in the first place? The answer to this is provided by Sutherland in the first two sentences of the long passage from *White Collar Crime* just cited. He notes that the ranks of white-collar criminals are not recruited from juvenile delinquents, but that as yet white-collar offenders are filled with idealism and thoughtfulness and must therefore be inducted into crime. In other words, the white-collar offender was formerly good (or else he would not be white-collar) and must somehow be "turned." It was not that business attracted bad people, but that "thoughtful" people were turned into criminal offenders. Borrowing from Everett C. Hughes (1962), Vaughan (1992: p. 124) argued that one of the "enduring puzzles" for white-collar crime scholars is to explain why "good people do dirty work," why seemingly upstanding members of the community and business world resort to crime and regulatory infractions resulting in financial and frequently physical damage to others? The answer was that the organizational climate or culture of businesses turned normally good people bad.

Not all scholars have dismissed the possibility that personality traits or an individual's psychological makeup are unimportant for understanding white-collar/corporate crime. Gross (1978: 67), for example, has argued that those who "make it to the top of large-scale organizations" have distinctive personal characteristics such as ambitiousness, shrewdness, and moral flexibility. The latter is defined as the ability of the manager, out of professional self-interest, to change his/her own moral beliefs should they conflict with those of the organization. Coleman (1987), Weisburd et al. (1991), and Wheeler (1992) have also put forth theoretical accounts of white-collar crime that attribute it in at least some part to the psychological characteristics of managers and executives such as love of risk, aversion to failure, and a strong ambition or desire to be both materially and professionally successful. More recently, Gottfredson and Hirschi (1990) have offered a general theory of crime that accounts for both street and white-collar offending in terms of a stable individual characteristic they label self-control, which is essentially the ability of persons to resist quick and easy gratification and to think in terms of long-term consequences. They have argued that, like street criminals, white-collar and corporate offenders are on average more impulsive than nonoffenders, as shown by their tendency to grab immediate rewards at the expense of later costs.

If it is acknowledged that white-collar and corporate crime may be due to organizational features such as a firm's culture or to personality/individual characteristics such as one's attraction to risk or tendency to act impulsively (or both), then it must also be recognized that there is the inevitable possibility that certain persons may be attracted to certain industries or firms. For example, those who have a greater tolerance for risky behavior may be attracted to firms or industries that have a history or culture of "cutting corners" or conducting their business activities right up to and just over the line of illegality. Those who are impulsive or ambitious may be attracted to companies that reward meeting financial goals at the expense of sound business ethics. Long ago, Gross (1978: 65) noted that there may be such a selection process at work in the creation of corporate crime:

> Since we maintain that organizations are criminogenic, we are led to examine the question of whether there exists in organizations *a set of selective processes* which propel certain kinds of persons to positions of influence, or which require of those in positions of influence kinds of behavior which, under conditions of difficulty in goal attainment, may result in crime (emphasis added).

If there are assortative mating processes or "selective processes" at work, and firms with lax moral cultures attract those with less demanding systems of personal morality, then a daunting inferential problem is created for those who wish to ascribe white-collar/corporate crime to the cultural features of the organization. A form of "selection bias" is introduced because it is hard to separate the effect of the culture from the personal attributes of those attracted to such a business culture in the first place. The problem of selection bias is, then, a serious issue for white-collar crime scholars who wish to make a causal inference about the effect of particular features of corporations, such as their moral or ethical climate. In this essay, we hope to illustrate this inferential problem, show how it is an issue with other criminological questions, such as the causal impact of adolescent employment on involvement in delinquency and other problem behaviors, and what scholars in these other areas can contribute to the study of white-collar crime.

Organization Culture as a Cause of White-Collar Crime

While the idea that there is a culture within certain businesses or firms that not only merely tolerates but supports the violation of regulatory and criminal laws may have originated with Sutherland, it certainly did not end with him. In a study of violations in the shoe manufacturing industry, Lane (1953: p. 159) noted both the empirical regularities that any theory of white-collar crime had to account for and one such explanation based upon the normative or cultural climate within the industry:

> An analysis of the rates of violation of labor relations laws in the shoe industry gives some support to the differential association hypothesis. This may be found in the fact that in some shoe-manufacturing communities none of the shoe firms violate whereas in other shoe-manufacturing communities almost half of the firms get into trouble with the law. There may be several reasons for this, but it seems fairly conclusive that one of the reasons is the difference in attitude toward the law, the government, and the morality of legality.[3]

In discussing two general models of organizational crime, Needleman and Needleman (1979: p. 517) used virtually the same approach as Sutherland some 40 years earlier. They noted that appeals to the characteristics of individuals are unlikely to be satisfactory and that:

> Only fairly recently have sociologists become sensitive to the idea that at least some criminal behavior usefully may be viewed not as personal deviance, but rather as a predictable product of the individual's membership in or contact with certain organizational systems, typically industries or professions. Such systems are said to be *criminogenic* (citation omitted, emphasis in original) in the sense that features of their internal structures—economic, legal, organizational and normative—play a role in generating criminal activity within the system, *independent at least to some degree from the criminal's personal motives* (emphasis added).

Similarly, Braithwaite (1989) has argued that, in response to the demands of criminal law and regulatory requirements, businesses develop a distinctive normative position—either a "culture of compliance" or a "culture of resistance" to such demands (see Clinard and Yeager 1980 for a similar view). The reason there is variation in offending rates both across and within business concerns, then, is that there is variation in an ethical climate or culture (Hunt et al. 1984; Jackall 1988; Shover and Bryant 1993; Victor and Cullen 1987) which approves of such conduct, and is not due to any differences in the kinds of persons that are attracted to different kinds of firms. We would add that an important implication of this is that the learning of cultural norms of misconduct within a business or industry *causes* violation of the criminal law and regulatory rules.

---

[3] In a related vein, Hartung (1950) argued that Sutherland's theory was one of the few viable explanations for violations in the Detroit wholesale meat industry that he studied.

The notion that the culture of the organization is an important causal factor in explaining variation in white-collar offending subsequently became a common staple in this area of criminological theorizing and research. In his analysis of antitrust violations within the heavy electrical equipment industry, Geis (1967; Geis and Meier 1977: p. 123) found fraud to be what he called "an established way of life" and that price fixing was prescribed behavior that met with approval if committed but with penalties by superiors if avoided. Similar kinds of cultural inducements to violate laws by members of business have been found in the automobile industry (Farberman 1975; Leonard and Weber 1970), the liquor industry (Denzin 1977), and the aerospace industry (Vaughan 1996, 1998). In addition to this swell of empirical studies about the importance of ethical climate or corporate culture, recent theoretical accounts of white-collar crime widely refer to the normative characteristics of organizations as a leading factor in causing corporate and white-collar crime (Hawkins 2002; Shover and Hochstetler 2006).

To be clear, criminologists interested in occupational and corporate offending have argued that an important component of any business organization is its culture or ethical climate. A business provides its employees with a set of normative guidelines that prescribe unethical or illegal behavior under certain conditions, and also establish a stock of incentives and sanctions intended to secure compliance with these norms. Empirical evidence that such norms are at work consists of the fact that some industries have higher rates of criminal and regulatory infractions than others, and within a given industry some firms offend more than others. Such empirical regularities, it is explained, cannot be due to the different motivational stances of individual actors, but to the cultural conditions existing within industries and individual firms.

The idea that it is not the characteristics of individuals but the characteristics of the situations or organizations within which individuals find themselves that foster criminal conduct has been a prominent feature of other areas of theoretical criminology. For example, those interested in studying the neighborhood origins of crime are adamant that emergent properties of communities create fertile soil for criminal conduct. That is, crime rates are higher in some neighborhoods than others not because some neighborhoods attract bad people (a compositional effect), but because people are made bad or worse because of the conditions existing within those neighborhoods (a contextual effect). For example, crime-ridden communities may lack strong social ties or social capital, or may otherwise suffer from weakened collective efficacy (Sampson et al. 1997).

Similarly, those interested in studying delinquency and youth crime have concluded for years that working too many hours during the school year, usually in "dead-end" service and retail jobs that constitute the majority of the youth labor market, is criminogenic. The argument put forth is that youth employment is undesirable not only because it pulls young people away from more beneficial social activities (e.g., studying, sports, school clubs, volunteer work), but also because the conditions under which they work are detrimental to their healthy development. In other words, youth jobs are criminogenic—they turn normally prosocial teens into antisocial ones. An alternative explanation, that intensive work during

the school year may be correlated with delinquent conduct and other problem behaviors (e.g., drinking and drug use) simply because young people at higher risk
for such behaviors self-select themselves into school-time employment, has been
largely dismissed until quite recently. As it turns out, in spite of extensive theorizing
and decades of competent research, it is likely *not true* that employment during the
school year is criminogenic. Researchers working with observational rather than
experimental data made causal inferences about the effect of adolescent employment conditions and likely made an erroneous inference. As a result, public policy
efforts to reduce the work hours of youth may be based on invalid social scientific
research.[4]

With research on the adolescent employment–crime relationship as a case study,
we would like to offer some caution to white-collar crime researchers who may also
have jumped prematurely to erroneous conclusions about the criminogenic effect
of an organization's climate—in this case its cultural or ethical climate. In both the
study of corporate crime and the adolescent labor market, researchers have been
led to conclude on the basis of observational data that a particular environment is
"criminogenic."[5] Corporate crime researchers have concluded that certain work or
business cultures have a causal effect on the level of offending by members of the
business, while youth employment researchers have for years believed that working
too many hours during the school year in dead-end jobs causes crime and other
self-destructive behaviors. In the area of youth employment, the causal inference

---

[4] This is an area of empirical research that, surprisingly enough, has been an impetus for active (yet
unresolved) legislation in the US Congress. On the basis of evidence about the possible harmful
effects of intensive employment, the National Research Council (1998) proposed that the federal
government limits work for young people aged 16 and 17, a group that is presently allowed to
work as many hours as they choose under federal child labor law (and under most state child labor
laws). The NRC's recommendation formed the basis for the Youth Worker Protection Act (H.R.
3193), which was introduced in the 108th Congress (2003–2004) by Representative Tom Lantos of
California. The bill was cosponsored by 31 members of the House and endorsed by the AFL-CIO,
the Child Labor Coalition, and the National Education Association, among others. The bill died
in committee but was resubmitted in the 109th Congress (2005–2006) as H.R. 2870, where it was
also tabled without resolution. As of this writing, the bill has not yet been resubmitted in the 110th
Congress (2007–2008). If eventually approved as drafted, the bill would amend the federal Fair
Labor Standards Act of 1938 to limit the work intensity of 16 and 17 year olds to no more than 20 h
per week during the school year (or 40 h during the summer). The choice of a 20-h work week as
the threshold is not merely arbitrary. It was believed at the time that social scientific research had
established a consistent, positive correlation between working more than 20 h per week while
in high school and a variety of problematic and developmentally unhealthy behaviors, including
crime.
[5] The same kind of problem plagues research on the role of community or neighborhood characteristics in causing crime. In fact, one of the leading researchers in this area has written that selection
bias is the "biggest challenge traditionally put to neighborhood-level research" (Sampson 2006).
The inferential problem here is the same as we have identified for adolescent employment and
white-collar crime research. Neighborhood researchers would like to infer that characteristics of
communities influence the levels of crime in such areas. The competing explanation is that some
kinds of neighborhoods may have high rates of crimes because they attract the wrong kind of
people.

now appears to be invalid, and we caution that similar inferential errors may pose a problem for research on white-collar crime. This is because, just as working long hours during the school year is more attractive to underachieving students than to overachieving ones, different industries with different ethical cultures may be differentially attractive to different employees. Employees with some pre-existing personal attribute, such as impulsivity or desire for control, may self-select themselves into firms or businesses that have a tradition of tolerating the consequences of such traits. We elaborate it in the next two sections.

Research on the Adolescent Employment–Crime Relationship

Literally dozens of peer-reviewed studies in the last 25 years have investigated the relationship between youth employment and delinquent behavior. The first systematic studies of this question were conducted by Greenberger et al. (1981) and Bachman et al. (1981). Relying on data from a sample of 10th and 11th graders in Orange County, California, high schools, Greenberger et al. (1981) found that work status (a dichotomous measure of working vs. not working) was unrelated to substance use although time spent in the workplace (the product of hours per week and length of employment) was a consistent predictor of elevated substance use—particularly excessive alcohol and marijuana use. Steinberg et al. (1982) followed up the nonworkers from this study, and found that youths spending more time in the workplace 1 year later had a higher risk of cigarette and marijuana use than youths who remained nonworkers.

Bachman et al. (1981) analyzed data from the 1975–1979 cohorts of the Monitoring the Future Survey—annual, representative samples of high school seniors—finding that the number of weekly work hours predicted higher cigarette, alcohol, and marijuana use among students. Follow-up studies using more recent cohorts from Monitoring the Future have confirmed the positive correlation between work intensity and substance use (including behavior as serious as cocaine use), and have shown similarly adverse effects of work intensity on theft, interpersonal aggression, and getting into trouble with police (Bachman et al. 2003; Bachman and Schulenberg 1993; Safron et al. 2001).

In his investigation of 11th grade males from the Youth in Transition Survey, Agnew (1986) found that the number of weekly work hours was positively associated with a general delinquency scale as well as its component subscales of interpersonal aggression (fighting, gang fighting, robbery, aggression against parents) and property offending (petty and major larceny, shoplifting, trespassing, arson, vandalism). These findings were robust to a number of control variables for other work characteristics including hourly pay, skill level, job satisfaction, and length of employment (none of which were consistently related to delinquency). Steinberg and Dornbusch (1991) collected data from high-school students in California and Wisconsin, finding that longer work hours were associated with higher rates of minor delinquency (theft, carrying a weapon, vandalism, using phony ID). In a follow-up study, Steinberg et al. (1993) reported that, controlling for prior problem behavior, nonworkers who entered the labor market 1 year later at high intensity (over 20 hours per week) reported higher levels of substance use, minor delinquency, and school misconduct than nonworkers who remained out of the labor market.

Mortimer et al. (1996) found that youths from St. Paul, Minnesota, who worked intensively were consistently more likely to drink alcohol during high school (see also McMorris and Uggen 2000; Staff and Uggen 2003). Cullen et al. (1997) used a sample of enrolled youths from the National Youth Survey to show that work intensity was associated with increased crime risk even after controlling for prior delinquency as well as other job characteristics (e.g., wages, job stability, and job changes). Mihalic and Elliott (1997) found that, among enrolled youths in the same survey, those nonworking respondents who entered the labor market at high intensity 1 year later reported higher levels of alcohol and drug use compared to those who entered the labor market at no more than 20 hours per week or who remained nonworkers.

Wright et al. (1997) examined the relationship between work intensity and delinquency among enrolled 12–18 year olds in the National Survey of Families and Households. Their analysis revealed that work intensity was associated with increased problem behavior (school misbehavior, official delinquency, and parent reports of substance use and aggression) after controlling for a number of delinquency risk factors. Their analysis also indicated more pronounced work intensity effects among high-risk males; that is, work intensity was criminogenic predominately among males with at least four risk factors for delinquency (e.g., parental criminality, family mobility, large household, low income, nonintact home, poor school performance).

In sum, the results from these and numerous other studies indicate that there is a robust, positive correlation between work involvement and juvenile crime and problem behavior. In addition, there is consensus surrounding the fact that work intensity, rather than working per se, is the crucial dimension for understanding this relationship. In other words, those youths who spend more time in the workplace each week have consistently higher risk of antisocial behavior. In no small measure, the foregoing empirical findings seem counterintuitive. How is it that something which appears as valuable as working for pay can produce such harmful effects as delinquency and substance use? There were two accounts offered as to why working during the school year might be harmful for adolescents. One suggestion is that intensive employment pulls young people away from more developmentally healthy activities, particularly school-related pursuits.[6] The second, with which we will be concerned here, is that the work environment for youths is itself harmful or criminogenic (for reviews of these and other

---

[6] This is essentially a control theory argument. Critics of adolescent employment have argued that by spending time working for pay, youths are pulled away from school and the educational commitments (higher education) and conventional involvements (studying, school athletics, clubs) that go with these commitments. In addition, working youth may spend fewer hours with their families, and their new-found income may free them from the close monitoring of their parents, especially if this income affords them the opportunity to pay for an automobile.

perspectives, see Greenberger and Steinberg 1986; Mortimer 2003). This latter explanation shares an interesting parallel with white-collar crime research, especially Sutherland's theoretical concepts of differential association and differential social organization.

Differential Association, Differential Social Organization, and the Adolescent Workplace

The argument that adolescent work is criminogenic was most elaborately developed by Greenberger and Steinberg (1986) in their book, *When Teenagers Work: The Psychological and Social Costs of Adolescent Employment.* They argued that the conditions under which youths work create an environment that is developmentally counterproductive. Most of the jobs in which adolescents are employed are low-end service and retail sector jobs. These jobs are repetitive, require very few skills, provide few opportunities to learn new skills or develop potential, and all too frequently involve unchallenging and unrewarding tasks. Working while in high school is also thought by critics of youth employment to involve great stress as adolescents confront the challenges of balancing expectations from parents, teachers, employers, and customers, with increasing and sometimes competing demands on their time. Moreover, these work expectations increase during a period of the life span when youth are as yet unprepared to handle many of the demands and stressors. In sum, the argument is that the conditions under which youths work are criminogenic ones—both working and working a great many hours during the school year puts them at risk for delinquent behavior.

In addition to the fact that the adolescent workplace may place undue stress on young people who are insufficiently mature to deal with that stress, the adolescent workplace is the one domain other than the school where youth come into contact with a wide circle of young people for an extended period of time. However, the adolescent workplace differs from the high school in two important respects. First, the adolescent workplace is far less age segregated than the high school, meaning that young workers are likely to come into more frequent contact with older adolescents and young adults. Second, because there are few enrollment or certification requirements for young people in the workplace, the other youth with which they do come into contact are also more likely to include high-school dropouts. Thus, working youth are likely to come into contact with individuals they would never encounter in the halls of the high school. This is to say that, for the "typical" adolescent worker (read, a suburban, middle-class white youth) in a "typical" adolescent job (read, a low-wage, low-skill, service occupation), same-age and older coworkers are likely to be less-than-exceptional role models for conventional, law-abiding behavior. Moreover, because supervisors in workplaces dominated by young people are often not much older than adolescent workers themselves, a climate of laxity and norm flexibility may prevail.

The adolescent workplace itself may be an environment ripe with a culture whose norms are consistent with violation of the law. Ruggiero (1984) has argued that working youth are not likely to learn the value of money as a result of where and with whom they work, but instead learn a very crass and materialistic conception both of money and employment in general. Youngsters learn that money is earned simply to support their lifestyle of leisure. In addition, they learn that workplace theft and vandalism is rampant, tolerated, and supported by other employees. Echoing this concern, Greenberger and Steinberg (1986: 140–141) argued that:

> [W]orking may promote the adoption of deviant attitude and behaviors—at least in certain realms. In particular, working youngsters may become more tolerant of unethical activities in the workplace itself. They are, we know, privy to a variety of deviant, unethical, or irresponsible behaviors perpetrated by both employers and employees.

Sutherland's (1947) theory of differential association provides a convenient way to explain how the adolescent workplace may constitute an environment conducive to misconduct. For Sutherland, deviant behavior is an expression of definitions favorable to such behavior, and these definitions are learned in association with others in intimate relationships. In studies of adolescence, conventional wisdom is that the most important relationships are with parents, teachers, and peers. However, given the amount of time that many youth commit to working, coworkers (encompassing fellow employees and supervisors) represent an additional "intimate group" that potentially provides definitions for behavior, and which may in fact compete with these other sources.[7] In addition, the adolescent workplace constitutes a unique social and moral order unto itself, in much the same way as the organizational climate of interest to white-collar crime researchers.

In short, the adolescent workplace may alter the balance of definitions favorable and unfavorable to misconduct in the workplace. Ruggiero et al. (1982), for example, found that certain characteristics of the adolescent work environment (e.g., closeness among coworkers) were predictive of occupational deviance. Interestingly, differential associations with unconventional coworkers may also tip the balance of law-violating definitions in situations outside of work. Wright and Cullen (2000) found that coworker misconduct was predictive of a youth's own misconduct, *both inside and outside of the workplace*. Specifically, the extent to which a youth's coworkers engaged in a variety of deviant behaviors on the job (e.g., padding time cards, purposely short-changing customers, theft) was related to a youth's own workplace deviance as well as his or her delinquency and substance use outside of work. Therefore, if the typical youth job is one that puts adolescents in contact with a more variable moral order and less conventional (on average) coworkers,

---

[7] In terms of mere duration, we might even say that, for some working youth, coworkers are a more important source of definitions than teachers. Whereas school-going youth spend about 30 h per week in the company of teachers, about a quarter of working youth are employed full time at over 35 h per week in their senior year of high school.

then spending more time in the workplace each week will likely increase deviant behavior both at work and outside of work.

The Selection Problem and Causal Inference

Although extant literature produced an impressively consistent set of findings about the linkage between adolescent work intensity and antisocial behavior, it could not be unambiguously concluded that this linkage reflects the causal effect of employment on behavior. In other words, although empirical research leaves no doubt about the *presence* of a positive correlation between work intensity and delinquent behavior, there remains considerable ambiguity about its *causal significance*. Experimental studies could provide some insight into causal linkages because they would ensure that variation in work patterns is randomly induced (or in econometric parlance, "exogenous"). In the absence of such studies, however, it is possible that observed work effects are spurious—youth predisposed to delinquent behavior may be precisely those who are most likely to work long hours while in school. This is the problem of *self-selection*, or the idea that working adolescents (or adolescents that work at high intensity) are systematically different with respect to characteristics that are correlated with antisocial behavior. Quite simply, the selection argument contends that adolescent workplaces do not genuinely cause adolescent misbehavior, they differentially attract misbehaving adolescents. Failure to account for these characteristics results in confounding the relationship between youth work and antisocial behavior in predictable ways, introducing the problem of selection bias. Studies that attempt to address this problem by controlling a variety of variables correlated with youth employment and crime only provide valid estimates of causal work effects if all the sources of joint variation in work and crime are measured—a rather strong requirement and one that is unlikely to be met in practice.[8] Therefore, the implication is that prior researchers may have mistaken self-selection for the causal impact of working, meaning that the adverse "work effect" so often observed in empirical research is, in fact, a selection artifact.

Indeed, there are empirical reasons to believe that youths self-select themselves into the workplace. Longitudinal research suggests that school disengagement, family withdrawal, affiliation with antisocial peers, and delinquent behavior *precede* work involvement (Bachman and Schulenberg 1993; Entwisle et al. 2000; Gottfredson 1985; Greenberger et al. 1981; Mihalic and Elliott 1997; Mortimer 2003;

---

[8] It is convenient to think of youth employment (or intensive employment) as a "treatment" thought to induce some response in antisocial behavior. For individuals who work, the "treatment effect" on the outcome of interest is the difference between two quantities: (1) the observed rate of delinquency of workers with due recognition of sampling error; and (2) their rate of delinquency had they not worked. The latter quantity, called the counterfactual (because it is, quite literally, "counter to fact"), cannot be directly observed because as a matter of logic we cannot observe an individual's delinquency in two mutually exclusive states. Thus, counterfactual delinquency must be inferred based on the delinquency rate of nonworkers. The validity of this inference depends crucially on the validity of statistical adjustments that are made to account for systematic pre-employment differences between workers and nonworkers.

Ploeger 1997; Schoenhals et al. 1998; Staff and Uggen 2003; Steinberg et al. 1993). Researchers have been aware of this pernicious selection problem and have made conscientious efforts to account for pre-employment differences, usually by including observed covariates in their multivariate regression models. In doing so, they have found that the positive relationship between work intensity and antisocial behavior is markedly reduced after controlling these differences in a regression framework (Bachman and Schulenberg 1993; Mihalic and Elliott 1997; Staff and Uggen 2003) or, more recently, altogether eliminated when using more sophisticated panel models (Apel et al. 2006; Paternoster et al. 2003).

Even more recent research employing a variation on propensity score matching has confirmed that previously reported findings of a strong positive relationship between intensive youth employment and antisocial behavior is entirely a selection artifact, rather than a genuine causal effect. For example, Apel et al. (2007) constructed latent-class trajectories of substance use and delinquency from ages 12 to 15 for youths who had no history of employment prior to age 16. Within each of these trajectories, they then evaluated the effect of the transition to intensive employment at age 16 on antisocial behavior at the same age. They found that the positive association between intensive work and antisocial behavior disappeared for all groups, and that the (weighted) average effect across all trajectory groups was neither significantly nor substantively distinguishable from zero. The unambiguous conclusion from this and other research, then, is that youth who work during the school year (and especially those who work intensively) are more involved in a wide sweep of problem behaviors not, as previous researchers had concluded, due to the causal effect of adolescent employment—that working makes good kids bad—but instead due to pre-existing differences between working and nonworking adolescents. Before they even enter the labor force in high school those who eventually work long hours are at elevated risk of antisocial behavior. [9]

We suspect that similar confounding is present in studies of the effect of corporate climate on regulatory and law violation. Gross (1978) very early on noted that there is self-selection of particular kinds of people (he specifically noted the ambitious, the shrewd, and the morally flexible) into particular kinds of firms. It should not be too difficult to come up with other time-stable individual traits, such as impulsivity

---

[9] Brame et al. (2004) attempted to quantify the uncertainty about the basis for valid estimates of the causal impact of adolescent employment on delinquent behavior. The purpose of their analysis was to evaluate the sensitivity of estimates of the "work effect" to plausible assumptions about (1) the effect of an unobserved "crime trait" on the probability of employment, (2) the effect of the unobserved crime trait on the probability of delinquent behavior, and (3) the prevalence of the unobserved crime trait in the population. Their sensitivity analysis was incapable of identifying the *sign* of the work effect on crime, let alone its magnitude. In other words, they could not determine with confidence whether the correlation between employment and delinquency was positive, zero, or negative. All three possibilities were consistent with the data, depending on what assumptions they were willing to adopt. Importantly, they concluded that if the unobserved crime trait increased the probability of employment and also increased the probability of delinquent behavior—and both assertions are consistent with the evidence—the estimated work effect was essentially zero and could actually be shown to be negative.

(Gottfredson and Hirschi 1990) or a desire for control (Piquero et al. 2005), that lead particular persons to select particular firms or industries as more comfortable environments within which to work. These individual traits may be positively correlated with the propensity to avail oneself of opportunities for personal or corporate gain. Along these lines, Dill et al. (1962) found that executives who discovered a lack of harmony between their values and those of the company for whom they worked were more likely to leave that company. Bass and Eldridge (1973) found that ambitious managers were more likely to make decisions that favored saving their company money than a more ethical but less economically beneficial decision. These findings suggest that the issue of selection bias is a distinct possibility in white-collar crime research.

An important book by Weisburd and colleagues (2001), entitled *White-Collar Crime and Criminal Careers*, is a unique study that incorporates information on the social backgrounds of convicted white-collar offenders. They found that their white-collar offender sample was indeed different from the typical street offender sample with respect to race, age, education, employment history, age of onset of "official" criminality, career length, and frequency of offending. However, in other important respects there was little to distinguish their white-collar offenders, on average, from the prototypical street offender. For example, an arrest history prior to the instant offense was quite common. The sample also exhibited a surprisingly heterogeneous offense history (including arrests for violent offenses), as well as the usual inverse correlation between age of onset and arrest frequency. Moreover, the "chronic" offenders (3+ arrests) in this study evidenced a history of social instability and unconventionality that well characterizes the backgrounds of street criminals, including unsteady employment, marital breakup, and substance abuse.[10] For at least some white-collar offenders, then, it appears to be the case that the workplace is nothing more than one additional setting within which they put their deviant impulses into action when the opportunity arises. For these individuals, the organizational climate does not appear to provide "definitions favorable to laws violation" that do not already exist. Instead, the organization may simply provide access to the situational requisites necessary to carry out specific white-collar offenses.

Thus, evidence from some white-collar crime research harmonizes with the view that individuals with a long-standing propensity for deviance and criminality are more likely to commit white-collar crime, possibly irrespective of the organizational and normative climates in which they are employed. This implies that white-collar crime scholarship would benefit from explicit consideration of the occupational and career choices that individuals make, particularly as they pertain to those firms and industries known to be more heavily involved in regulatory and law violations.

---

[10] Equally interesting, we believe, is Weisburd's (2001) finding of a great deal of heterogeneity in their sample of white-collar offenders. Only their subsample of antitrust violators appeared to fit the profile of the stereotypical white-collar offender (e.g., white, male, older, married, highly educated, high-status occupation, financially very well-off, first-time offender). Their findings as a whole seem to argue in favor of a perspective that views white-collar offenders as different in degree rather than kind vis-à-vis street offenders.

Note that it is not our intention to imply that such selection processes explain all of the apparent "climate effects" of organizations on law violation, only that processes of self-selection are very likely indeed to be relevant and are thus worthy of close attention by white-collar crime researchers.[11] Nevertheless, it is worth recalling that prior youth employment studies were virtually unanimous that adolescent working conditions were criminogenic, but in the last 5 years we have acquired a much better understanding of the source of the relationship between youth employment and crime. Characteristics of the adolescent workplace were indelibly confounded with characteristics of adolescent workers, *well before they began working*. Indeed, we now know that the criminogenic effect of high-intensity employment is more apparent than real because of the way that high-risk youth select themselves into high-risk work patterns. The supposed climate effect of youth work on delinquent activity appears to be nothing more than a selection effect after all.

Conclusion

Since its inception, theoretical and empirical work in the white-collar crime tradition has taken a close look at organizational culture as a key explanatory and causal variable. In the most famous statement on the topic, Sutherland (1949) proposed that a normative climate exists in certain industries or firms that implicitly approves of illegal conduct and explicitly rewards compliance with law-violating norms. He termed these proscriptions "definitions favorable to law violation," and further proposed that said norms are learned by employees during the course of business, just as individuals would learn norms related to, say, playing basketball. Accordingly, certain organizational climates are criminogenic independent of the individuals employed in them. By virtue of mere (differential) association with deviant others in the workplace and exposure to an organizational climate implicitly supportive of deviance, otherwise upstanding, law-abiding individuals acquire attitudes and behaviors that are conducive to illegal conduct (Shover and Hochstetler 2006; Vaughan 1998).

---

[11] A version of the former perspective gained some notoriety in the work of Hirschi and Gottfredson 1987, 1989; also Gottfredson and Hirschi 1990: pp. 180–201). To be sure, their claim was that white-collar crime is not unique with respect to its causes, leaving little to distinguish it from other forms of lawbreaking, notably street crime, as well as behaviors "analogous" to crime, such as auto accidents. White-collar crime is only distinctive to the extent that its opportunity requirements are different than for street crime. They argued that their theory of low self-control was sufficiently general to account for all criminal offending, white-collar, and otherwise. Obviously, their claims were met with a good deal of resistance, as indicated by the critiques of Steffensmeier (1989) and Reed and Yeager (1996). We make no such sweeping theoretical claims in this chapter, but we hasten to add that we do see validity in the critique that white-collar crime research has not conclusively demonstrated that the organizational climate is independent of those employed in it, and that it has an effect on individual behavior independent of an individual's underlying proclivities.

This idea shares interesting parallels with some empirical and theoretical research on the relationship between youth employment and delinquent behavior. Virtually all adolescents gain work experience before they graduate from high school, and many spend a nontrivial amount of time working each week. Moreover, an intensive work commitment has been found to have a consistently positive correlation with a variety of problem behaviors, leading some observers to comment that the work environment itself may be conducive to bad behavior (i.e., criminogenic) and leading to calls for federal action to limit youth work involvement. However, upon closer inspection, there is reason to believe that youth already inclined to be antisocial select themselves into work situations that are "intensive," and there is little recent evidence to suggest that these work situations have genuine causal effects on delinquency and substance use.

It thus seems that youth employment researchers, until recently, have drawn conclusions that we now deem to be erroneous. Although a compelling case can indeed be made about why the adolescent workplace could be criminogenic (using similar conceptual tools employed in white-collar crime research), the reality appears to be that this correlation is, in fact, a spurious one. Youth with a measurable propensity to engage in antisocial behavior are simply more likely to work, and to work longer hours each week, and it is this propensity rather than the work environment per se that is the fundamental cause of their antisocial behavior. This important insight from research on the youth employment–crime relationship may perhaps serve as a cautionary tale for studies of white-collar crime that insist on the existence of an autonomous normative climate that causally influences individual behavior.

References

Agnew, R. (1986). Work and delinquency among juveniles attending school. *Journal of Criminal Justice*, 9, 19–41.

Apel, R., Paternoster, R., Bushway, S.D., and Brame, R. (2006). A job isn't just a job: the differential impact of formal vs. informal work on adolescent problem behavior. *Crime and Delinquency*, 52, 333–369.

Apel, R., Bushway, S., Brame, R., Haviland, A.M., Nagin, D.S., and Paternoster, R. (2007). Unpacking the relationship between adolescent employment and antisocial behavior: a matched samples comparison. *Criminology*, 45, 67–97.

Bachman, J.G. and Schulenberg, J. (1993). How part-time work intensity relates to drug use, problem behavior, time use, and satisfaction among high school seniors: are these consequences or merely correlates? *Developmental Psychology*, 29, 220–235.

Bachman, J.G., Johnston, L.D., and O'Malley, P.M. (1981). Smoking, drinking, and drug use among American high school students: correlates and trends, 1975–1979. *American Journal of Public Health*, 71, 59–69.

Bachman, J.G., Safron, D.J., Sy, S.R., and Schulenberg, J.E. (2003). Wishing to work: new perspectives on how adolescents' part-time work intensity is linked to educational disengagement, substance use, and other problem behaviours. *International Journal of Behavioral Development*, 27, 301–315.

Bass, B.M. and Eldridge, L.D. (1973). Accelerated managers' objectives in twelve countries. *Industrial Relations*, 12, 158–171.

Braithwaite, J. (1989). Criminological theory and organizational crime. *Justice Quarterly*, 6, 333–358.

Brame, R., Bushway, S.D., Paternoster, R., and Apel, R. (2004). Assessing the effect of adolescent employment on involvement in criminal activity. *Journal of Contemporary Criminal Justice*, 20, 236–256.

Clinard, M.B. and Yeager, P.C. (1980). *Corporate Crime*. New York: Free Press.

Coleman, J.W. (1987). Toward an integrated theory of white-collar crime. *American Journal of Sociology*, 93, 406–439.

Cullen, F.T., Williams, N., and Wright, J.P. (1997). Work conditions and juvenile delinquency: is youth employment criminogenic? *Criminal Justice Policy Review*, 8, 119–143.

Denzin, N. (1977). Notes on the criminogenic hypothesis: a case study of the American liquor industry. *American Sociological Review*, 42, 905–920.

Dill, W.R., Hilton, T.L., and Reitman, W.R. (1962). *The New Managers*. Englewood Cliffs, NJ: Prentice-Hall.

Entwisle, D.R., Alexander, K.L., and Olson, L.S. (2000). Early work histories of urban youth. *American Sociological Review*, 65, 279–297.

Farberman, H. (1975). A criminogenic market structure: the automobile industry. *Sociological Quarterly*, 16, 438–457.

Geis, G. (1967). The heavy electrical equipment anti-trust cases of 1961. In M. Clinard and R. Quinney (Eds.), *Criminal Behavior Systems* (pp. 139 -150). New York: Holt, Rinehart and Winston.

Geis, G. and Meier, R.F. (1977). *White-Collar Crime* (Revised Edition). New York: Free Press.

Gottfredson, D.C. (1985). Youth employment, crime, and schooling: a longitudinal study of a national sample. *Developmental Psychology*, 21, 419–432.

Gottfredson, M.R. and Hirschi, T. (1990). *A General Theory of Crime*. Stanford, CA: Stanford University Press.

Greenberger, E. and Steinberg, L.D. (1986). *When Teenagers Work: The Psychological and Social Costs of Adolescent Employment*. New York: Basic Books.

Greenberger, E., Steinberg, L.D., and Vaux, A. (1981). Adolescents who work: heath and behavioral consequences of job stress. *Developmental Psychology*, 17, 691–703.

Gross, E. (1978). Organizational crime: a theoretical perspective. *Studies in Symbolic Interaction*, 1, 55–85.

Hartung, F.E. (1950). White-collar offenses in the wholesale meat industry in Detroit. *American Journal of Sociology*, 56, 25–34.

Hawkins, K. (2002). *Law as Last Resort*. New York: Oxford University Press.

Hirschi, T. & Gottfredson, M.R. (1987). Causes of white-collar crime. *Criminology*, 25, 949–974.

Hirschi, T. and Gottfredson, M.R. (1989). The significance of white-collar crime for a general theory of crime. *Criminology*, 27, 359–371.

Hughes, E.C. (1962). Good people and dirty work. *Social Problems*, 10, 3–11.

Hunt, S.D., Chonko, L.B., and Wilcox, J.B. (1984). Ethical problems of marketing researchers. *Journal of Marketing Research*, 21 304–324.

Jackall, R. (1988). *Moral Mazes*. New York: Oxford University Press.

Lane, R.E. (1953). Why business men violate the law. *Journal of Criminal Law, Criminology, and Police Science*, 44, 151–165.

Laub, J.H. and Sampson, R.J. (1991). The Sutherland-Glueck debate: on the sociology of criminological knowledge. *American Journal of Sociology*, 96, 1402–1440.

Leonard, W.N. & Weber, M.G. (1970). Automakers and dealers: a study of criminogenic market forces. *Law and Society Review*, 4, 407–424.

McMorris, B. and Uggen, C. (2000). Alcohol and employment in the transition to adulthood. *Journal of Health and Social Behavior*, 41, 276–294.

Mihalic, S.W. and Elliott, D. (1997). Short- and long-term consequences of adolescent work. *Youth and Society*, 28, 464–498.

Mortimer, J.T. (2003). *Working and Growing Up in America*. Cambridge, MA: Harvard University Press.

Mortimer, J.T., Finch, M.D., Ryu, S., Shanahan, M.J., and Call, K.T. (1996). The effects of work intensity on adolescent mental health, achievement, and behavioral adjustment: new evidence from a prospective study. *Child Development*, 67, 1243–1261.

National Research Council. (1998). *Protecting Youth at Work: Health, Safety, and Development of Working Children and Adolescents in the United States*. Washington, DC: National Academy Press.

Needleman, M.L. and Needleman, C. (1979). Organizational crime: two models of criminogenesis. *Sociological Quarterly*, 20, 517–528.

Paternoster, R., Bushway, S., Brame, R., and Apel, R. (2003). The effect of teenage employment on delinquency and problem behaviors. *Social Forces*, 82, 297–335.

Piquero, N.L., Exum, M.L., and Simpson, S.S. (2005). Integrating the desire-for-control and rational choice in a corporate crime context. *Justice Quarterly*, 22, 252–280.

Ploeger, M. (1997). Youth employment and delinquency: reconsidering a problematic relationship. *Criminology*, 35, 659–675.

Reed, G.E. and Yeager, P.C. (1996). Organizational offending and neoclassical criminology: challenging the reach of a general theory of crime. *Criminology*, 34, 357–382.

Ruggiero, M. (1984). Work as an impetus to delinquency: an examination of theoretical and empirical connections. Unpublished Ph.D. dissertation, University of California, Irvine.

Ruggiero, M., Greenberger, E., and Steinberg, L.D. (1982). Occupational deviance among adolescent workers. *Youth and Society*, 13, 423–448.

Safron, D.J., Schulenberg, J.E., and Bachman, J.G. (2001). Part-time work and hurried adolescence: the links among work intensity, social activities, health behaviors, and substance use. *Journal of Health and Social Behavior*, 42, 425–449.

Sampson, R.J. (2006). How does community context matter? Social mechanisms and the explanation of crime rates. In P.H. Wikström & R.J. Sampson (Eds.), *The Explanation of Crime: Context, Mechanisms and Development* (pp. 31–60). New York: Cambridge University Press.

Sampson, R.J., Raudenbush, S., and Earls, F. (1997). Neighborhoods and violent crime: a multilevel study of collective efficacy. *Science*, 277, 918–924.

Schoenhals, M., Tienda, M., and Schneider, B. (1998). The educational and personal consequences of adolescent employment. *Social Forces*, 77, 723–762.

Shover, N. and Bryant, K.M. (1993). Theoretical explanations of corporate crime. In M.B. Blankenship (Ed.), *Understanding Corporate Criminality* (pp. 141–176). New York: Garland.

Shover, N. and Hochstetler, A. (2006). *Choosing White-Collar Crime*. New York: Cambridge University Press.

Staff, J. and Uggen, C. (2003). The fruits of good work: early work experiences and adolescent deviance. *Journal of Research in Crime and Delinquency*, 40, 263–290.

Steffensmeier, D. (1989). On the causes of "white-collar" crime: an assessment of Hirschi and Gottfredson's claims. *Criminology*, 27, 345–358.

Steinberg, L. and Dornbusch, S.M. (1991). Negative correlates of part-time work in adolescence: replication and elaboration. *Developmental Psychology*, 17, 304–313.

Steinberg, L., Fegley, S., and Dornbusch, S.M. (1993). Negative impact of part-time work on adolescent adjustment: evidence from a longitudinal study. *Developmental Psychology*, 29, 171–180.

Steinberg, L.D., Greenberger, E., Garduque, L., Ruggiero, M., and Vaux, A. (1982). Effects of working on adolescent development. *Developmental Psychology*, 18, 385–395.

Sutherland, E.H. (1940). White-collar criminality. *American Sociological Review*, 5, 1–12.

Sutherland, E.H. (1947). *Principles of Criminology* (4th ed.). Chicago: J.B. Lippincott.

Sutherland, E.H. (1949). *White Collar Crime*. New York: Dryden Press.

Sutherland, E.H. (1983). *White Collar Crime* (uncut version). New Haven, CT: Yale University Press.

Vaughan, D. (1992). The macro-micro connection in white-collar crime theory. In K. Schlegal and D. Weisburd (Eds.), *White-Collar Crime Reconsidered* (pp. 124–145). Boston: Northeastern University Press.

Vaughan, D. (1996). *The Challenger Launch Decision: Risky Technology, Culture, and Deviance at NASA*. Chicago: University of Chicago Press.

Vaughan, D. (1998). Rational choice, situated action, and the social control of organizations. *Law and Society Review*, 32, 23–61.

Victor, B. and Cullen, J. (1987). A theory and measure of ethical climate in organizations. *Research in Corporate Social Performance and Policy*, 9, 51–71.

Weisburd, D., Wheeler, S., Waring, E., and Bode, N. (1991). *Crimes of the Middle Classes: White-Collar Offenders in the Federal Courts*. New Haven: Yale University Press.

Weisburd, D., Waring, E., and Chayet, E.F. (2001). *White-Collar Crime and Criminal Careers*. New York: Cambridge University Press.

Wheeler, S. (1992). The problem of white-collar crime motivation. In K. Schlegal & D. Weisburd (Eds.), *White-Collar Crime Reconsidered* (pp. 108–123). Boston: Northeastern University Press.

Wright, J.P. and Cullen, F.T. (2000). Juvenile involvement in occupational delinquency. *Criminology*, 38, 863–896.

Wright, J.P., Cullen, F.T., and Williams, N. (1997). Working while in high school and delinquent involvement: implications for social policy. *Crime and Delinquency*, 43, 203–221.

General Strain Theory and White-Collar Crime

Robert Agnew, Nicole Leeper Piquero, and Francis T. Cullen

Abstract This paper applies general strain theory (GST) to the explanation of white-collar crime, including (a) occupational crimes committed by higher class individuals, (b) economic offenses such as fraud and embezzlement, which are committed by lower as well as higher class individuals, and (c) corporate crimes. Several strains or stressors are said to be especially relevant to the explanation of such crimes, including the blockage of economic goals, the experience of a range of other economic problems, the inability of achieve status goals, and a variety of work-related stressors. Whether these strains result in white-collar crime, however, is said to be influenced by such things as coping skills and resources, social support, opportunities for white-collar crime, social control, the perceived costs and benefits of white-collar crime, and association with criminal others.

Strain theories were developed to explain what was thought to be the much higher rate of crime among lower class individuals. According to the classic strain theories of Merton (1938), Cohen (1955), and Cloward and Ohlin (1960), individuals from all social classes are encouraged to pursue the goal of monetary success or middle-class status. Lower class individuals, however, frequently have trouble achieving these goals through legitimate channels. The frustration resulting from this goal blockage drives some of these individuals to crime. Crime may be used to achieve monetary goals, obtain status in the eyes of one's peers, seek revenge against the perceived source of goal blockage or other targets, and alleviate frustration and other negative emotions (through illicit drug use). Given these arguments, it may seem that strain theory has little to say about the causes of white-collar crime (see Waring et al. 1995; Wheeler 1992:109). In fact, the existence of white-collar offending is sometimes taken as evidence against strain theory (see Agnew 2000; Curran and Renzetti 2001).

Strain theory, however, is actually quite relevant to the explanation of white-collar crime. Although it was not a central theme in his work, Merton (1957; 1968) argued that higher class individuals may also experience goal blockage and respond

R. Agnew (✉)
Department of Sociology, 1555 Dickey Drive, Emory University, Atlanta, GA 30322, USA
e-mail: bagnew@emory.edu

S.S. Simpson, D. Weisburd (eds.), *The Criminology of White-Collar Crime*,
DOI 10.1007/978-0-387-09502-8_3, © Springer Science+Business Media, LLC 2009

with crime, including white-collar crime (also see Waring et al. 1995). Several theorists have elaborated on this argument, more fully describing the reasons why higher class individuals may pursue goals beyond their reach (e.g., Braithwaite 1992; Messner and Rosenfeld 2001; Passas, 1997). And the inability to achieve economic goals is frequently offered as an explanation for white-collar crime by researchers (e.g., Braithwaite 1992; Clinard and Yeager 1980; Jamieson 1994; Simpson 1986; Simpson and Koper 1997; Simpson et al. 1998; Vaughan 1982, 1992; Waring et al. 1995). In particular, economic strain is said to be an important cause of white-collar crimes committed strictly for personal gain, such as embezzlement, as well as corporate crimes, such as antitrust violations.

This paper draws on and extends such arguments by applying general strain theory (GST) to the explanation of white-collar crime (Agnew 1992, 2006). GST incorporates the arguments of classic strain theory and provides a vehicle for systematically describing the central themes in the research on strain and white-collar crimes. At the same time, GST allows us to build on the prior literature in several important ways. In particular, GST more fully describes the nature of economic strain and provides much guidance on the proper measurement of such strain. GST also points to additional types of strain that may contribute to white-collar crime, including a range of work-related strains. Finally, GST points to a range of factors that increase the likelihood that individuals will react to strains with crime. Certain of these factors increase the likelihood of both "street" and white-collar crimes, while others increase the likelihood of just white-collar crime.

The chapter begins by describing the different definitions of white-collar crime. Drawing on these definitions, the paper applies GST to the explanation of (a) occupational crimes committed by higher class individuals; (b) certain types of economic crimes, such as fraud and embezzlement, which are committed by lower as well as higher class individuals; and (c) corporate crimes. Because it is a general theory, GST attempts to explain all types of white-collar crime. The chapter then describes the major types of strain that may contribute to these white-collar crimes. The focus is on economic strain, since most white-collar crimes have the primary aim of increasing monetary gain or minimizing monetary loss. Finally, those factors that increase the likelihood that individuals will respond to strains with crime, especially white-collar crime, are described.

Defining White-Collar Crime

There is much debate over how to define white-collar crime (for overviews, see Geis 1992; Shover and Wright 2001; Shapiro 1990; Weisburd and Waring 2001). Some definitions focus on crimes committed by upper class or upper status individuals, particularly crimes committed during the course of their occupation. Sutherland, for example, defined white-collar crime as "crime committed by a person of respectability and high social status in the course of his occupation" (1949:9). Other definitions focus more on the nature of the offense rather than the offender. Wheeler et al. (1982:642), for example, define white-collar crime as "economic offenses committed through the use of some combination of fraud, deception, or collusion" (also see Shapiro 1990; Weisburd and Waring 2001). Such offenses include antitrust offenses, securities fraud, mail and wire fraud, false claims and statements, credit and lending institution fraud, bank embezzlement, income tax fraud, and bribery. Researchers who employ definitions of this type typically find that while white-collar offenders are of higher status on average than "street crime" offenders, a substantial percentage of white-collar criminals are of lower social status. For example, when Weisburd and Waring (2001:24) focused on credit fraud, false claims, and mail fraud offenders, they found that "fewer than half [were] steadily employed, and between fifteen and twenty percent of each category [were] unemployed at the time of their offenses" (also see Croall 1989; Gottfredson and Hirschi 1990). Using some of the same data (Weisburd et al. 1991), Daly (1989) found that about one fifth of the female white-collar offenders had as their primary source of support welfare or unemployment benefits. Further, most of the employed female offenders were clerical workers.

Still others distinguish individual from organizational offending (see Reiss and Tonry 1993). Organizational offending is viewed as a subcategory of white-collar crime and is distinguished by the fact that it is committed at least in part to serve organizational goals and that it occurs within an organizational context. Clinard and Quinney's (1973:189) definition of corporate crime illustrates these points: "offenses committed by corporate officials for their corporation and the offenses of the corporation itself." Examples of organizational crime include fixing prices, financial frauds, the creation and maintenance of hazardous working conditions, environmental pollution, and selling unsafe products. Some criminologists focus on a broad array of organizations, including government agencies, nonprofit agencies, and private businesses (e.g., Holtfreter 2005), but most limit their focus to corporations (see Croall 1989). Also, some criminologists limit their focus to violations of the criminal law, while others argue that violations of the civil and administrative law should also be considered (see the discussions in Clinard and Yeager 1980; Pearce 2001; Sutherland 1949).

This paper does not favor one definition over another. Rather, it argues that GST can help explain white-collar crime no matter how it is defined. It is, however, sometimes important to distinguish between the different definitions or types of white-collar crime. The strains that prompt different types of white-collar crime sometimes differ. Also, the factors that condition the effect of strains on white-collar crime sometimes differ by the type of crime. For that reason, the discussion below frequently distinguishes between the explanation of (a) occupational crimes committed by higher class individuals, (b) economic offenses of the type described above, many of which are committed by lower class individuals, and (c) corporate crimes. Further, at one point a distinction is made between offenses that target the organization where the offender works and those that do not.

In all cases, however, the core arguments of GST are the same. Certain strains increase the likelihood of white-collar crime. Whether individuals cope with these strains through white-collar crime, however, depends on the characteristics of these individuals and their environments. In particular, it depends on those characteristics that affect the ability to cope in a legal versus criminal manner, the costs of criminal coping, and the disposition for criminal coping. Also, in all cases the focus is on explaining the behavior of individuals. This is true even with respect to corporate crime, with the focus here being on the behavior of corporate officials (who sometimes take the interests of the corporation into account).

Types of Strain Contributing to White-Collar Crime

According to GST, strains refer to events or conditions disliked by individuals (Agnew 1992, 2006). Strains may involve (a) the inability to achieve valued goals, (b) the actual or threatened loss of positively valued stimuli (e.g., material possessions, friends), and (c) the actual or threatened presentation of negatively valued stimuli (e.g., verbal and physical abuse). GST has primarily focused on the explanation of "street" crime (see Langton and Piquero 2007 for an exception). Those specific strains contributing to such crime include parental rejection, harsh/erratic parental discipline, child abuse and neglect, abusive peer relations, work in the secondary labor market, chronic unemployment, marital problems, criminal victimization, homelessness, and discriminatory treatment (see Agnew 2006).

GST would also predict that strains contribute to white-collar crime, although it should not be assumed that the strains which increase street crime will have a similar effect on white-collar crime. Agnew (2006:79) has recently argued that certain strains are more conducive to some types of crime than others. This is because certain strains are more readily resolved through particular types of crime. Economic strains, for example, are more easily resolved through income-generating crimes than through aggressive acts. Also, there is some evidence that strains which occur in a particular domain, such as the family, are more likely to result in crimes in that domain (DeCoster and Kort-Butler 2006). The strains described below are believed to be especially relevant to white-collar crime. These strains include economic and status-related strains, which are readily resolved through most white-collar crimes. They also include work-related strains, since white-collar crimes are generally work related.[1] Each strain is described and its potential relationship to one or more types of white-collar crime is discussed.

---

[1] It should be noted, however, that there is also limited evidence for "crossover" effects, with strains occurring in one domain (e.g., family) increasing the likelihood of crimes in another domain (e.g., work) (DeCoster and Kort-Butler 2006; Grebner et al. 2005). For that reason, researchers should also determine whether additional strains of the type listed by Agnew (2006: Chapter 3) increase the likelihood of white-collar crime.

The Blockage of Economic Goals

GST would predict that individuals and corporations (i.e., corporate managers) are more likely to turn to white-collar crime when they have trouble achieving their economic goals through legitimate channels. Many white-collar crime researchers, drawing on Merton (1938), make the same argument. And certain data are compatible with this argument. Several studies have examined the motives of white-collar offenders, typically samples of convicted offenders. Some of these offenders state that they were motivated by a desire for financial gain, although they more often state that their offense was motivated by the (more socially acceptable) desire to prevent financial loss and the hardship it might cause (see below; Daly 1989; Weisburd and Waring 2001). No study, however, has attempted to directly measure the blockage of economic goals in a sample of both offenders and nonoffenders and determine whether this blockage increases the likelihood of white-collar crime.

Researchers examining corporate crime frequently find that such crime is related to financial problems (e.g., Clinard and Yeager 1980; Coleman 1987; Coleman and Ramos 1998:19; Geis and Salinger 1998; Jamieson 1994; Jenkins and Braithwaite 1993; Simpson 1986, 2002; Simpson and Koper 1997; Simpson and Piquero 2002; Staw and Szwajkowski 1975). Although the data are somewhat mixed, studies suggest that corporate crime is more common in for-profit companies, companies with relatively low profits, companies with declining profits, companies in depressed industries, and companies suffering from other types of financial problems (e.g., low sales relative to assets, small or negative difference between assets and liabilities, perceived threats from competitors). The experience of financial problems, however, is a rough surrogate for goal blockage. For example, some firms with low profits levels may be meeting their (limited) economic goals, while some firms with high profit levels may not be meeting their (lofty) economic goals.

GST can contribute to the research in this area by offering guidance on the conceptualization and measurement of goal blockage. Three lines of inquiry seem especially important to consider.

First, goal blockage should be conceptualized in terms of the gap between expected or "minimally acceptable" economic goals and actual achievements. Criminologists investigating "street crimes" have typically measured goal blockage in terms of the gap between aspirations and expectations, and they have usually focused on educational and occupational goals. This gap does not increase the likelihood of crime (Agnew 2000; Agnew et al. 1996). GST explains this in several ways (Agnew 1992, 1995, 1997, 2006; Agnew et al. 1996). Most notably, aspirations or ideal goals have something of the utopian in them, and so the expected failure to achieve aspirations is not taken seriously. The actual failure to achieve expected or minimally acceptable goals is more likely to generate the distress that fosters crime. Measuring the goals and achievements of individuals is relatively straightforward (Agnew 1992, 1997; Agnew et al. 1996). Researchers might measure corporate goals through the examination of corporate documents and/or interviews with key corporate officials. It is important to consider a range of related economic goals, including profitability, sales volume, market share, and the acquisition of resources such as personnel and real estate (Clinard and Yeager 1980: 48; Vaughan 1982).

Second, the magnitude of goal blockage should be measured. Magnitude is a function of the centrality of economic goals, the duration and frequency of the goal blockage, and the size of the gap between goals and achievements (Agnew 2001). The centrality of economic goals should be measured by asking individuals about the absolute and relative importance they attach to a range of goals. In the case of corporations, researchers might again rely on corporate documents and interviews with corporate officials. Anecdotal accounts suggest that economic goals are given much higher priority in some corporations than others, with executives in some companies being under extreme pressure to achieve a certain profit level and evaluated almost exclusively based on profits (Geis and Salinger 1998; Jamieson 1994; Pearce 2001). Estimates of the duration and frequency of goal blockage should not only focus on prior goal blockage, but also on the expected duration of goal blockage into the future. It is unclear how to best measure the size of the gap between goals and achievements (see Agnew 1997, 2001; Agnew et al. 1996). One might consider the absolute size of the gap (e.g., the difference in dollars between expected and actual income), the relative size of the gap (e.g., this difference expressed as a percentage of the individual's current income), and/or the size of the gap compared to various referents – such as the individual's previous gap, the gap of the individual's comparison others, and cultural beliefs regarding what is a large versus small gap. Similar measures are available for corporations (e.g., profitability compared to previous years, compared to other companies in the same industry, compared to the expectations of shareholders or other key groups). Researchers should experiment with these different methods in order to determine which method or combination of methods best predicts distress and offending – keeping in mind that there may be individual and organizational differences in this area (the social comparison and relative deprivation literatures provide some guidance here, see Agnew 1992, 1997, 1999; Passas 1997).

Third, the perceived injustice of the goal blockage should be measured. Blockages viewed as unjust are more conducive to crime for several reasons, including the fact that they are more likely to generate emotions such as anger (see Agnew 1992, 2001, 2006). Individuals experiencing the goal blockage or knowledgeable others can be asked to rate the injustice of the blockage. In addition, it is useful to devote some attention to those factors that influence perceptions of injustice. According to Agnew (2001), strains are more likely to be seen as unjust if they involve the voluntary and intentional violation of relevant justice norms. Agnew discusses those factors that influence the individual's perceptions in these areas. Also, certain of the literature on organizations and work stress has focused on perceptions of injustice and their determinants in the economic arena (Cropanzano et al. 2005; Tsutsumi and Kawakami 2004).

When the gap between economic expectations and achievements is high in magnitude and perceived as unjust, individuals should experience much anger and frustration. These emotions create pressure for corrective action and increase the predisposition for crime. Among other things, anger and frustration energize the individual for action, lower inhibitions, and create a desire for revenge. This goal blockage also reduces ties to conventional society, since the core goals of the individual (or corporation) are not being satisfied through conventional means. Further, this goal blockage fosters the belief that crime is justified or excusable and promotes association with deviant others (see Agnew 2006). Individuals in such circumstances, then, are more likely to turn to crime, particularly income-generating crime.

Goal Blockage and the Various Types of White-Collar Crime

The inability to achieve economic goals is more common among lower than higher class individuals (Agnew 2000, Agnew et al. 1996). This might cause some to question the extent to which these arguments apply to white-collar crime. There is, however, reason to believe that the blockage of economic goals has much relevance to the explanation of (a) particular white-collar offenses, such as fraud and embezzlement; (b) occupational offending by higher class individuals; and (c) corporate crime.

First, as noted above, some white-collar offenses are committed by lower class individuals. It is reasonable to suppose that many of these individuals experience trouble realizing their economic expectations or minimally acceptable goals. Studies of white-collar offenders, in fact, find that such individuals frequently mention economic problems as the source of their offending (Daly 1989; Weisburd and Waring 2001; Weisburd et al. 1991).

Second, the blockage of economic goals may help explain the commission of occupational crimes by higher class individuals. Higher class individuals, by definition, possess abundant financial resources. However, they may also pursue economic goals beyond their reach. Several reasons have been suggested for this. The cultural system in the United States encourages all individuals, rich as well as poor, to pursue goals beyond their reach (Agnew 1997; Coleman 1987; Durkheim 1951; Merton 1964; Messner and Rosenfeld 2001:63–64; Passas 1997; Schoepfer and Piquero 2006; see Daly 1989 on gender differences in this area). As Merton (1968: 190) states, "In the American Dream there is no final stopping point. The measure of 'monetary success' is conveniently indefinite and relative. At each income level... Americans want just about twenty-five percent more (but of course this 'just a bit more' continues to operate once it is obtained)." Higher class individuals may select even more privileged others as reference groups, also causing them pursue goals beyond their reach (Agnew et al. 1996; Coleman and Ramos 1998; Passas 1997). The selection of more privileged others as referents may be especially likely during periods of rapid economic growth and/or high rates of social mobility (e.g., Durkheim 1951; Passas 1997). The achievement of wealth, in itself, may foster the pursuit of lofty goals since basic needs are being satisfied and the power associated with wealth leads to an increase in expectations (Braithwaite 1992:80; Durkheim 1951). Finally, certain personality traits may lead individuals to set unrealistic goals. Piquero et al. (2005) suggest that this is the case with individuals who have a high "desire for control." Such individuals overestimate their own abilities and believe they can control everything around them, which often leads them to develop unrealistic expectations (also see Wheeler 1992). Higher class individuals, then, may pursue goals beyond their reach for several reasons. This may help explain why social class has only a weak to moderate association with individuals' level of satisfaction with their monetary status (Agnew et al. 1996).

Third, corporations (i.e., corporate managers) may have trouble achieving their economic goals. As several commentators have noted, the primary goal of corporations is profit (e.g., Clinard and Yeager 1980; Cohen 1997; Coleman 1987; Jamieson 1994; Simpson and Koper 1997; Vaughan 1982). And as Pearce (2001:40) states, the managers of corporations "experience pressure to achieve high profits from the company's major shareholders and major creditors, from stock market evaluations of the corporation's performance vis-a-vis their competitors, and because their own interests are linked with the company's since significant components of their own remuneration is related to profit returns and/or is in shares in the company." It has been suggested that some corporations (or managers) may be more likely than others to set unrealistic or "greedy" economic goals – although more research is needed in this area (Clinard 1983; Clinard and Yeager 1980; Coleman 1987; Shover and Wright 2001:255–256; Simpson and Koper 1997; Vaughn 1982). Corporations may also have trouble achieving more reasonable economic goals through legitimate channels. There are a variety of reasons for this, including economic downturns, competition from others, a lack of resources, technological changes, changes in the law, and a variety of problems internal to the corporation (Baucus and Near 1991; Croall 1989; Probst 2005; Simpson 1986; Simpson and Koper 1997; Simpson et al. 1998; Vaughan 1982). Again, more research is needed in this area, including research on whether certain types of corporations are more vulnerable to economic problems than others (see Simpson and Koper 1997).

In sum, there is good reason to believe that the inability to achieve economic goals may be an important cause of white-collar crime, no matter how defined. Much care, however, needs to be taken in the conceptualization and measurement of such goal blockage.

The Actual or Threatened Loss of Money/Possessions/Services; and the Actual or Threatened Presentation of Negative Stimuli Related to Economic Problems

GST builds on the classic strain theories of Merton and others by arguing that goal blockage is only one of three major types of strain. As indicated, strain may also involve the actual or threatened loss of positively valued stimuli and the presentation of negatively valued stimuli. In these areas, GST would predict that individuals and corporations are more likely to engage in white-collar crime when they experience the actual or threatened loss of money, possessions, or services, as well as the actual or threatened presentation of negatively valued stimuli related to economic problems (e.g., pressure from creditors, the need to work two jobs). These two types of strain are treated together because it if often difficult to distinguish between them in practice. Suppose, for example, that a worker is laid off. This may be viewed as both the loss of something positive (income) and the presentation of something negative (unemployment). For the sake of convenience, these strains are collectively referred to as "economic problems." Individuals and corporations experiencing economic problems may engage in white-collar crime to protect or retrieve valued stimuli, to prevent the presentation of negative stimuli, and to seek revenge. This type of strain is said to be especially conducive to crime because it frequently involves ongoing difficulties and major changes in lifestyle, which are more difficult to ignore or define away than the inability to achieve economic goals, especially distant goals (also see Wheeler 1992).

White-collar crime researchers have devoted some attention to this type of strain. In one of the best studies in this area, Daly (1989) found that financial need for themselves or their families was the most common motive for offending among a sample of convicted white-collar criminals (also see Braithwaite 1992; Coleman and Ramos 1998:10–11; Cressey 1953; Langton and Piquero 2007; Schoepfer and Piquero 2006; Weisburd and Waring 2001). Economic problems have also been linked to corporate offending. Researchers have noted that corporate actors are sometimes explicitly or implicitly threatened with job loss or limited advancement unless they engage in corporate crime (e.g., Coleman 1987: Shover and Wright 2001). For example, Coleman and Ramos (1998:18) report that an executive who took a strong stand against the manufacture of an unsafe car was told: "You're not a member of the team. Shut up or go looking for another job." Further, as indicated above, quantitative studies tend to suggest that a range of corporate economic problems increase the likelihood of offending. Case studies of corporate offending confirm this point (e.g., Baker and Faulker 2003; Black 2005). While some corporate officials may be pressured into crime by their supervisors, others may engage in crime out of a genuine desire to prevent or reverse economic losses on the part of the corporation. These officials may be stakeholders in the corporation who want to protect their privileged position or they may be concerned about the hardship others might suffer.

White-collar crime, then, may result not only from the inability to satisfy economic goals, but also from the experience or threat of economic problems. Researchers, therefore, should attempt to carefully measure both types of strain.[2] And just as GST can provide advice on how to better measure goal blockage, it can point to ways to more systematically measure economic problems. In particular, several studies provide models for the measurement of economic problems (e.g., Agnew et al. forthcoming; Conger et al. 1992, 2002; Elder and Caspi 1988). These studies have examined the extent to which individuals and their families

---

[2] Some measures of economic problems, such as declining profits, are closely related to measures of goal blockage. This is not a serious problem, however. The aim is not to clearly distinguish between the two types of strain, but rather to develop a comprehensive set of measures that will allow us to better explain white-collar crime.

(a) cannot meet their basic needs, such as the needs for food, shelter, and medical care; (b) cannot purchase desired goods and services; (c) have had to make undesirable adjustments in response to financial problems, such as giving up medical insurance and taking second jobs; and (d) have fallen behind in paying bills. These economic problems contribute to street crime in juveniles (Agnew et al. forthcoming). White-collar crime researchers might draw on the above research to more systematically measure this type of strain. Such researchers, however, should expand the list of economic problems that are considered so as to more fully measure problems experienced by higher class individuals (e.g., loss of wealth, business failure) and corporations (e.g., reduction in assets, increase in liabilities, loss of personnel). Interviews with white-collar offenders and corporate managers can help researchers better describe the specific economic problems that are of concern. Further, researchers should attempt to measure both the magnitude and perceived injustice of such problems.

Economic Problems and the Various Types of White-Collar Crime

Economic problems are generally more common among lower class individuals (Agnew 2006), so one may again wonder how relevant this type of strain is to the explanation of white-collar crime. As before, it can be argued that some white-collar offenders are from lower class and routinely experience economic problems. In this area, Langton and Piquero (2007) found that lower class white-collar offenders were in fact more likely to report financial motivations – such as economic hardship – for their offending.

Economic problems, however, also frequently affect higher class individuals (see Agnew et al. forthcoming). The strong emphasis on consumerism in the United States leads many middle- and higher class individuals to spend beyond their means (Dunaway et al. 2000; Passas 1997). This is reflected, for example, in the rising rate of debt among the middle class (National Mortgage News 2006). Higher class individuals are not immune to financial crises brought on by such things as major health problems, economic downturns, and unemployment (Fox and Chancey 1998). And higher class individuals may be even more susceptible to certain types of economic problems, such as business losses, downturns in the stock market, and threats of job loss if they do not engage in corporate offending. Data provide some support for these arguments.

Agnew et al (forthcoming) employed a scale examining 16 economic problems (e.g., moved to cheaper living quarters, postponed medical care, had a creditor call to demand payment, borrowed money from friends or relatives). The correlation between these problems and family income was weak ($r = -0.14$), and many higher income people experienced several of these problems. For example, 19% of the individuals with family incomes over $70,000 experienced three or more economic problems. Reflecting this fact, studies have found that white-collar offenders in the higher classes sometimes explain their crime in terms of financial need or hardship (Willott et al. 2001; Zietz 1981). To illustrate, many of the upper middle class male offenders in Willott et al.'s (2001) study explained their white-collar crimes by stating that an economic recession created serious financial problems for them and they wanted to protect their families, employees, and others from hardship.

Finally, this type of strain is relevant to corporate/organizational crime. As indicated, corporate officials may be pressured into engaging in corporate crime through the threat of termination or limited opportunities for advancement. And corporations themselves may of course experience a range of economic problems.

The Blockage of Status Goals

Strain theorists such as Cohen (1955, 1997) have argued that individuals not only desire economic success, but status as well – with status involving the respect and admiration of others. Individuals unable to obtain status through legal channels may turn to illegal channels. Studies, for example, suggest that some lower class individuals seek to enhance their status by adopting a tough demeanor and responding to even minor shows of disrespect with violence (Anderson 1999; Brezina et al. 2005). Many white-collar workers already have much status in the eyes of the larger society. Certain of these workers, however, may develop status goals beyond their reach, usually for the same reasons they develop economic goals beyond their reach. Also, many white-collar workers may turn to crime when their status is threatened (Wheeler 1992).

Given their background and social environment, most such workers do not attempt to achieve status through physical toughness. Rather, they are deeply immersed in the "culture of competition" said to characterize our economic system (Coleman 1987). Therefore, they attempt to achieve status by using illegal means to achieve success in this competitive struggle. In the words of Coleman and Ramos (1998:12): "Along with the desire for great wealth goes the desire to prove oneself by 'winning' the competitive struggles that play such a prominent role in our economic system. And this desire to be 'a winner' provides another powerful motivation for deviant behavior irrespective of any financial gain that may be involved." Individuals may prove themselves to be winners by using illegal means to advance their own position or the position of the corporation with which they are associated. There is limited data for this argument, with some white-collar offenders claiming that they offended out of a concern about their standing in their profession (Willott et al. 2001).

Work Stress

A range of work-related strains may also contribute to white-collar crime, particularly crimes against the worker's company (e.g., embezzlement, employee theft). This is especially the case if such strains are viewed as unjust (see Cropanzano et al. 2005 for a discussion of justice in the workplace). These strains may create anger, thereby lowering inhibitions and creating a desire for revenge, particularly against the source of the strains or related targets. These strains also reduce one's attachment and commitment to the company, again increasing the likelihood of crime – particularly against the company. In addition, these strains foster beliefs that justify or excuse crime, particularly against the company (see Beugre 1998). In particular, crime is seen as a way to "right" a wrong and obtain revenge against a deserving target. And if these strains are shared with other workers, they may contribute to the development of subcultures that hold beliefs favorable to white-collar crime.

There is a large literature on work-related strains or stresses (for overviews and selected studies, see Barling et al. 2005; Beehr and Glazer 2005; Chen and Spector 1992; Grebner et al. 2005; Hollinger and Clark 1983; Kelloway et al. 2005; Marchand et al. 2005; Schat and Kelloway 2005; Tsutsumi and Kawakami 2004; Van Der Doef and Maes 1999). Researchers have identified the major types of work stress, and they include role ambiguity (unclear job expectations), role conflicts (incompatible job demands, conflict between job and family demands), role overloads (too much work, lack of personnel or other resources to complete work), high job demands in combination with low control, insufficient rewards for ones efforts, job insecurity, unpleasant working conditions (e.g., repetitive work, low levels of skill utilization, and decision authority), and interpersonal problems – including discriminatory treatment and physical, sexual, and psychological harassment.

Evidence suggests that these types of stress contribute to a range of negative outcomes, including negative emotions, job dissatisfaction, alcohol use, and selected crimes – such as drug use, workplace aggression, and employee theft (see above cited references). With the exception of employee theft, however, there is little research on the effect of these workplace strains on white-collar offending. In the area of employee theft, Wheeler (1992:118) reports that among the white-collar offenders he studied are "occasional cases of revenge seekers, who are unhappy with the way they have been treated by their companies and who justify stealing from them." And Coleman (1987) reports that workers engaging in employee theft commonly justify their crime by claiming they deserve what they have taken since their employers exploit them (also see Hollinger and Clark 1983; Langton et al. 2006). While workplace stressors may be most conducive to crimes directed against the individual's employer, they may sometimes contribute to corporate crimes as well. In particular, individuals facing role overloads may engage in corporate crime in an effort to satisfy the excessive demands of their supervisors.

Work-related strains are more common among lower class workers. Again, however, many such workers engage in white-collar crime. Further, many higher class workers experience such strains (Marchand et al. 2005). In addition, corporations may experience the organizational equivalent of work-related strains. Corporations, for example, may be treated in a negative and unjust manner by others – including other corporations and government agencies. Braithwaite's (1989) work on regulation is relevant here, with there being some evidence that regulations seen as excessive or unreasonable may prompt corporate defiance, including offending (also see Clinard and Yeager 1980; Coleman 1987).

A Note on Subjective, Vicarious, and Anticipated Strains

Objective Versus Subjective Strains

GST states that it is important to consider the distinction between objective and subjective strains (Agnew 2001, 2006). Objective strains refer to events and conditions that are disliked by most people in a given group, while subjective strains refer to events and conditions that are disliked by the people experiencing them. Individuals frequently differ in their subjective evaluation of the same objective strains. For example, two individuals may both experience unemployment, but one may evaluate their unemployment in a much more negative manner than the other. Not surprisingly, there is some evidence that subjective strains are more strongly related to crime than objective strains (Agnew et al. 1996; Froggio and Agnew 2007). It is therefore important to measure subjective strains. This is easily done at the individual level, with respondents being asked how much they dislike the particular events and conditions they have experienced. This may be done at the corporate level by interviewing corporate officials and examining corporate documents. At the same time, it is important to measure the experience of objective strains as well and to investigate those factors that influence the subjective reaction to these strains – including personality traits (e.g., negative emotionality), coping skills and resources (e.g., financial resources), social supports, and beliefs (see Agnew 2001). This allows researchers to link the circumstances of individuals to their subjective states, thereby dramatically improving our ability to explain and control crime.

Anticipated Strains

GST states that crime may result not only from experienced strains, but also from the anticipation that strains may be experienced in the future (Agnew et al. 2002). Individuals and corporations may engage in white-collar crime to prevent or mitigate such strains or seek revenge against those who might inflict them. The concept of anticipated strain may be particularly relevant to white-collar crime, because corporations and many white-collar workers devote much effort to the prediction and management of their future economic state. In this area, the "fear of falling" has been identified as a type of anticipated strain that may have much relevance to white-collar crime. It is said that many white-collar workers become fearful that they might lose the financial success and status they have achieved, and they sometimes engage in crime to prevent this anticipated loss (Wheeler 1992). In the words of Weisburd et al. (1991:224): "the motivation for their crime is not selfish ego gratification, but rather the fear of falling – of losing what they have worked so hard to gain." Also, it has been said that high levels of environmental uncertainty, such as that associated with a complex or rapidly changing environment, may motivate corporate crime. Uncertainty makes planning difficult and thus poses a threat to future profits. Corporate officials may engage in actions such as price fixing in order to reduce uncertainty and ensure their future economic well-being (Clinard and Yeager 1980:49–50; Staw and Szwajkowski 1975).

Vicarious Strains

Finally, GST states that vicarious strains may sometimes lead to crime (Agnew et al. 2002). Vicarious strains refer to the strains experienced by close others, such as family and coworkers, and others with whom that the individual strongly identifies. In this area, some white-collar offenders state that their crimes were motivated not so much by their own strain or anticipation of strain, but by their desire to protect family, friends, and employees from hardship (e.g., Daly 1989; Willott et al. 2001). This is especially true of female offenders. Researchers, then, should not only ask individuals about the strains they are experiencing, but also about the strains of close and referent others. Individuals who report little personal strain may nevertheless engage in crime to protect others from hardship.

The concept of vicarious strain may also help us better understand the motivation for corporate crime. As Simpson (2002:8) states, corporate crimes "have little to do with an individual employee's personal needs but a lot to do with organizational contingencies, priorities, and needs." Offenders, of course, may nevertheless benefit from such crimes, particularly if they are stakeholders in the corporation or the crimes advance their position in the corporation. And these benefits may form part of their motivation for the crime. However, it is possible that some individuals so closely identify with the corporations in which they work that they vicariously experience the strains of the corporation. That is, they become genuinely upset when their corporation encounters economic or other problems – even if such problems have little personal effect on them. This vicarious strain may also form part of the motivation for corporate offending.

Summary

In sum, there is reason to believe that several strains increase the likelihood of white-collar offending. These strains include the inability to achieve economic goals through legal channels; the experience of a range of economic problems, with these problems involving actual or threatened losses and the presentation of negative stimuli; the inability to achieve status goals; and several work-related strains. These strains are most likely to result in white-collar crime when they are high in magnitude and perceived as unjust. And these strains may result in a variety of white-collar crimes, including occupational crimes by higher class individuals, particular economic crimes such as fraud and embezzlement – often committed by lower class individuals, and corporate crimes. As noted, specific strains may be more relevant to some types of white-collar crime than others. For example, the economic strains that explain white-collar offenses by lower class individuals differ somewhat from those that explain the occupational crimes of higher class individuals and corporate crimes.

Conditioning Factors

While these strains increase the likelihood of crime, GST recognizes that most individuals experiencing these strains do *not* respond with crime. Most individuals cope with these strains in a legal manner or simply endure them. As a consequence, GST devotes much attention to those factors that increase the likelihood of criminal coping. GST, however, does not devote much attention to why individuals cope with one type of crime versus another. Therefore, we must further describe why some individuals respond to these strains with white-collar crime rather than street crimes, such as larceny and burglary. This final section draws on GST and the white-collar crime research to list those factors that increase the likelihood that strained individuals will engage in offending and – in the case of certain factors – white-collar offending.

Poor Conventional Coping Skills and Resources

Crime is more likely if individuals lack the skills and resources to cope with strains in a legal manner. Such skills/resources include problem-solving skills, financial resources, and selected personality traits – such as high constraint and low negative emotionality (Agnew 2006; Agnew et al. 2002). Certain of these coping skills and resources vary substantially among lower class individuals and so may play a large role in conditioning the effects of strains on crime in this group. These skills and resources, however, may not vary as much among higher class individuals and corporate officials. As a consequence, they may play a more limited role in conditioning the effect of strains on crime in these groups (for related discussions, see Beehr and Glazer 2005; Benson and Moore 1992; Coleman and Ramos 1998:10; Piquero et al. 2005; Simpson and Piquero 2002; Walters and Geyer 2004).

Other coping skills and resources may be more relevant to higher class individuals and corporate officials. For example, Piquero et al. (2005) argue that many corporate officials have a high "desire for control;" that is, they are "assertive, decisive, and active... seek to influence others... [and] prefer to avoid unpleasant situations or failures by manipulating events to ensure desired outcomes" (Burger and Cooper 1979:383). Piquero et al. argue that such individuals are more likely to respond to strains with corporate offending, in part because of their strong fear of failure and their willingness to take risks. Related personality traits, such as "egocentricity" and a "hunger for power" may also play an important role in conditioning the effect of strains in these groups (see Friedrichs 1996:216). Likewise, the business skills and corporate resources available to higher class individuals and corporate managers may condition the effects of strains on offending. For example, it has been argued that corporate offending frequently occurs when managers feel much pressure from top administrators to achieve particular goals, but lack the resources necessary to achieve these goals (Jenkins and Braithwaite 1993).

Researchers have explored the direct effects of certain of the above coping skills and resources on white-collar offending (see the above cited studies), but no study has examined whether these traits condition the effect of strains on white-collar crime.

Low Conventional Social Support

Criminal coping is also more likely when strained individuals are unable to turn to others for assistance in legal coping. Such assistance or support includes emotional support, information or advice, and direct assistance – such as financial assistance (Agnew 2006; Cullen 1994). This support may come from such others as family members, friends, coworkers, supervisors, and government agencies. The literature on work stress confirms the importance of social support, with some studies suggesting that work stress is less likely to result in negative outcomes when social support is high (see Beehr and Glazer 1995, Van Der Doef and Maes 1999; also see Agnew 2006). There is also some limited evidence for the importance of social support in explaining white-collar crime. A central theme in certain of the white-collar crime research is that offending is most likely when individuals experience serious financial strains *and* they are unable to turn to others for help (Cressey 1953)

Opportunity

Strained individuals who are unable to cope in a legal manner cannot engage in white-collar crime unless they have the opportunity to do so (see Piquero and Piquero 2001; Shover and Wright 2001; Vaughn 1982). Opportunity is here defined as "a circumstance where that behavior is possible" (Tittle 1995:169). The opportunities to engage in certain white-collar crimes, such as passing bad checks, are fairly widespread among the adult population. The opportunities for other white-collar crimes are more limited, with such crimes requiring a white-collar occupation – sometimes a high status occupation in a corporation.

Criminal Coping Skills and Resources

The inability to cope in a legal manner does not guarantee criminal coping – even if the opportunity for crime is available (Cloward and Ohlin 1960; Cullen 1984). Criminal coping often requires or is made easier by the possession of certain criminal coping skills and resources. For example, it is easier to successfully engage in many street crimes if one is physically strong and agile, possesses what Agnew (2006:97–98) calls "criminal self-efficacy," and has some knowledge about how to best commit crimes such as robbery and drug selling. Most higher class individuals and corporate officials lack these skills and resources. Many such individuals, however, have the skills and resources to engage in a range of white-collar offenses. These skills and resources may have been acquired as part of their occupational socialization. In some cases, such individuals may receive deliberate instruction in the techniques of white-collar crime (more below). As such, theses individuals are less likely to respond to strains with street crimes and more likely to respond with white-collar crimes. Some lower class individuals, however, may have the skills and resources to engage in both street crimes and certain white-collar crimes, such as fraud and embezzlement. And Weisburd and Waring (2001) found that some of the lower class offenders in their study did in fact engage in a range of offenses, both street and white-collar.

Low Social Control

Strained individuals may be unable to legally cope, may have opportunities for white-collar crime, and may have the skills and resources to take advantage of these opportunities. Nevertheless, they may still refrain from white-collar crime. One reason for this is they have too much to lose through crime. Criminal coping is therefore more likely among those with little to lose; that is, those low in social control. Individuals low in social control have a low attachment to conventional others and institutions, such as family, community, and work. They have a low commitment to conventional society. In particular, they have poor reputations, little involvement in their communities, and are unemployed or work in poorly paid jobs in the secondary labor market. And they are amoral in their beliefs regarding white-collar crime. Based on these arguments, we would predict that a given strain is more likely to lead to white-collar crime among lower class individuals than among higher class individuals, holding opportunity constant. These arguments, however, are less easily applied to the explanation of offending among higher class individuals and corporate offenders.

As several researchers have noted, higher class and corporate offenders appear to be high in most forms of social control (e.g., Reed and Yeager 1996; Weisburd et al. 1991; Wheeler 1992). For example, Piquero et al. (2005:262) state that corporate offenders tend to be "highly trained, properly ambitious, and conventionally socialized individuals who strain to manage the ethical and legal dilemmas they face." Likewise, Wheeler (1992:109) states that "many white-collar offenders have led lives not only unmarked by prior trouble with the law, but characterized by positive contributions to family and community life." Social control, however, may still aid in the explanation of offending among such individuals. In particular, higher class offenders may be low in certain forms of social control, such as attachment to work and beliefs condemning white-collar crime.

Low Perceived Costs and High Benefits of the Crime

Individuals tend to consider the costs and benefits associated with the crimes they are contemplating. Criminal coping is more likely when the perceived costs are low and the benefits are high. The benefits of the crime include both monetary benefits and psychological benefits, such as pleasure and excitement. The costs of the crime include feelings of guilt and shame and the likelihood of sanction from family, friends, employers, and government agencies. Many of these factors have direct effects on white-collar offending (Coleman and Ramos 1998; Paternoster and Simpson 1996; Piquero et al. 2005; Simpson 2002; Simpson and Piquero 2002; Simpson et al. 1998). Researchers, however, have not devoted much attention to whether these factors condition the effect of strains on offending (although see Paternoster and Simpson, 1996).

Perceptions of the costs and benefits of white-collar crime are likely influenced by certain individual, organizational, and social characteristics (Clinard and Yeager 1980; Monacan and Quinn 2006). To give a few examples: (1) Wright et al. (1999) suggest that while higher class individuals have more to lose by engaging in crime, they may believe they are better able to resist the sanctioning efforts of others – particularly the efforts of government agencies. This belief may be a function of such things as their reputations in the community, connections to powerful others, and assess to good legal advice and representation. (2) Individuals who work in large, highly diversified organizations may believe that the likelihood of sanction is lower because it is more difficult to monitor employee behavior in such organizations. Further, there may be a greater "diffusion of responsibility" in such organizations – which can alleviate feelings of guilt. (3) The managers and/or workers in some organizations may be more tolerant of white-collar crime; in fact, they may encourage and reward crime in certain circumstances (see below; Paternoster and Simpson 1992). Again, this influences perceptions of costs and benefits. (4) White-collar offending is less subject to legal sanction during certain times and in certain places (see Coleman 1987; Black 2005). So a range of individual and environmental factors may reduce the perceived costs and/or increase the perceived benefits of crime, thereby increasing the likelihood that individuals will cope with strains through crime. There is no systematic data in this area, although certain case studies support this idea (e.g., Black 2005).

Beliefs Favorable to White-Collar Crime/Association with Criminal Others

Finally, individuals should be more likely to cope through white-collar crime when they associate with white-collar criminals and hold beliefs favorable to white-collar crime. Data indicate that such beliefs increase the likelihood of white-collar offending and that white-collar offenders commonly hold such beliefs (Benson 1985; Clinard and Yeager 1980; Coleman 1987; Hochstetler and Copes 2001; Piquero et al. 2005; Reed and Yeager 1996; Simpson 2002; Simpson et al. 1998; Simpson and Piquero 2002; Vaughn 1982). In certain cases, white-collar crimes may be defined as generally acceptable, but it is more often the case that such offenses are defined as justifiable or excusable in particular circumstances. In particular, such beliefs frequently define offenses as justifiable/excusable in response to a range of strains. Offenses, for example, are said to be justifiable/excusable if they are necessary to protect family members, employees, or stockholders from financial hardship. To illustrate, one of the executives involved in the heavy electric price-fixing case in the 1960s stated "I thought we were more or less working on a survival basis in order to make enough to keep our plant and our employees" (Geis 1977).

Coping through white-collar crime is also more likely when individuals associate with others who engage in and favor such crime. These others may teach beliefs favorable to white-collar crime, teach techniques of crime commission, provide models for crime, apply pressure to engage in crime, provide assistance in committing crime, and differentially reinforce crime (Clinard and Yeager 1980; Coleman 1987; Coleman and Ramos 1998; Reed and Yeager 1996). These criminal groups may develop within an organization, across organizations, and in particular fields. The origin of these criminal groups is often explained in terms of strain theory (e.g., Hochstetler and Copes 2001; Vaughan 1997). For example, Coleman and Ramos (1998:28) explain such groups in terms of goal blockage: "When presented with highly attractive deviant opportunities and a relative absence of attractive legitimate opportunities, subcultures are likely to develop and perpetuate rationalizations for pursuing those deviant opportunities." Braithwaite (1989:127–133) explains such groups in terms of the presentation of negative stimuli, arguing that punitive policies by regulatory agencies often breed "cultures of opposition" in corporations that support law breaking.

Summary

In sum, people experiencing the strains listed earlier are most likely to engage in white-collar crime when they (a) lack the skills and resources for legal coping and for street crime, (b) do not receive support from conventional others, (c) have the opportunity to engage in white-collar crime, (d) possess the skills and resources for white-collar crime, (e) are low in social control (have little to lose), (f) perceive the costs of white-collar crime as low and the benefits as high, (g) hold beliefs favorable to white-collar crime, and (h) associate with others supportive of such crime. Not all of these factors are necessary for criminal coping to occur, most simply increase the likelihood of criminal coping.

It should be noted that the individual's standing on these factors is frequently influenced by socio-demographic characteristics. Some evidence suggests that males are more likely than females to possess certain of these factors, such as opportunities for many types of white-collar crime and association with others who support such crime (Daly 1989). The relationship between social class and these characteristics is mixed. For example, lower class individuals are more likely to possess poor coping skills/resource and be low in social control, while higher class individuals are more likely to possess opportunities for many types of white-collar crime. On balance, lower class individuals are probably more inclined to criminal coping than higher class individuals. Higher class individuals, however, are more likely to have the opportunity to engage in many types of white-collar crime, especially corporate crime. And opportunity is the one conditioning factor that is *necessary* for white-collar offending.

Conclusion

GST has much to contribute to the understanding of white-collar crime, including (a) occupational crimes by higher class individuals, (b) particular economic offenses, such as fraud and embezzlement, which are often committed by lower class individuals, and (c) corporate crimes. Certain strain theorists and researchers have argued that these crimes are more likely when individuals are unable to achieve their economic goals through legal channels. GST incorporates this argument, but also extends it in certain fundamental ways:

- GST provides much advice on how to better conceptualize and measure the blockage of economic goals. In particular, economic goals should be conceptualized in terms of the gap between *expected* or *minimally acceptable* goals and *actual achievements*; the magnitude of goal blockage should be measured (i.e., the centrality of economic goals, the duration/frequency of goal blockage, the size of the goal blockage); and the perceived injustice of the goal blockage should be considered. Several specific recommendations for measurement were offered.
- GST notes that lower class individuals, higher class individuals, and corporations/corporate managers may experience the blockage of economic goals, with there being some discussion of the origins and manifestations of goal blockage in these different groups.
- GST also focuses on types of economic strain other than goal blockage. In particular, GST points to a range of economic problems that involve the loss of positively valued stimuli and the presentation of negatively valued stimuli. These problems vary somewhat depending on whether the focus is on lower class individuals, higher class individuals, or corporations. Examples of such problems include trouble paying bills, downturns in the stock market, and reductions in assets.
- GST notes that while economic strains may be the primary source of white-collar crime, other strains may also contribute to such crime. These strains include the inability to achieve status goals and a broad range of work-related stressors, such as conflicts between job and family, high job demands in combination with low control, interpersonal problems at work, and excessive/unreasonable government regulations.
- GST makes several key points about the conceptualization and measurement of all strains. In particular, GST points to the importance of distinguishing between objective and subjective strains, experienced and anticipated strains, and personal and vicarious strains.

- GST provides the most complete account of those factors that influence the likelihood that individuals will respond to strains with crime, including white-collar crime. Such factors include conventional and criminal coping skills and resources, social support, opportunities for white-collar crime, social control, the perceived costs and benefits of white-collar crime, beliefs regarding white-collar crime, and association with criminal others. While researchers have examined the direct effect of certain of these factors on white-collar crime, they have not devoted much attention to whether these factors condition the effect of strains on white-collar crime. This is a major omission, since the commission of white-collar crime is not simply a function of the strains experienced by individuals. Rather, it is a function of both strains and the factors that condition the reaction to strains.

In sum, GST can contribute much to the analysis of white-collar crime. At the same time, it is also important to note that the analysis of white-collar crime contributes to the development of GST.

- GST is intended to be a general theory of crime, but up to now it has been applied almost exclusively to explanation of "street" crime. As Benson and Moore (1992) demonstrated with respect to self-control theory, "general" theories of crime often experience serious problems when applied to the explanation of white-collar crime. The application of GST to white-collar crime in this paper is therefore an important extension of the theory – suggesting that GST *may* in fact be more general in its applicability than previous research has suggested. Empirical research, however, is of course necessary to verify the many claims made about GST and white-collar crime.
- GST claims that lower class individuals are more likely to experience most of those strains conducive to crime (see Agnew 2006). This paper does not dispute that claim, but it tempers it somewhat by emphasizing that higher class individuals and corporations also experience selected strains conducive to crime. Further, this paper more fully describes the strains faced by these groups and the sources of these strains. As such, this paper challenges the perception that strain theory is only relevant to the explanation of offending by lower class individuals.
- This paper provides one of the first illustrations of Agnew's (2006:79) recent argument that certain strains are more likely than others to lead to particular types of crime. In particular, the strains listed above were said to be especially relevant to white-collar crime because all are readily resolved through such crime and most are rooted in the work environment.
- Finally, this paper builds on GST by arguing that conditioning variables not only influence whether strained individuals cope with crime but, in selected cases, also influence the type of crime selected (see Cloward and Ohlin 1960; Cullen 1984). Several factors that increase the likelihood of coping through white-collar crime were listed, including the nature of one's criminal coping skills/resources, opportunities for white-collar crime, and association with other white-collar criminals.

The challenge is to test these ideas, something not easily done given the difficulties of collecting good data on white-collar crime. Nevertheless, numerous suggestions for future research were offered and, hopefully, sufficient motivation for pursuing these suggestions was provided.

References

Agnew, R. (1992). Foundation for a General Strain Theory of Crime and Delinquency. *Criminology*, 30, 47–87.

Agnew, R. (1995). The contribution of social-psychological strain theory to the explanation of crime and delinquency. In F. Adler and W. Laufer (Eds.), *The Legacy of Anomie Theory, Advances in Criminological Theory, Volume 6*. New Brunswick, NJ: Transaction.

Agnew, R. (1997). The nature and determinants of strain. In N.Passos and R. Agnew (Eds.), *The Future of Anomie Theory*. Boston: Northeastern University Press.

Agnew, R. (2000). Sources of criminality: Strain and subcultural theories. In J. Shelet (Ed.), *Criminology*. Belmont, CA: Wadsworth.

Agnew, R. (2001). Building on the Foundation of General Strain Theory: Specifying the Types of Strain Most Likely to Lead to Crime and Delinquency. *Journal of Research in Crime and Delinquency*, 38, 319–361.

Agnew, R. (2002). Experienced, Vicarious, and Anticipated Strain: An Exploratory Study Focusing on Physical Victimization and Delinquency. *Justice Quarterly*, 19, 603–632.

Agnew, R. (2006). *Pressured Into Crime: An Overview of General Strain Theory*. New York: Oxford University Press.

Agnew, R, Brezina, T., Wright, J. P., and Cullen, F. T. (2002). Strain, Personality Traits, and Delinquency: Extending General Strain Theory. *Criminology*, 40, 43–72.

Agnew, R, Cullen, F. T., Burton, V. S., Jr., Evans, T. D., and Dunaway, R. G. (1996). A New Test of Classic Strain Theory. *Justice Quarterly*, 13, 681–704.

Agnew, R., Matthews, S. K., Bucher, J., Welcher, A., and Keyes, C. (forthcoming). Socio-Economic Status, Economic Problems, and Delinquency." *Youth & Society*.

Anderson, E. (1999). *Code of the Street*. New York: W.W. Norton.

Baker, W. E., and Faulker, R. R. (2003). Diffusion of Fraud: Intermediate Economic Crime and Investor Dynamics. *Criminology*, 41, 1173–1206.

Barling, J. E., Kelloway, K, and Frone, M. R. (2005). *Handbook of Work Stress*. Thousand Oaks, CA: Sage.

Baucus, M. S., and Near, J. P. (1991). Can Illegal Behavior Be Predicted? An Event History Analysis. *Academy of Management Journal*, 34, 9–36.

Beehr, T. A., and Glazer, S. (2005). Organizational role stress." In J. Barling, E. K. Kelloway, and M. R. Frone (Eds.), *Handbook of Work Stress*. Thousand Oaks, CA: Sage.

Benson, M. L. (1985). Denying the Guilty Mind: Accounting for Involvement in a White-Collar Crime. *Criminology*, 23, 583–607.

Benson, M. L., and Moore, E. (1992). Are White-Collar and Common Offenders the Same? An Empirical and Theoretical Critiue of a Recently Proposed General Theory of Crime. *Journal of Research in Crime and Delinquency*, 29, 251–72.

Beugre, C. D. (1998). Understanding organizational insider-perpetrated workplace aggression. In P. A. Bambergher and W. J. Sonnenstuhl (Eds.), *Research in the Sociology of Organizations: Deviance On and Of Organizations, Volume 15*. Stamford, CT: JAI Press.

Black, W. (2005). Control Fraud as an Explanation for White-Collar Crime Waves: The Case of the Savings and Loan Debacle. *Crime, Law, & Social Change*, 43, 1–29.

Braithwaite, J. (1992). Poverty, power, and white-collar crime: Sutherland and the paradoxes on criminological theory. In K. Schlegel and D. Weisburd (Eds.), *White-Collar Crime Reconsidered*. Boston: Northeastern University Press.

Braithwaite, J. (1989). *Crime, Shame, and Reintegration*. Cambridge, England: Cambridge University Press.

Braithwaite, J. (1992). Poverty, power, and white-collar crime." In P. A. Bamberger and W. J. Sonnenstuhl (Eds.), *Research in the Sociology of Organizations: Deviance On and Of Organizations, Volume 15*. Stamford, CT: JAI Press.

Brezina, T., Agnew, R., Cullen, F. T., and Wright, J. P. (2005). The Code of the Street: A Quantitative Assessment of Elijah Anderson's Subculture of Violence Thesis and Its Contribution to Youth Violence. *Youth Violence and Juvenile Justice*, 2, 303–328.

Burger, J.M., and H.M. Cooper. (1979). The Desirability of Control. *Motivation and Emotion*, 3, 381–393.

Chen, P. Y., and Spector, P. E. (1992). Relationships of Work Stressors with Aggression, Withdrawal, Theft, and Substance Use: An Exploratory Study. *Journal of Occupational and Organizational Psychology*, 65, 177–184.

Clinard, M. (1983). *Corporate Ethics and Crime*. Beverly Hills, CA: Sage.

Clinard, M. B., and Quinney, R. (1973). *Criminal Behavior Systems: A Typology*. New York: Holt, Rinehart, and Winston.

Clinard, M. B., and Yeager, P. C. (1980). *Corporate Crime*. New York: Free Press.

Cloward, R. A., and Ohlin, L. E. (1960). *Delinquency and Opportunity*. New York: Free Press.

Cohen, A. K. (1955). *Delinquent Boys*. New York: Free Press.

Cohen, Albert K. 1997. An elaboration of anomie theory. In N.Passos and R. Agnew (Eds.), *The Future of Anomie Theory*. Boston: Northeastern University Press.

Coleman, J. (1987). Toward an Integrated Theory of White-Collar Crime. *American Journal of Sociology*, 93, 406–439.

Coleman, J. W., and Ramos, L. L. (1998). Subcultures and deviant behavior in the organizational context." In P. A. Bamberger and W. J. Sonnenstuhl (Eds.), *Research in the Sociology of Organizations: Deviance On and Of Organizations, Volume 15*. Stamford, CT: JAI Press.

Conger, R. D., Conger, K. J., Elder, G. H., Lorenz, F. O., Simons, R. L., and Whitbeck, L. B. (1992). A Family Process Model of Economic Hardship and Adjustment in Early Adolescent Boys. *Child Development*, 63, 526–541.

Conger, R.D., Wallace, L. E., Sun, Y., Simmons, R. L., McLoyd, V. C., and Brody, G. H. (2002). Economic Pressure in African American Families: A Replication and Extension of the Family Stress Model. *Developmental Psychology*, 38, 179–193.

Cressey, D. R. (1953). *Other People's Money: A Study in the Social Psychology of Embezzlement*. Glencoe, ILL: Free Press.

Croall, H. (1989). Who Is the White-Collar Criminal? *British Journal of Criminology*, 29, 157–174.

Cropanzano, R., Goldman, B. M., and Benson L. III. (2005). Organizational justice. In P. A. Bamberger and W. J. Sonnenstuhl (Eds.), *Research in the Sociology of Organizations: Deviance On and Of Organizations, Volume 15*. Stamford, CT: JAI Press.

Cullen, F. T. (1984). *Rethinking Crime and Deviance Theory*. Totowa, NJ: Rowman and Allanheld.

Cullen, F. T. (1994). Social Support As an Organizing Concept for Criminology. *Justice Quarterly*, 11, 527–559.

Curran, D. J., and Renzetti, C. M. (2001). *Theories of Crime*. Boston: Allyn and Bacon.

Daly, K. (1989). Gender and Varieties of White-Collar Crime. *Criminology*, 24, 769–794.

DeCoster, S. and Kort-Butler, L. (2006). How General Is General Strain Theory? *Journal of Research in Crime and Delinquency*, 43, 297–325.

Dunaway, R. G., Cullen, F. T., Burton, V. S., Jr., and Evans, T. D. (2000). The Myth of Social Class and Crime Revisited: An Examination of Class and Adult Criminality. *Criminology*, 38, 589–632.

Durkheim, E. (1951). *Suicide*. [1897]. New York: Free Press.

Elder, G. H., Jr., and Caspi, A. (1988). Economic Stress in Lives: Developmental Perspectives. *Journal of Social Issues*, 44, 25–45.

Fox, G. L., and Chancey, D. (1998). Sources of Economic Distress. *Journal of Family Issues*, 19, 725–749.

Friedrichs, D. O. (1996). *Trusted Criminals*. Belmont, CA: Wadsworth.

Froggio, G., and Agnew, R. (2007). The relationship between crime and 'objective" versus 'subjective' strains. *Journal of Criminal Justice, 35,* 81–87.

Geis, G. (1967). White-collar crime: The heavy electrical equipment antitrust cases of 1961. In Clinard. M. B., and Quinney, R. (Eds.), *Criminal Behavior Systems: A Typology.* New York: Holt, Rinehart, and Winston.

Geis, G. (1992). White-collar crime: What is it? In K. Schlegel and D. Weisburd (Eds.), *White-Collar Crime Reconsidered.* Boston: Northeastern University Press.

Geis, G., and Salinger, L. S. (1998). Antitrust and organizational deviance." In P. A. Bamberger and W. J. Sonnenstuhl (Eds.), *Research in the Sociology of Organizations: Deviance On and Of Organizations, Volume 15.* Stamford, CT: JAI Press.

Gottfredson, M. R., and Hirschi, T. (1990). *A General Theory of Crime.* Stanford, CA: Stanford University Press.

Grebner, S., Semmer, N. K., and Elfering, A. (2005). Working Conditions and Three Types of Well-Being: A Longitudinal Study with Self-Report and Rating Data. *Journal of Occupational Health Psychology,* 10, 31–43.

Hochstetler, A., and Copes, H. 2001. Organizational culture and organizational crime." In N. Shover and J. P. Wright (Eds.), *Crimes of Privilege: Readings in White-Collar Crime.* New York: Oxford University Press.

Hollinger, R., and Clark, J. (1983). *Theft by Employees.* Lanham, MD: Lexington.

Holtfreter, K.. (2005). Is Occupational Fraud "Typical" White-Collar Crime? A Comparison of Individual and Organizational Characteristics. *Journal of Criminal Justice,* 33, 353–365.

Jamieson, K. M. (1994). *The Organization of Corporate Crime.* Thousand Oaks, CA: Sage.

Jenkins, A., and Braithwaite, J. (1993). Profits, Pressure, and Corporate Lawbreaking. *Law and Social Change,* 20, 221–232.

Kelloway, E. K., Sivanathan, N., Francis, L., and Barling, J. (2005). Poor leadership. In Barling, J. E., Kelloway, K, and Frone, M. R. (Eds.), *Handbook of Work Stress.* Thousand Oaks, CA: Sage.

Langton, L., and Piquero, N. L. (2007). Can General Strain Theory Explain White-Collar Crime? A Preliminary Investigation of the Relationship between Strain and Select White-Collar Offenses. *Journal of Criminal Justice,* 35, 1–15.

Langton, L., Piquero, N. L., and Hollinger, R. C. (2006). An Empirical Test of the Relationship between Employee Theft and Low Self-Control. *Deviant Behavior,* 27, 537–565.

Marchand, A., Demers, A., and Durand, P. (2005). Does Work Really Cause Distress? The Contribution of Occupational Structure and Work Organization to the Experience of Psychological Distress. *Social Science & Medicine,* 61, 1–14.

Merton, R. (1938). Social Structure and Anomie. *American Sociological Review,* 3, 672–82.

Merton, R. K. (1964). Anomie, anomia, and social interaction: Contexts of deviant behavior. In Clinard, M. B. (Ed.), *Anomie and Deviant Behavior: A Discussion and Critique.* New York: Free Press.

Merton, R. (1968). *Social Theory and Social Structure.* New York: Free Press.

Messner, S. F., and Rosenfeld, R. (2001). *Crime and the American Dream.* Belmont, CA: Wadsworth.

National Mortgage News. (2006). Measuring the Extent of Middle-Class Debt. *National Mortgage News* 30, #33:10.

Passas, N. (1997). Anomie, Reference Groups, and Relative Deprivation. In N.Passos and R. Agnew (Eds.), *The Future of Anomie Theory.* Boston: Northeastern University Press.

Paternoster, R., and Simpson, S. (1992). "A rational choice theory of corporate crime." In Clarke, R.V., and Felson, *M. Routine Activity and Rational Choice.* New Brunswick, NJ; Transaction.

Paternoster, R., and Simpson, S. (1996). Sanction Threats and Appeals to Morality: Testing a Rational Choice Model of Corporate Crime. *Law and Society Review,* 30, 549–583.

Pearce, F. (2001). Crime and capitalist business corporations. In N. Shover and J. P. Wright (Eds.), *Crimes of Privilege: Readings in White-Collar Crime.* New York: Oxford University Press.

Piquero, N. L., Exum, M. L., and Simpson, S. S. (2005). Integrating the Desire-for-Control and Rational Choice in a Corporate Crime Context. *Justice Quarterly,* 22, 252–280.

Piquero, N. L., and Piquero, A. (2001). Characteristics and sources of white-collar crime. In N. Shover and J. P. Wright (Eds.), *Crimes of Privilege: Readings in White-Collar Crime.* New York: Oxford University Press.

Piquero, N. L., Tibbetts, S. G., and Blankenship, M. B. (2005). Examining the Role of Differential Association and Techniques of Neutralization in Explaining Corporate Crime. *Deviant Behavior,* 26, 159–188.

Probst, T. M. (2005). Economic stressors. In Barling, J. E., Kelloway, K, and Frone, M. R. (Eds.), *Handbook of Work Stress.* Thousand Oaks, CA: Sage.

Reed, G. E., and Yeager, P. C. (1996). Organizing Offending and Neoclassical Criminology: Challenging the Reach of a General Theory of Crime. *Criminology,* 34, 357–382.

Reiss, A. J., Jr., and Tonry, M. (1993). Organizational crime. In M. Tonry and A.J. Reiss, Jr. (Eds.), *Beyond the Law.* Chicago: University of Chicago Press.

Schat, A. C. H., and Kelloway, E. K. (2005). Workplace aggression. In Barling, J. E., Kelloway, K, and Frone, M. R. (Eds.), *Handbook of Work Stress.* Thousand Oaks, CA: Sage.

Schoepfer, A., and Piquero, N. L. (2006). Exploring White-Collar Crime and the American Dream: A Partial Test of Institutional Anomie Theory. *Journal of Criminal Justice,* 34, 227–235.

Shapiro, S. (1990). Collaring the Crime, Not the Criminal: Reconsidering the Concept of White-Collar Crime. *American Sociological Review,* 55, 346–365.

Shover, N., and Wright, J. P. (2001). *Crimes of Privilege: Readings in White-Collar Crime.* New York: Oxford University Press.

Simpson, S. S. (1986). The Decomposition of Antitrust: Testing a Multi-level, Longitudinal Model of Profit-Squeeze. *American Sociological Review,* 51, 859–875.

Simpson, S. S. (2002). *Corporate Crime, Law, and Social Control.* Cambridge, England: Cambridge University Press.

Simpson, S. S., and Koper, C. S. (1997). The Changing of the Guard: Top Management Characteristics, Organizational Strain, and Antitrust Offending. *Journal of Quantitative Criminology,* 13, 373–404.

Simpson, S. S., Paternoster, R., and Piquero, N. L. (1998). Exploring the micro-macro link in corporate crime research. In P. A. Bamberger and W. J. Sonnenstuhl (Eds.), *Research in the Sociology of Organizations: Deviance On and Of Organizations, Volume 15.* Stamford, CT: JAI Press.

Simpson, S. S., and Piquero, N. L. (2002). Low Self-Control, Organizational Theory, and Corporate Crime. *Law & Society Review,* 36:509–547.

Staw, B. M., and Szwajkowski, E. (1975). *Administrative Science Quarterly,* 20, 345–354.

Sutherland, E. (1949). *White-Collar Crime.* New York: The Dryden Press.

Tittle, C. R. (1995). *Control Balance: Toward A General Theory of Deviance.* Boulder, CO: Westview.

Tsutsumi, A., and Kawakami, N. (2004). A Review of Empirical Studies on the Model of Effort-Reward Imbalance at Work: Reducing Occupational Stress by Implementing a New Theory. *Social Science & Medicine,* 59, 2335–2359.

Doef, M., and Maes, S. (1999). The Job Demand-Control(-Support) Model and Psychological Well-Being: A Review of 20 Years of Empirical Research. *Work & Stress,* 13, 87–114.

Vaughan, D. (1982). *Controlling Unlawful Organizational Behavior.* Chicago: University of Chicago Press.

Vaughan, D. (1992). The micro/macro connection in 'white-collar crime' theory. In K. Schlegel and D. Weisburd (Eds.), *White-Collar Crime Reconsidered.* Boston: Northeastern University Press.

Vaughan, D. (1997). Anomie theory and organizations: Culture and the normalization of deviance at NASA." In N.Passos and R. Agnew (Eds.), *The Future of Anomie Theory.* Boston: Northeastern University Press.

Walters, G. D., and Geyer, M. D. (2004). Criminal Thinking and Identity in Male White-Collar Offenders. *Criminal Justice and Behavior,* 31, 263–281.

Waring, E., Weisburd, D., and Chayet, E. (1995). White-collar crime and anomie." In F. Adler and W. S. Laufer (Eds.), *The Legacy of Anomie Theory, Advances in Criminological Theory, Volume 6.* New Brunswick, NJ: Transaction.

Weisburd, D., Wheeler, S., Waring, E., and Bode, N. (1991). *Crimes of the Middle Classes*. New Haven, CT: Yale University Press.

Weisburd, D., and Waring, E. (2001). *White-Collar Crime and Criminal Careers*. Cambridge, England: Cambridge University Press.

Wheeler, S. (1992). The problem of white-collar crime motivation. In P. A. Bamberger and W. J. Sonnenstuhl (Eds.), *Research in the Sociology of Organizations: Deviance On and Of Organizations, Volume 15*. Stamford, CT: JAI Press.

Wheeler, S., Weisburd, D., and Bode, N. (1982). Sentencing the White-Collar Offender: Rhetoric and Reality." *American Sociological Review*, 47, 641–659.

Willott, S., Griffin, C., and Torrance, M. (2001). Snakes and Ladders: Upper-Middle Class Male Offenders Talk About Economic Crime. *Criminology*, 39, 441–466.

Wright, B. R. E., Caspi, A., Moffitt, T. E., Meich, R. A., and Silva, P. A. (1999). Reconsidering the Relationship between SES and Delinquency: Causation but No Correlation. Criminology, 37, 175–194.

Zietz, D. (1981). *Women Who Embezzle or Defraud: A Study of Convicted Felons*. New York: Praeger.

Part II
Emergent Themes and Methodological Issues

Persistent Heterogeneity or State Dependence? An Analysis of Occupational Safety and Health Act Violations

Sally S. Simpson and Natalie Schell

Abstract Persistent heterogeneity and state dependence explain the persistence of criminal offending over time in two distinct ways. The first asserts that offending is persistent over time due to a stable individual trait while the latter suggests that offending has a causal relationship with future crime because it increases the risk of negative consequences. In this chapter, we examine Occupational Safety and Health Act (OSHA) violations to assess which of these explanations is more consistent with corporate crime over time. Using fixed-effects time series analysis (which controls for unobserved heterogeneity), we find an inhibitory effect associated with OSHA inspections, thus challenging the persistent heterogeneity explanation.

Introduction

One of the most persistent findings in criminology is the link between prior and future offending (Nagin and Farrington, 1992). This relationship is so consistent that it has lead some to suggest that an underlying time-stable trait within individuals causes persistence in criminal behavior over time (Gottfredson and Hirschi, 1990). Yet, even though early antisocial behavior is the best predictor of illegality in later life, most antisocial children do not grow up to become antisocial adults (Robins, 1978). Thus, change is possible (Sampson and Laub, 1993; Laub and Sampson, 2003). This alternative point of view suggests that prior crime has a "causal" relationship with future offending in that criminal activity changes an individual's relationships with significant others at that same time that it increases the risk of negative consequences (e.g., victimization, social stigmatization, poor academic performance) – essentially "knifing off" legitimate opportunities as the individual slips into a downward spiral of cumulative disadvantage (Sampson and

S.S. Simpson (✉)
Department of Criminology and Criminal Justice at the University of Maryland/College Park, MD, USA
e-mail: ssimpson@crim.umd.edu

This research was funded, in part, by a grant awarded to the senior author from the National Institute of Justice (2001IJCX0020). Interpretations and points of view are those of the authors.

S.S. Simpson, D. Weisburd (eds.), *The Criminology of White-Collar Crime*,
DOI 10.1007/978-0-387-09502-8_4, © Springer Science+Business Media, LLC 2009

Laub 1993, 2005). However, an individual's downward trajectory and criminogenic lifestyle can reverse itself under a variety of different scenarios. For instance, marriage to the right person, military service, or cognitive transformations can break the link between prior and future crime (Giordano et al., 2002; Bouffard, 2003; Laub and Sampson, 2003).

In the criminology literature, the time-stable explanation for continuity is defined as "persistence heterogeneity" and the criminogenic effects of past crime on future crime is referred to as "state dependence" (Nagin and Paternoster, 1991). Although the empirical evidence is mixed regarding which of these two positions is more persuasive (or whether both have merit), one point is perfectly clear – empirical tests of these arguments draw exclusively from studies of individual offenders and usually focus on traditional street offenders (see Weisburd et al., 2001 for a more inclusive approach). This is true even though continuity of offending over time is characteristic of corporations as well. Longitudinal studies of corporate crime show that in a sample of corporations most offenders are recidivists but a small cohort of firms typically "owns" or is responsible for a substantial share of the total amount of crime committed (Sutherland, 1983, Clinard and Yeager, 1980, Simpson, 1999; Simpson et al., 2007). Research has also shown that many firms comply with the law with some moving well beyond "mere compliance" to set higher standards of behavior (Harrington, 1988, Cohen, 1998, Arora and Cason, 1996, King and Lenox, 2000, Gibbs, 2006). What is less clear is whether these observed relationships reflect general patterns or are specific to particular types of illegality (e.g., antitrust, environmental, fraud, and so forth) or time period.

In this chapter, we hope to shed some light on the following research questions. First, is there an empirical relationship between prior crime and future crime when we examine Occupational Safety and Health violations in a sample of corporations studied during the 1990s? Second, if there is a relationship, is it consistent with persistent heterogeneity or state dependence? Finally, do observed relationships vary by the period of time under study? To answer these questions, we focus on a group of US-based corporations that were studied as part of an environmental crime research project (Simpson et al., 2007). These firms operated in four basic manufacturing industries including pulp, paper, steel, and oil refining. We measure corporate offending using official reports of violations collected from the Occupational Safety and Health Administration.

There is a great deal of debate in the corporate crime literature, and in criminology more generally, whether theory and empirical work focused around individuals can be applied to aggregate units of analysis (e.g., neighborhoods, terrorist organizations). In this paper, we inform that debate with our empirical exploration of state dependence and persistent heterogeneity. Our work is also important, however, to the ongoing discussions regarding the relationship between legal interventions and recidivism, especially regulatory interventions (such as those brought by Occupational Safety and Health Act (OSHA)) that lack the punitive salience of criminal law. Do regulatory measures increase or decrease the risk of future crime? Either outcome is consistent with a state dependence argument because it suggests that criminal involvement leads to cumulative disadvantage (perhaps through labeling) or that companies respond to sanctions in a prosocial manner (deterrence or reha-bilitation).

In the next section, we apply the key concepts (state dependence and persistent heterogeneity) to corporate offending. This is followed with a description of the research problem and how we approach it. The section concludes with a brief defi-nition of corporate crime.

The Research Problem and Current Study

Relative to traditional crime, there are few systematic and quantitative studies of corporate offending. Of those that do exist, a majority focus on antitrust violations (Staw and Szwajkowski, 1975, Asch and Seneca, 1976, Simpson, 1986, 1987). Less attention has been paid to other types of corporate offenses (see Sutherland, 1983; Clinard and Yeager, 1980; Alexander and Cohen, 1996 for exceptions). Thus, one of our goals is to widen the scope of offenses investigated with a focus on safety and health violations (OSHA). Consistent with our focus on persistent heterogeneity and state dependence, we are interested in the relationship between prior "criminal" history and later crime at the company level. The empirical literature (albeit sparse) typically has found a positive association between prior and future offending, but why and how these are related is subject to speculation (Baucus and Near, 1991, Simpson and Koper, 1997). The complications and dependencies created by earlier violations can produce a corporate culture that supports illegal behavior (Finney and Lesieur, 1982, Vaughan, 1983), raise the visibility of offending companies to regula-tory agencies, and negatively affect firm economic stability due to potentially costly fines and restitution, and restrict where or the conditions under which a company can do business – all of which affect a firm's ability to remain law abiding in the future. In this sense, prior offending is viewed as an enduring social circumstance ("state dependence") that increases the risk of future crime (see, e.g., Nagin and Paternoster, 1991).

As noted, the state dependence perspective is in direct contrast to the view that prior offending is a measure of persistent heterogeneity, a stable trait or charac-teristic of the individual (or, in this case, corporation) that is associated with both past and future offending (Gottfredson and Hirschi, 1990). A corporation setup for criminal purposes, for instance, would clearly explain why crime at time one (T_1) would predict crime at time two (T_2). Similarly, because certain industries or mar-kets are more risky and challenging than others (e.g., venture capital compared with automobile manufacturing), they may attract businesses that are less risk averse. This company trait would increase the firm's overall propensity to offend over time. Or, as Apel and Paternoster (this volume, p. 18) suggest, there are assortative mating processes though which individuals "may be attracted to certain industries or firms. For example, those who have a greater tolerance for risky behavior may be attracted to firms or industries that have a history or culture of 'cutting corners' or conducting their business activities right up to and just over the line of illegality. Those who are impulsive or ambitious may be attracted to companies that reward meeting financial goals at the expense of sound business ethics."

Although we do not know the actual causal mechanism linking past with future crime, our plan is to explore whether a firm's prior OSHA violation history predicts its current offending and if this relationship is affected when other variables are included in the analysis. If the relationship is positive and unaffected by the inclusion of other variables, we can conclude that persistent heterogeneity is a better explanation for corporate offending over time. Conversely, if the relationship between priors and current offending is negative or changes in a substantial way (e.g., from positive to negative or from a significant relationship to insignificance), the evidence will favor state dependence over persistence heterogeneity.

Before moving to a description of our research design and data analysis, it is important to define corporate crime. There is no universally agreed-upon definition for corporate crime, but researchers should adopt a definition that is consistent with their research problem (Friedrichs, 2002).

Defining Corporate Crime

The debate surrounding the definition of corporate crime usually focuses on whether it should be an offense- or offender-based definition and whether it should include all illegal behavior or just criminal behavior (Sutherland, 1983, Tappan, 1977, Clinard and Yeager, 1980, Shapiro, 1990). Also in dispute is whether the definition should encompass the behavior of corporations, the individuals employed by them, or both.

For this research, we rely on the definition provided by Clinard and Yeager (1980:16). Corporate crime is "any act committed by corporations that is punished by the state, regardless of whether it is punished under administrative, civil, or criminal law." This definition provides the best fit for our data because it is an offense-based definition that encompasses a wide range of behaviors including, tax and securities violations, intentional pollution of the environment, numerous anticompetitive behaviors (e.g., price fixing), and the focus of this study: knowingly failing to provide a safe work environment. It focuses on acts committed by corporations, which is what OSHA investigates, and it widens the net of illegal behaviors to include any act by corporations punishable by the state rather than simply those acts punishable by criminal law. This is integral to this study since OSHA enforcement is based on administrative, and not criminal, penalties.

In the next section, we provide a brief introduction to OSHA and its inspection procedures, violations, and fines. The data and analytic methods used are described next followed by our results and conclusions.

The Occupational Safety and Health Administration

Since its creation in 1971, the mission of OSHA has been to ensure safe and healthful workplaces in America through enforcement of OSHA regulations. OSHA enforces workplace safety through inspections and fines, and is authorized to conduct workplace inspections and investigations to determine whether employers are complying with standards issued by the agency. Inspections are conducted for four main reasons. First, accidents are reported to OSHA by employers and receive high priority for inspections when they result in death or hospitalization of three or more employees. Complaints and referrals by employees generate inspections and are second in priority to accidents. OSHA policies give all employees the right to request an OSHA inspection if they believe a standard is being violated. Third, OSHA places the next priority on programmed inspections. These general schedule inspections can be aimed at specific high-hazard industries, workplaces, occupations or health substances, or they can be randomly selected. Planned inspections generally result in a bias toward larger corporations being inspected more often than small corporations (Scholz and Gray, 1990, Ruser and Smith, 1990, Weil, 1991, 1996). Finally, inspections can also originate from the need to follow-up a previous inspection that resulted in a citation (U.S. Department of Labor, 2002). These inspections can result in one or more violations, which range in seriousness and carry various fines; these violation types will be discussed more fully in the data and methods section.

OSHA inspections were not stable during the time period of interest for this study. In the early 1990s, the number of annual inspections was fairly constant at roughly 40,000 per year. Amid threatened budget cuts and an emphasis on egregious violations (which monopolized resources), inspections fell steeply in 1995 to 29,000 annually and continued to decline in 1996 until they reached 24,259, the lowest level in OSHA's history. A partial recovery occurred in 1997–2000, bringing inspections up to 36,613 in 2000 (Siskind, 2002). We believe this change in OSHA inspections could have an important effect on corporate offending.

Enforcement activity and company behavior can also be affected by "the spirit of the times" or period under study. For instance, regulators are affected by political considerations, social movements against corporate crime, enforcement budgets, and changes in the law, among other factors (Katz, 1980; Cullen et al., 1987). These same conditions can also influence firm decision making. If top managers believe that regulatory agencies are under attack by government (e.g., the Reagan era) that knowledge may affect their perceptions of sanction likelihood (discovery and prosecution). Thus, empirical relationships may be modified by the time period under consideration.

In their study of risk assessment and OSHA enforcement, Scholz and Gray (1990) found that firms monitor OSHA enforcement activity relevant to their circumstances and respond in ways to decrease injury rates when enforcement risk increases. There is evidence, then, that firms observe OSHA inspection levels in order to make rational choice decisions about safety and health matters. To the extent that firms are aware of fewer inspections, we expect that they would have greater incentive to violate OSHA regulations. As mentioned above, due to budget cuts and policy changes there was considerable variability in OSHA inspections and violations during the time period of interest. The first four years (1993–1996) of this study were marked by a steep decline in overall inspections while the second four years

(1997–2000) were noted for the partial recovery in overall inspections. This knowledge of OSHA budget cuts and policies during the 1990s, leads us to anticipate "period" effects.

Sample and Methodology

The original sample of companies was created as part of a grant funded by the National Institute of Justice to examine corporate environmental compliance. The sampling frame consisted of a universe of public companies within four SIC industry codes (oil, steel, pulp, and paper) in 1995. Economic and other relevant information was collected using Ward's Business Directory, Standard and Poor's Industrial Compustat, and Mergent Online, formerly Financial Information System (FIS) Online. The companies were then located in the Directory of Corporate Affiliations and all plants, mills, and subsidiaries owned by that corporation were identified and added to the database. These companies were linked to EPA facility records. Additional facilities and companies were added using the Toxic Release Inventory database maintained by the EPA and from the Permit Compliance System database.

These procedures produced a list of 104 companies that own and operate facilities subject to OSHA regulations, but upon closer inspection we discovered substantial overlap between firms in the pulp and paper industry. These firm redundancies were eliminated, reducing our list to 80 unique businesses. We were unable to find any economic data for 11 of these companies and another 14 firms did not have economic information for more than 3 years of the study period. Subsequent investigation found that four of these business entities were subsidiaries of other companies in the sample, so violation data for these four subsidiaries were counted as violations by the parent companies. All firms with fewer than 3 years of inspection/ violation data were dropped from the sample. These decision rules resulted in a final sample of 55 companies. Of these 55 companies, 23 operate in the pulp and paper industries, 16 in the oil industry, with another 16 located in the steel industry. It is unfortunate that we could not follow more of the sample, but we did compare firms in our sample with those for which we had limited economic information and violation data. There were no substantial observed differences between the two groups.

Dependent Variables

This study utilizes violation data collected from the OSHA Management Information System (MIS), which is used by the agency to track enforcement and compliance and is available online. OSHA violation data are collected for all violating facilities listed under the firm name in OSHA's Management Information System for the years 1990–2000. Although enforcement actions target the facility, we aggregate up to the company level to tap into the firm economic data. Thus, all citations received by a company's facilities are counted as violations by that company.

Table 1 OSHA violation types

Violation type	Description	Minimum fine	Maximum fine
Other	Related to job safety and health but would not result in death or serious physical harm	$0	$1000
Serious	Substantial probability that death or serious physical harm could result	$1500	$7000
Willful	Intentionally and knowingly committed	$5000	$70000
Repeat	Upon reinspection, similar violation is found	$5000	$70000
Unclassified	Reclassification of willful or repeat violations to purge company of averse public reaction	$5000	$70000

The main dependent variable of interest (OSHA offending) is operationalized as a count of all violations per company per year, including repeat, willful, serious, other, and unclassified offenses (see Table 1 for a definition of each violation type). An examination of the different offense types showed numerous "serious" and "other" offenses, but only a handful of repeat, willful, and unclassified violations. Preliminary analyses revealed that there were too few of the latter to analyze as a separate category of offenses (only 12% of all violations). Therefore, we combine all offenses into one category (Total Offenses) for our analyses.

Prior-Offending Variable

A measure of prior offending was created by lagging 1 year of each company's previous count of total violations. This measure was used to investigate whether there is a positive relationship (as hypothesized) between prior and current offending.

Control Variables

One of the most common explanations for corporate offending is firm level profit squeeze. Companies are thought to engage in illegal behavior during periods of economic hardship as a way to increase profits (e.g., price fixing) or decrease costs (e.g., reduce OSHA-mandated expenditures). Therefore, it is important to control for economic indicators in our analysis. Economic data at the firm level were collected from Mergent Online for the years 1993–2000. Financial indicators of firm's performance include current assets, total assets, total liabilities, total stockholder's equity, total sales, and total net income. Following Clinard and Yeager (1980, p. 128), firm profitability was measured by dividing net income by the total sales of the firm; efficiency by dividing a firm's total sales by its assets; and liquidity ("a firm's working capital") is calculated as the difference between current assets and current liabilities, divided by total corporate assets. These three ratios measure different aspects of firm performance and are commonly used to assess financial performance. Profit and performance measures are lagged by 1 year.

As is the case with all official crime statistics, it is difficult to disentangle whether official offense records actually measure the behavior of criminals or that of enforcement agents. Thus, in this study we improve on previous research by controlling for agency behavior. One unique aspect of OSHA enforcement is that workers can be powerful regulatory actors. Employees may initiate an OSHA inspection by filing a complaint, and, consistent with regulations, workers can accompany the inspector throughout the inspection process. Unionized employees have been shown to take advantage of these rights more than nonunionized workers (Weil, 1991, 1996). In addition, labor unions can use their political power to affect which companies get inspected more often. For instance, research shows that unions lobby OSHA to inspect nonunion firms more heavily (Bartel and Thomas, 1985). Therefore, including information regarding union membership should help us distinguish the inspection behavior of OSHA from the offending behavior of companies in our analysis. While we recognize that this is not a perfect measure of agency activity, we believe that it is a reasonable proxy based on the empirical literature. Data on union membership are collected from the OSHA MIS but are provided at the facility level. We aggregated this measure up to the company level by calculating the percent of the company's inspected facilities that were unionized.

Another control variable included in the analysis is the total number of inspections OSHA conducted of each company each year. Since we use counts of violations rather than rates, this variable is used to control for OSHA's opportunity to find violations at each company. We also include dummy variables for each year of the study to control for unmeasured effects on the dependent variables that occurred during any given year of the study. Variable descriptions, averaged for years 1993–2000, are shown in Table 2.

Table 2 Variable descriptions, averaged for years 1993–2000

Variables	Minimum	Maximum	Mean	Std. deviation
Profitability	−0.38570	1.03644	0.0227631	0.08107160
Efficiency	0.00000	4.29853	1.1477233	0.61398813
Liquidity	−1.00424	0.43745	0.0866198	0.11363177
Union membership	0.00	1.00	0.8264	0.31562
Number of inspections	0.00	22.00	3.0530	3.74193
1993	0.00	1.00	0.1250	0.33109
1994	0.00	1.00	0.1250	0.33109
1995	0.00	1.00	0.1250	0.33109
1996	0.00	1.00	0.1250	0.33109
1997	0.00	1.00	0.1250	0.33109
1998	0.00	1.00	0.1250	0.33109
1999	0.00	1.00	0.1250	0.33109
2000	0.00	1.00	0.1250	0.33109
Total violations	0.00	161.00	9.2651	18.02272

Statistical Procedure

Most corporate crime studies rely on cross-sectional analyses, even those that have time-series data (Clinard and Yeager, 1980; Simpson, 1986; Alexander and Cohen, 1996). Because we have longitudinal data, we take advantage of this fact by utilizing a panel design (specifically, a fixed-effects time series analysis). This design provides a more rigorous test of our research expectations by looking at *within* company changes in offending. The fixed-effects method models unobserved heterogeneity explicitly as a time constant intercept for each company in the sample. The approach absorbs all company-specific factors that are constant over the 8-year time period. Thus, we do not need to control for company size, whether a facility is under federal versus state OSHA policies, or the primary industry in which a company operates (variables commonly used in other cross-sectional studies) because these attributes of the company are relatively constant over time and are accounted for in the fixed-effects model. For our model, we report the overall R^2 and F-tests.

Our review of OSHA history revealed important differences over time with regard to changes in resources, regulatory philosophy, and inspection frequency during the 1990s. Therefore, we split the data into two 4-year periods for analysis and present our results separately by time period. We also begin our empirical investigation with a look at the bivariate correlations for our main variables of interest. The correlation coefficients for all the variables (aggregated across years) are reported in Table 3.

Table 3 Correlation matrix, means, and standard deviations of variables ($N = 335$)[+]

	Total violations	Profitability	Efficiency	Liquidity	Priors	Union	Number of Inspections
Profitability	−0.013	1					
Efficiency	−0.015	−0.027	1				
Liquidity	−0.019	0.083	0.142**	1			
Priors	0.130*	0.043	−0.022	−0.066	1		
Union	0.053	−0.071	−0.085	−0.138**	0.088	1	
Number of inspections	0.504**	−0.007	−0.141**	−0.125*	0.275**	0.127*	1
1993	0.085	0.024	−0.024	0.024	0.043	−0.001	0.052
1994	0.094	0.018	−0.014	0.020	0.077	0.002	0.120*
1995	0.026	0.008	−0.023	0.028	0.086	−0.075	0.021
1996	−0.025	0.123*	0.068	0.064	0.017	−0.013	−0.027
1997	0.033	0.021	0.047	−0.004	−0.035	0.047	−0.027
1998	−0.100*	−0.062	0.017	−0.007	0.024	0.011	−0.091
1999	−0.053	−0.071	−0.072	−0.018	−0.111*	0.007	−0.035
2000	−0.073	−0.041	−0.028	−0.088	−0.063	0.025	−0.020

[+] $p < 0.10$
[*] $p < 0.05$
[**] $p < 0.01$ (Two-tail test)

Results

Bivariate Results

As expected, there is a modest positive and significant ($r = 0.130$, $p < 0.05$) relationship between prior offending and later crime. Prior offending also is related to the number of times a firm is inspected (0.275, $p < 0.05$). Given that priors are lagged by 1 year, this correlation suggests that prior offending increases the risk of subsequent OSHA inspections. The correlation matrix also shows that all of our firm economic measures are inversely, though not significantly, related to total violations. Unionized workplaces are associated with more violations as research by Weil (1991, 1996) would predict, but the correlation is neither strong nor significant. Not surprisingly, the number of inspections is strongly correlated with total violations ($r = 0.504$, $p < 0.01$). We also see that inspections are negatively and significantly related to efficiency ($r = -0.141$, $p < 0.05$) and liquidity ($r = -0.125$, $p < 0.01$). Thus, companies fairing poorly on two out of three profit measures received more inspections than the better performing companies. Also, inspections are positively correlated with union membership ($r = 0.127$, $p < 0.05$), which means that companies with a higher percentage of union members received more inspections. Finally, it appears that offenses are positively correlated with earlier time periods (1993, 1994) but negatively with later years (1998, 1999, 2000).

Correlations among the independent variables are not high, so multicollinearity is not apt to be a serious problem in our multivariate models and they provide some support for our expected relationships. Priors are modestly related to later violations, inspections are positively related to total violations, unionized workplaces are inspected more often than nonunionized firms (indicating a more proactive role for unionized workers), and it appears that there were fewer OSHA inspections later in the decade than earlier. However, the correlations do not measure change *within* companies over time. So these patterns may not hold when we move to our fixed-effects panel analyses. Further, the data are unclear as to whether there may be period effects worth exploring. Therefore, before turning to our multivariate analysis, we ran one-way ANOVA mean differences tests for inspections and violations during the two different time periods. The results (in Table 4) show significant mean differences for inspections and total violations between the two time periods at the 0.05 level thus justifying splitting the sample into separate time periods for further analysis.

Fixed-Effects Results

During both eras of the 1990s (1993–1996 and 1997–2000), prior offending predicted current OSHA violations; however, the effect is opposite of what was hypothesized and counter to the observed relationship in the *cross-sectional correlations*. Controlling for unobserved heterogeneity, companies with prior violations actually

Table 4 One-way ANOVA test for differences between period one (1993–1996) and period two (1997–2000)

Variable		Sum of squares	Degrees of freedom	Mean square	F-test
Number of inspections	Between groups	73.889	1	73.889	5.332*
	Within groups	5722.945	413	13.857	
	Total	5796.834	414		
Total violations	Between groups	2011.259	1	2011.259	6.271*
	Within groups	132463.584	413	320.735	
	Total	134474.843	414		

$+p < 0.10$
$*p < 0.05$
$**p < 0.01$

Table 5 Panel analysis, current offending on priors by era ($N = 150$)

	Total violations 1993–1996 (Std. coef.)	Total violations 1997–2000 (Std. coef.)
Priors	−0.274(0.093)**	−0.315(0.100)**
R^2 Overall	0.01	0.019
F-test	8.68**	9.87**

$**p < 0.01$

have fewer OSHA offenses in subsequent years (see Table 5). Prior violations are negatively and significantly related to OSHA violations. Recall that the panel model absorbs all unmeasured company specific characteristics that are stable over time. Thus, these models provide a much more rigorous test of our research hypotheses than do cross-sectional time series approaches. Indeed, these results imply an inhibition effect associated with OSHA enforcement.[1]

Our results also show that the observed relationship between priors and future offending is relatively unaltered when additional variables are added to the model in a stepwise manner (comparing models from Table 5 to those in Tables 6 and 7).[2] The inhibition effect is somewhat weakened during the 1997–2000 era compared with the earlier time, but the relationship remains significant ($p < 0.05$). Our suggestion that OSHA enforcement has an opprobrious impact on future offending is reinforced by the consistent positive relationship between inspections and violations.

---

[1] The negative relationship might imply a deterrent or rehabilitative effect. It is not possible in this study, with these variables, to determine which explanation is more accurate.

[2] The panel analysis was conducted for each era in two ways. First, all independent variables in the model were analyzed simultaneously. Then, each variable was added to the analysis to see if it changed the relationship between priors and current offending. The step-wise models are reported in Tables 6 and 7, but these results do not differ in any meaningful way from the simultaneous models.

Table 6 Panel fixed-effects model, stepwise ($N = 150$) current OSHA offending on priors with control variables

Era (1993–1996)	Total OSHA violations (Std. coef.)
Priors	−0.267(0.080)**
Profitability	4.104 (5.219)
Efficiency	−11.597 (10.872)
Liquidity	−79.975 (48.567)
Number of inspections	3.855(0.784)**
Union	3.969 (5.374)
1994	Dropped
1995	1.707 (3.326)
1996	1.708 (4.831)
R^2 overall	0.141
F-test	5.86**

$^* p < 0.05$
$^{**} p < 0.01$

Table 7 Panel fixed-effects model, stepwise ($N = 150$) current OSHA offending on priors with control variables

ERA (1997–2000)	Total OSHA violations (Std. coef.)
Priors	−0.303(0.121)*
Profitability	−31.836(24.082)
Efficiency	−5.768(6.537)
Liquidity	28.559 (31.120)
Number of inspections	2.215(0.476)**
Union	−5.512(5.126)
1998	−4.963(2.419)*
1999	−6.765(5.181)
2000	−5.745(3.627)
R^2 overall	0.121
F-test	5.54**

$^* p < 0.05$
$^{**} p < 0.01$

Companies subject to more inspections have higher violation counts across the board (by era).

The fixed-effects time series analysis suggests more of a dynamic relationship between enforcement and offending than a static one. Inspections are linked to violation discovery that lowers the risk of future violations. This interpretation is consistent with a state dependence argument. In fact, other than the positive bivariate correlation between prior offending and total violations (using aggregate cross-sectional measures over time), there is little evidence to support persistent heterogeneity. Moreover, while our analysis of variance (ANOVA) results shown in Table 4 suggest potentially important differences in how OSHA inspected companies might affect firm offending over time, the panel models reveal few substantive differences between the eras. Inspections are a strong predictor of a firm's total offending regardless of era, priors remain negative and significant between models, and few of the other control variables have much of an effect (other than 1998 showing a significant negative effect in the 1997–2000 analysis). Unionized firms have more OSHA offenses than nonunionized companies during the first part of the decade and this effect changes direction in 1997–2000. However, since neither of these relationships is significant, the sign switching between time periods should be interpreted cautiously.

Discussion and Conclusion

Our main goal in this study was to examine the impact of prior violations on future offending using a sample of corporate offenders. Drawing from state dependence and population heterogeneity perspectives developed from studies of traditional offenders, we thought that firms with prior offending records would commit more violations in the future. Data from other corporate offending studies, based on descriptive accounts or cross-sectional analysis, lead us to believe this would be the case. We discovered that a positive relationship did exist between prior and current offending, but this was true *only* if we looked at the relationship using cross-sectional analysis. When the relationship was modeled as a dynamic process within companies, we found that priors had a negative and significant effect on offending over time.

This negative relationship suggests that enforcement (i.e., being caught and "processed") lowers the level of future OSHA offending. Given that our analysis controls for any differences in the number of inspections over time, we conclude that some kind of crime inhibition process is at work (whether that process is deterrence or rehabilitation is unclear). This finding is important as policy makers and regulators struggle to identify and implement the appropriate regulatory mix of punishment and cooperation for corporate offenders. Our results suggest that regulators are doing something right. Change is possible. Importantly, our findings are also consistent with what criminologists have learned about the impact of legal sanctions on crime more generally, i.e., the *risk of discovery* (certainty) lowers reoffending probabilities more than *the severity of the punishment*. Although OSHA has received much criticism for its relatively low fine amounts, the inspection itself (and the potential for getting caught) appears to inhibit recidivism.

We began this research by suggesting that the jury is still out as to whether theories and empirical analysis that inform our understanding of individuals are also applicable to aggregates. We found it relatively easy to fit the theoretical concepts of state dependence and persistent heterogeneity to empirical findings in the corporate crime literature. Similarly, we incorporated a robust panel design, developed from longitudinal and cohort studies of individuals over the life course, to test expected relationships. Our aggregate level analyses did not find evidence that individual traits and characteristics through selection into particular companies positively affect a firm's crime rate over time. Nor did we find that a criminal record necessarily produces a downward spiral into chronic crime. Instead, we found more of a positive dynamic process – one that suggests that individuals within firms are susceptible to regulatory persuasion or punishment. It may be that our aggregate level data simply are unable to identify companies that "attract" high-risk employees or that official counts of violations simply fail to uncover a substantial amount of hidden crime (and thus bias our results). Or, as Gottfredson and Hirschi (1990) have suggested, corporate decision makers will tend on average to rank higher on self-control than the traditional offender. Therefore, while there may be some predisposition to offend, it may be situationally induced and less impulsive (and perhaps linked to a different trait than self-control – such as hubris or desire for control, see Piquero et al., 2005). However, we do know that prior violations increase the risk of future inspections. Thus, companies with risky employees should be more apt to be tracked over time than less criminogenic firms. So our results should be fairly robust to this charge. We will have more confidence in our findings when we can assess individual level data in conjunction with that collected at the firm level.

Finally, we want to note some limitations with our study. First, because our data were not collected specifically for this study, the companies we followed did not change from one primary industry to another over time. It was not possible, therefore, to model industry effects in our fixed-effect panel analysis. Because other studies have found industry characteristics to be even more important than those measured at the firm, our inability to model industry variables is a significant shortcoming that should be addressed in future studies. Finally, perhaps the greatest limitation of this study rests with the small sample size and consequent reduction of statistical power in the analysis. More definitive results will emerge from larger and more diverse samples. However, the sum of our evidence challenges the idea that firms have a stable underlying trait or characteristic that increases criminal propensity.

References

Alexander, C. and Cohen, M. (1996). New Evidence on the Origins of Corporate Crime. *Managerial and Decision Economics*: 17, 421–435.

Arora, S. and Cason, T.N. (1996). Why do Firms Volunteer to Exceed Environmental Regulations? Understanding Participation in EPA's 33/50 Program. *Land Economics*: 72(4), 413–432.

Asch, P. and Seneca, J.J. (1976). Is Collusion Profitable? *The Review of Economics and Statistics*: 58(1), 1–12.

Bartel, A.P. and Thomas, L.G. (1985). Direct and Indirect Effects of Regulation: A New Look at OSHA's Impact. *Journal of Law and Economics*: 28, 1–25.

Baucus, M.S. and Near, J.P. (1991). Can Illegal Corporate Behavior Be Predicted? An Event History Analysis. *Academy of Management Journal*: 34(1), 9–36.

Bouffard, L.A. (2003). Examining the Relationship between Military Service and Criminal Behavior during the Vietnam Era. *Criminology*: 41, 491–510.

Clinard, M.B. and Yeager, P.C. (1980). *Corporate Crime*. New York City: The Free Press.

Cohen, M.A. (1998). Monitoring and enforcement of environmental policy. *International Yearbook of Environmental and Resource Economics*: 3, 1–48.

Cullen, F. T., Maakestad, W.G. and Cavender, G. (1987). Corporate Crime Under Attack: The Ford Pinto Case and Beyond. Cincinnnati, OH: Anderson Publishing Co.

Finney, H.C. and Lesieur, H.R. (1982). A Contingency Theory of Organizational Crime. In Bacharach, S. B. (Ed.) Research in the Sociology of Organizations. Greenwich: JAI Press, Inc. (pp. 255–299).

Friedrichs, D.O. (2002). Occupational Crime, occupational deviance, and workplace crime: Sorting out the difference. *Criminal Justice* 2: 243–256.

Gibbs, C. E. (2006). *Corporate Citizenship, Sanctions, and Environmental Crime*. Doctoral Dissertation, University of Maryland, College Park.

Giordano, P.C., Cernkovich, S.A. and Rudolph J.L. (2002). "Gender, Crime, and Desistance: Toward a Theory of Cognitive Transformation." *American Journal of Sociology* 107:990–1064.

Gottfredson, M.R. and Hirschi, T. (1990). A General Theory of Crime. Stanford University Press.

Harrington, W. (1988). Enforcement Leverage When Penalties are Restricted. *Journal of Public Economics*: 37, 29–53.

Katz, J. (1980). "The Social Movement Against White-Collar Crime," in Egon Bittner and Sheldon Messinger (eds)., Criminology Review Yearbook: 2. Beverly Hills, CA: Sage Publications.

King, A.A. and Lenox, M.J. (2000). Industry Self-Regulation without Sanctions: The Chemical Industry's Responsible Care Program. *Academy of Management Journal*: 43 (4), 698–716.

Laub, J.H. and Sampson, R.J. (2003). Shared Beginnings, Divergent Lives. Cambridge, MA: Harvard Univ. Press.

Nagin, D.S. and Paternoster, R. (1991). On the Relationship of Past to Future Participation in Crime. Criminology 29: 163–198.

Nagin, D.S. and Farrington, D.P. (1992). "The Stability of Criminal Potential from Childhood to Adulthood." Criminology 30:235–260.

Piquero, N. L., Exum, M. L., and Simpson, S. S. (2005). Integrating the Desire-for-Control and Rational Choice in a Corporate Crime Context. *Justice Quarterly,* 22, 252–280.

Ruser, J.W. and Smith, R.S. (1990). Reestimating OSHA's Effects: Have the Data Changed? *The Journal of Human Resources*: 26(2), 212–2.

Sampson, R.J. and Laub, J.H. (1993). Crime in the Making: Pathways and Turning Points Through Life. (Chapters 1–3, skim Chapters 4–5).

Sampson, R.J. and Laub, J.H. editors (2005). Developmental Criminology and Its Discontents: Trajectories of Crime from Childhood to Old Age. The Annals of the American Academy of Political and Social Science, Volume 602, November.

Scholz, J.T. and Gray, W.B. (1990). OSHA Enforcement and Workplace Injuries: A Behavioral Approach to Risk Assessment. *Journal of Risk and Uncertainty*: 3, 283–305.

Shapiro, S.P. (1990). Collaring the Crime, Not the Criminal: Reconsidering the Concept of White-Collar Crime. *American Sociological Review*: 55, 346–365.

Simpson, S.S. (1986). The Decomposition of Antitrust: Testing a Multi-Level, Longitudinal Model of Profit-Squeeze. *American Sociological Review*: 51, 859–875.

Simpson, S.S. (1987). Cycles of Illegality: Antitrust Violations in Corporate America. *Social Forces*: 65(4), 943–963.

Simpson, S.S. (1999) "Corporate Crime." Review Essay. Craig Calhoun and George Ritzer (eds.), *Social Problems*. New York: McGraw-Hill.

Simpson, S.S., Garner, J. and Gibbs, C. (2007), Why Do Corporations Obey Environmental Law? National Institute of Justice. Washington, DC: U.S. Department of Justice.

Simpson, S.S. and Koper, C.S. (1997). The Changing of the Guard: Top Management Characteristics, Organizational Strain, and Antitrust Offending. *Journal of Quantitative Criminology*: 13(4), 373–404.

Siskind, F. (2002). 20th Century OSHA Enforcement Data. Online. Available: www.dol.gov/asp.

Staw, B.M. and Szwajkowski, E. (1975). The Scarcity-Munificence Component of Organizational Environments and the Commission of Illegal Acts. *Administrative Science Quarterly*: 20(3), 345–354.

Sutherland, E. H. (1983) White Collar Crime. New Haven: Yale University Press.

Tappan, P.W. (1977). Who is the Criminal? In Geis, G. and Meier, R.F. (Eds.) White Collar Crime. New York: The Free Press, pp. 272–282.

U.S. Department of Labor (2002) "OSHA Inspections," Occupational Safety and Health Administration Publication 2098, www.osha.gov (accessed November 2003).

Vaughan, D. (1983). Controlling Unlawful Organizational Behavior. Chicago: The University of Chicago, 1983.

Weil, D. (1991). Enforcing OSHA: The Role of Labor Unions. *Industrial Relations*: 30(1), 20–36.

Weil, D. (1996). If OSHA is so bad, why is compliance so good? *RAND Journal of Economics*: 27(3), 618–640.

Weisburd, D., E. Waring and E.F. Chayet (2001). White-Collar Crime and Criminal Careers. New York: Cambridge University Press.

White-Collar Crimes and the Fear of Crime: A Review

Michael Levi

Abstract The focus of this chapter is 'fear of crime' and – within severe data limitations and conceptual controversies – it interrogates the variations in fear of different forms of crime, white-collar and other. It begins by examining the state of 'fear of crime' policy and what we might mean by 'fear' in this sort of arena; goes on to review fears of and concerns about those white-collar crimes that have been researched; and ends with a discussion of their implications for thinking and policy about fear of crime generally and about what we can learn about it from studying fears about white-collar crimes. Despite real fears and even more real consequences of frauds, there is relatively little 'read across' between fear of white-collar and of many other crimes: the embeddedness of fraud in voluntary interactive routines seems to be accompanied by a lack of visceral reactions of 'stranger danger' fear within the general population, but the precise causal mechanisms remain unclear.

Introduction

This book as a whole confronts the extent to which explanations, patterns, and the control of 'crime' are generic or particular, either excluding or including white-collar crimes of various kinds; it also examines what white-collar criminology and mainstream criminology (without white-collar crimes) can learn from each other. The focus of this chapter is 'fear of crime' and – within severe data limitations and conceptual controversies – it interrogates the variations in fear of different forms of crime, white-collar and other. It begins by examining the state of 'fear of crime' policy and what we might mean by 'fear' in this sort of arena; goes on to review fears of and concerns about those white-collar crimes that have been researched; and ends with a discussion of their implications for thinking and policy about fear of crime generally and about what we can learn about it from studying fears about white-collar crimes.

M. Levi (✉)
Cardiff University, Wales, UK
e-mail: levi@cardiff.ac.uk

S.S. Simpson, D. Weisburd (eds.), *The Criminology of White-Collar Crime*,
DOI 10.1007/978-0-387-09502-8_5, © Springer Science+Business Media, LLC 2009

It seems appropriate at the beginning to highlight one important difference between fraud and other property crimes, and one that reduces very significantly the similarities between fear of fraud and fear of other crimes. With the exception of some 'stealth frauds' like the copying of data from credit cards and illegal electronic funds transfers, people hand over their property to fraudsters voluntarily, under the mistaken apprehension that they are transacting business – purchasing or selling goods, saving or investing or merely transferring funds – in their own interests. Thus, trust in business processes, in institutions and/or in people is a key element in fraud in a way that is absent from many burglaries, theft of and from vehicles, robberies, etc. Victim management in face-to-face situations may also be present in nonfraud offenses for gain – for example, robbery – and indeed, Sutherland (1937) stressed the importance of *social* skills in professional thefts in which victims and offenders meet. By no means all fraudsters meet their individual, corporate or governmental victims face to face. However, it is interesting to conduct a thought experiment on what we could do to manage a modern economy and survive old age if we were fearful that every transaction we undertook might be fraudulent.[1]

Fraud is, of course, present in other sorts of relationships that may give rise to crime. These include espionage (commercial or national/ideological), which arguably can be committed by psychologically 'normal' people, and other offences including white-collar ones that may be more likely committed by the sociopathic (Babiak and Hare, 2006). Manipulative behavior can occur not just for financial gain or espionage, but also for direct interpersonal or Internet-based 'grooming' of underage persons, and in adult relationships to gain opportunities for predatory date rape and violence within marriage. In such cases, success requires the initial nonevocation of fear or the disarming of suspicions. Our perception that we have more to fear from 'outsiders' whose aggressive intent or lack of self-control is manifest rather than from people we (physically) know and *seem* 'ok' makes us more vulnerable to manipulators: whether this perception is wholly socialized or is in any degree 'natural' remains moot, but victim cognition and conduct is important in facilitating fraud.

Fraudsters flourish where either we are not fearful of being deceived or the fraudsters have social engineering techniques that deceptively allay our fears. If the above conditions do not apply, then fraud could not happen outside of technological simulation which fools machines (such as the copying of magnetic stripe data and their re-encoding onto blank plastic) or our visual senses, like adulterated or counterfeit 'organic'/prepackaged foodstuffs, or car parts, whose authenticity we cannot judge by mere inspection. Paradoxically, the very fact that some fraudsters persuade us that we have lost money legitimately rather than fraudulently may reduce both 'fear of fraud' and the subjective impact of victimization among those who 'actually' have been defrauded.

---

[1] Or, for that matter, how we would function if we believed that every organization we dealt with might go into liquidation without compensation for creditors, even if it were managed honestly but unfortunately/incompetently.

Two important if all too often latent themes in 'fear of crime' are (i) what do our measures capture? and (ii) why do we judge the probabilities and impacts of different crimes in the way that we do? We can of course simply map out and contrast the levels of concern and fear about different crimes: but though interesting, this is not theoretically satisfying, as we often want to know how and why these arise. Fear, worry, and trust are concepts that are not just free floating or common sense, but are typified in three different theoretical traditions that apply to all offenses involving material or symbolic gain.[2] The Foucaultian tradition, following in the steps of the conflict theorists and also feminism, articulates *fear* and its management in the context of economic and ideological reasons (including the hegemony of masculinity and power). Weberians articulate the conditions under which rational calculation comes to the fore – impersonal organizations and markets – that include notions of personal responsibility and thus inevitably some degree of *worry* about the costs and benefits of different options for action. Durkheimians point to conditions for solidarity which are also the conditions for *trust*, basically the sense that we all belong to the same community: this is a mirage created and exploited by fraudsters, especially within close cultural or faith communities where pyramid selling and fraudulent investment schemes can easily spread. As the sorcerer *Comus* declaims in Milton's masque of that name:

> I, under fair pretence of friendly ends,
> And well-placed words of glozing courtesy,
> Baited with reasons not unplausible,
> Wind me into the easy-hearted man,
> And hug him into snares.

The Correlates of and Influences on Fear of Crimes

Terminology is important. It is appropriate to differentiate generalized concerns and worries from concrete 'fear' – defined in the Oxford English Dictionary online as, *inter alia*, 'The emotion of pain or uneasiness caused by the sense of impending danger, or by the prospect of some possible evil' and 'Apprehensive feeling towards anything regarded as a source of danger, or towards a person regarded as able to inflict injury or punishment' (see further, Gabriel and Greve, 2003; Jackson, 2004).

Fear is not necessarily based wholly on rationality. In a 'rational' world, one might expect (i) fear among nonvictims to be related to expected victimization risks and expected impact (which varies according to emotional/physical 'vulnerability'), and (ii) fear among crime victims to be related to these plus the actual impact of past experiences. (What the multiplier is empirically between expected risk/probability and expected impact, however, remains easier to theorize than to predict consistently.) Although most of us might want to avoid the things that cause

---

[2] I am grateful to Nicholas Dorn for this insight.

us fear, this is not always possible, since they may be embedded in our physical environment and be hard to escape, given our financial means and entitlements (e.g., to travel to safer environments).[3] Research excluding white-collar crimes indicates that personal crime victimization increases the fear of both personal and property crime, whereas property crime victimization only increases the fear of property crime (Rountree 1998). This might be a question applied to white-collar victimization, though this has not been investigated to date. Although their research predates '9/11' – which has transformed the security agenda via enhanced fears – the most serious crimes do not necessarily generate the highest fear (LaGrange and Ferraro 1987; Warr, 2001), perhaps because they are correctly seen to be less frequent.[4] Killias (1990) argues that fear is determined by three factors: *exposure* to nonnegligible risk; the ability to *control* exposure (protective measures and the ability to escape);[5] and the anticipation of how *serious the consequences* might be. However, in his analysis, control is seen in terms of vulnerability to physical attack. Are there any lessons here for fear of fraud? The equivalent in fraud might be the ability to control risks of identity invasion/take-over/card 'skimming'[6] (for individuals) or illicit qualifications/unauthorized financial transfers/credit control evasion for both staff and business functions (for business). One might further refine this to stress the importance of *perceptions* of the ability to control exposure, since we are not here predicting probabilities of victimization but rather fear of it.

We know comparatively little about the relationship between detailed exposure to the risk of victimization and fear, or its connection with lifestyles and routine activities. For example, if senior citizens (or women of whatever age) seldom go

---

[3] Consider the case of people living near toxic waste dumps in North America or in Bhopal, India (caused by environmental crimes); those living in public housing projects with very high crime rates; or in Darfur and other extremely risky spots without the right to travel to other countries. Of course, those embedded in a culture of masculinity and/or with particular sorts of personalities might seek out danger and challenges, so risk avoidance is far from universal. See Coates and Herbert (2008) for a research paper on the impact of testosterone and cortisol on stimulating risk-taking behavior that may lead to white-collar crimes: this may lead to victimization and/or to offending. In a sense, these are the opposite of fear.

[4] One might reasonably question whether levels of physical harm caused by terrorist attacks are higher than those from other violent crimes, from 'ordinary' homicides to health and safety at work violations and dangerous driving causing death: see Levi et al. (2007b). However, levels and forms of media representation and political action are very different. This serves to point up the difference between statistical risk and the phenomenology of 'the risk society'.

[5] Though a better way of thinking about this would be to recast it in terms of *perceptions* of the ability to control exposure, rather than the more objective measure of ability implied by Killias.

[6] 'Skimming' refers to the copying of information from the magnetic stripe on payment cards and their re-encoding onto other cards of varying degrees of realism, depending on the context in which they are used. In many parts of the world (especially Europe), skimming of domestic cards for domestic use is made pointless, since the cards work only when the microchip on the cards is activated by the correct PIN. In the United States, however, the economics of the card industry is different and the copying of magnetic stripe data on US-issued cards anywhere in the world is therefore profitable.

out much at night because of fear of crime (or so they say), it is not surprising that they are not mugged or raped by strangers very often; by contrast, young men who go out nightly are exposed to risk for much longer and much more frequently than their mere numbers would suggest. What are the analogies in the world of fraud? If people do not use the Internet (whether because of fear of fraud or anxiety about using technology), no 'phishermen'[7] can inveigle their online banking passwords, though they then cannot avail themselves of facilities and reduced prices that increasingly one can get only through the net. The importance of the electronic web to consumer and investment fraud can be overstated: avoiding it altogether still may not protect people from telemarketers' phone calls; from pyramid-selling webs whose rewards are based on recruiting friends into schemes; from local religious authority figures offering them 'unbeatable' returns on investments; from the regular impressive-looking letters informing them they have won the Spanish or some other lottery prize (even though they have never entered for it); or from the unwanted 'preapproved' personalized credit card offers that come through the mail but may not be shredded by recipients,[8] and thus may provide 'identity fraudsters' with good personal information that they can use for other credit applications, even if they do not make use of the offer directly.

Technically, a review of the link between fear and victimization might want to take into account the frequency of exposure to potential crime events rather than mere numbers per 100,000 population category: but such refined data are seldom available, for fraud or for any other offenses (and would be particularly difficult with cyber threats taken as an aggregate).[9] Paradoxically, as with people in high-crime areas who may be less fearful and even less often victimized than are strangers in those locations because they 'know their area,' frequent Internet users logically should be less susceptible to victimization from 'phishing' and other harmful e-mails, since if they get so many e-mails from banks where they do *not* hold accounts, they should be equally skeptical (fearful?) of those that appear to come from their bank. They also might actually read *and absorb* the warnings on their banks' websites that the bank *never* asks people online for passwords or confidential personal details. Such warnings are partly circumvented nowadays by fraudsters who have moved to 'vishing': they seek to allay suspicions by telling potential victims not to fill in security details online but rather to telephone the bank security department at a particular number, which happens to be their own fake bank telephone number rather than

---

[7] 'Phishing' means electronically simulating a legitimate business or government actor in order to persuade people to give their personal financial or other information. A common example is the e-mails that many of us receive telling us to update our security for a variety of online banks (at almost all of which we do not have accounts) or eBay.

[8] If they *are* responded to, this may contribute to the debt mountains, which have contributed to the subprime-related panics that led to major interest rate interventions by central banks in the United States and Europe, increasing 'moral hazard' by reducing the risks to imprudent lenders and borrowers alike.

[9] Imagine, for instance, that one were to look at payment card fraud risks per total number of times that cards were used, or even as a ratio of numbers of payment cards, rather than numbers of cardholders.

that of the target's actual bank. However, we know that some people are repeat victims of such scams (OFT, 2006; Titus and Gover, 2001), and that some citizens (disproportionately, senior ones) send a number of checks to fraudulent firms or throw good money after bad, like desperate gamblers trying to recoup their losses. Unlike the victims of repeat domestic violence or burglary, who may find it difficult to move and reduce their risks, these multiple fraud victims could say no and avoid victimization, but they are insufficiently fearful and/or have some personality that makes them vulnerable to repeat victimization.

To the extent that fear relates to perceptions of inability to control events, we might seek to differentiate fraud fears along those lines. Titus and Gover (2001: 135) helpfully divide personal frauds into those involving:

- 'No cooperation: A woman discovers in her monthly credit card statement that she has been the victim of an identity fraud, having done nothing to facilitate the crime.
- Some cooperation: A man responds to a "cold" phone call and contributes to a charity without investigating and learning that it was phony.
- Considerable cooperation: Having responded to an ad for a fabulous investment opportunity and been victimized in a Ponzi scam, a man is burned again in a recovery scam. Over a period of years, a woman loses many thousands of dollars in a series of one-in-five scams but continues to participate.'

The first may lead people to try to control risk by subscribing to account monitoring services; the second remains undetected and has a neutral effect unless the authorities learn about it from other sources and inform donors; the third may lead to the fearful avoiding victimization, provided they correctly identify the warning signs.[10] Australian research has found that older people who interact with their community feel safer than those who are isolated. Simply providing written information without social contact can sometimes increase levels of fear (James et al. 2003), but elderly consumers of fraud advice would need to be assured that those who are providing the information are acting legitimately.

Fear and the Media

An important link in the chain between actual risks of different crimes and fears thereof is the role of the media. Wall (2008) has examined the way that the media have shaped our images of 'cybercrimes.' However, the link between fear and exposure to crime stories is not clear cut. Otherwise, given the significant frequency with which fraud and corruption cases are reported in the 'quality' newspapers in the United Kingdom and (though researched less systematically) in the United States

---

[10] They may, of course, become ultracautious and see many 'false positive' indicators, in which case both they and the economy may suffer financially; on an alternative welfare model, they may 'buy local,' stimulating the local economy and arguably create more sense of community, benefiting them and others in their area.

(Levi, 2006, 2008), one might have expected fear of fraud to be quite high.[11] Nor is the reporting of white-collar crimes always unsensational. Ironically, though liberal UK media sometimes are very critical of some estimates of the terrorist threat, there seems to be little skepticism about high and rising 'cost of fraud' or 'cost of money laundering' figures; likewise with 'data' on some 'organized crimes' such as people trafficking. The extent to which such data increase people's (including business executives') fear of such crimes remains obscure, however. The link between risk and the 'actual' incidence/ prevalence of crime is also often obscured: thus a stolen business laptop with thousands or millions of people's financial or other personal data on it becomes massive 'identity theft,' and this in turn becomes 'identity fraud,' despite the often proportionately modest criminal usage of such data (personal interviews with industry and police). Parallels outside white-collar crimes would be the interchangeability in the media of 'Internet pornography' and 'pedophilia.'[12] These are part of a wider theme of the politics of fear (Gardner, 2008).

Skogan (1995) argued that the political genesis of 'fear of crime' during the late 1960s was stimulated by a 'fear of blacks,' fear of crime being an indirect way of expressing racial worries (see also, for the United Kingdom, Goodey, 1998, 2005). We will discuss later whether there are any parallels in the 'fear of white-collar crime' (or, since that category is itself highly diverse, of 'white-collar *crimes*'). However, illegal immigration has been an important theme in the coverage of 'organized crime' in the British media, and globally, Nigerians (and, in Francophone countries, Congolese) have come to 'stand for' fraud threats in the way that Jews once did in the European (and particularly Germanic) mindset.[13] Nevertheless, outside of Watergate

---

[11] An unexamined aspect of this issue is whether media stories principally tell us about 'just deserts' having been obtained or whether their motif is rather about crime existing/growing and being uncontained or unresolved. The former might be less fear inducing than the latter, though whether the dramaturgy and politics of 'law and order' ever allow that result is less clear. To the extent that – not least for defamation risk reasons – white-collar crime reporting takes place more after an arrest/raid/regulatory action has taken place than do events like violent assaults, then one might expect a larger proportion of frauds to be in the 'just deserts' category.

[12] To the extent that underage sexual portrayals involve real children and not artificial computer graphics, there is an undeniable connection between 'kiddie porn' and actual pedophilia: but given their numbers, it seems implausible that all such porn consumers directly commit offenses against underage persons. *A fortiori*, with adult sex fantasists.

[13] There is an older sociological 'fear of fraud' debate, exemplified in the work of those such as Ichheiser (1944) who were understandably absorbed by what underlay the social psychology of anti-Semitism. He argued that

"Gangsters" and "swindlers" may be considered. . .as two *personified symbols* of . . .fundamental forms of danger in social life. . . . Especially, in times like our own, characterized by deep economic insecurities, ideological confusion, fluidity and impenetrability of intricate social processes, by propaganda, advertising, adulteration of goods, the man in the street feels himself far more deeply threatened by those rather "invisible" social dangers than by overt coercion and violence. And he is getting more and more suspicious that those invisible processes by which he is threatened are – intentionally, and for someone's advantage, manipulated by some kind of swindlers "behind the scenes." Consequently the swindler. . .*becomes the main symbol of the predominant fear.*

(now around four decades old), very few frauds or other 'white-collar' crimes constitute 'signal crimes' which evoke and symbolize wider problems in society, for example, whereby seemingly 'low-level' crimes such as graffiti are amplified into indicators of a wider lack of community spirit or social decay (Innes, 2004).

Politicians are distressed by the lack of impact of objective crime reduction on public fears or satisfaction with their crime-fighting performance, but it would be political suicide to suggest explicitly that voters are 'irrational.' Whereas risk management has become a routine activity of all business and public sector discourses (including the police, when allocating their own scarce resources), politicians seem locked into a model in which they cannot speak of or spell out an 'acceptable level of crime' – at least for any type of crime that the public/media care about – for fear of being portrayed as callous. This is doubtless one reason for the popularity of terms like 'zero tolerance policing' which have been transmitted across the Atlantic, despite limited evidence for their impact on crime levels (Jones and Newburn, 2006a, 2006b). When fear itself becomes defined as a significant cost of crime, and especially when media coverage is treated as a proxy for public sentiments, this has serious consequences for public policy and for cost-benefit analysis of crime control measures (for which, see Cohen, 2005). It is likely that people are more afraid of being stabbed or shot in the streets of London or Los Angeles than they are of dying as a result of industrial accidents precipitated by unsafe management practices, even though the statistical risks of death via the latter (and of course the risks of death on the roads by careless or dangerous driving) are higher: but despite the best efforts of 'corporate safety crime' and 'road safety' moral entrepreneurs, both media coverage and public fears do not reflect these differential rates. The implications of this for financial white-collar crimes of different kinds will be examined conceptually, though data are sparse.

Interestingly, although there are an increasing number of studies estimating (and, more often, wildly guesstimating) the direct economic costs of fraud, especially to business (see Levi et al., 2007a, and Levi, 2008, for a review), and these studies get well publicized via the efforts of PR agencies acting for the survey firms, frauds other than 'identity frauds' have been largely bypassed in the 'fear of crime' debate. This bypassing occurs both in developed and developing countries (e.g., in the International Crime Victimization Surveys, henceforth ICVS, and its regional offshoots), though the fact that the ICVS ask about consumer fraud and corruption – issues usually left out of developed country studies – reflects the importance of those crimes to people's consciousness in developing countries. Another way of looking at the absolute and relative salience of corruption to concern about 'crime' is the role that anticorruption campaigns play in elections, not just in developing countries but also in some EU countries like Poland.[14] But these appear to reflect anger at corruption more than they do fear of it.

---

[14] There is a broader debate we might have about the ambiguity of attitudes to corruption in places such as Italy and Louisiana. Perhaps in their mindsets, the fear of idle, rule-bound and incompetent bureaucracy unable to get anything done and of consequent economic decline is even greater than the concern about corruption? However, this is too large a topic for this essay.

Some fears – the fear of assault, for example – arguably are 'natural,' but even in those cases, perceptions of the incidence, prevalence, and even the effects of particular harms may be based on misinformation (Gardner, 2008) or even disinformation (i.e., the deliberate production of misleading information). The economic interests of individual and commercial security businesses cause them to amplify risks and/or present them in a sensational and geographically undifferentiated way, for example, 'there is one burglary every 40 seconds.' In other cases, perceptions of harm are shaped by media treatment, and these are affected by the way that the conduct is portrayed, either as events or in the aftermath of criminal or other official actions. Visibility, bureaucratic and commercial interests, ideology, and media production values and routines all play their part in media representations of both white-collar and other crimes. One of the principal differences – which also may affect and reflect the visceral emotions of fear – is that except for pure celebrity reportage, most white-collar crimes require more space and time for the story to be told and more concentration by readers and viewers to follow these stories than do other forms of crime; and that space is in very short supply in tabloid newspapers and television news.[15]

Levi (2006, 2008) notes that media coverage of financial frauds focuses on celebrity people and corporations (as offenders, victims and/or negligent storers of our personal data), 'widows and orphans' frauds against the especially vulnerable, cases involving dramatic harms or activities such as disappearance/discovery, and hi-tech crimes ('preferably' committed by juveniles or 'the Russian Mafiya'). All of these forms of offending do exist, but their salience is not as great among actual fraud risks as their media representation would suggest. The growing money and consumer sections of newspapers and radio/television programs frequently contain warnings about more ordinary scams such as Nigerian 'advance fee' and telemarketing ones. However the *effects* of media representations are often neglected by academics in favor of analyses of how the media portrayal is constructed and what economic interests it serves. Ditton et al. (2004) note that although there is an intuitively attractive connection between (a) media reports and dramatizations of crime and (b) peoples' fear of crime, an actual relationship between media and fear has been discovered surprisingly infrequently; their mixed methods study indicated that respondents' perceptions and interpretations of the media are more important than the frequency of media consumption and/or any objective characteristics of media material. In the context of white-collar crimes, this is likely to be the case also, to the extent that the public are exposed at all to particular types of white-collar crime.

Fear of Fraud Among Individuals – Some Evidence

What do we know about 'fear of fraud' among individuals? Unfortunately, the evidence is sparse on most forms of white-collar crime and in most countries. Fear of

---

[15] One could draw here some distinctions here about corporate health and safety crimes, where the physical events can be dramatically independent of the 'who is criminally responsible for this, if anyone?' question.

fraud (and, for that matter, actual fraud victimization) has until recently not been included in conventional criminological surveys in the United States, though the specialist and much smaller sample surveys by the National White-Collar Crime Center include questions on it, as do e-crime and the Pew Internet and American Lifestyles (2006, 2007) surveys. The Pew (2006) survey discusses senior citizens' use of and vulnerability to the Internet, while the Pew (2007) report discusses the nuanced reactions to spam: 'Spam has not become a significant deterrent to the use of email, as some observers speculated it might...But... 55% of email users say they have lost trust in email because of spam.' It is not clear what the implications are of loss of trust in this context, other than as an uncosted emotional impact. The US National Crime Victimization Survey (Baum, 2006, 2007) now contains some interesting questions on the economic and practical consequences of ID theft (very broadly defined), but does not address the psychological effects or the effects on future commercial actions, nor fear as commonly understood.

Krone and Johnson (2007) have usefully examined Australian perceptions of the riskiness of Internet shopping: two thirds of people with Internet access who had not used it to make purchases cited (in)security of providing credit card details over the net as the reason.[16] For reasons of space, the consumer fraud questions asked in the International Crime Victimisation Surveys do not explore the fear dimension at all. Likewise, in an already burdensome questionnaire, the questions asked in the British Crime Survey (BCS) since 2002 (see the valuable study of fear of payment card fraud by Semmens, 2003) are too few to explore the more subtle dimensions of fear; and it is symbolic for the marginalization of fraud that 'mainstream' Home Office publications regarding worry about crime have not discussed the data on card crime, leaving the latter to specialist reports on fraud and technology crimes.[17] Indeed, frauds against individuals and the fear thereof appear to have been 'technologized,' unconsciously neglecting the risks and concerns posed by more traditional forms of deception. Remote transactions are not the exclusive preserve of the Net; nor is the Net the only significant plausible source of anxiety about fraud. Thus, although their careful analysis shows that offline payment card victimization – though still much larger in total losses – has been falling as online purchases have been rising, Krone and Johnson (2007) fail to make the point that nearly all the Australian

---

[16] Of those who had used the net to buy things, 2% claimed more money had been taken than authorized; 3% that goods/services paid for were not received; and – more ambiguously – 4% that goods were not as advertised, in quality or quantity.

[17] The questions are

1. As far as you know, including anything we have already talked about, since the first of January xxxx has anyone used your credit card or bank card, or your card details, such as your PIN, to buy things or withdraw cash without your permission?

   Yes No

2. How worried are you about someone using your credit card or bank card details, such as your PIN, to buy things or withdraw cash without your permission?

   Very/fairly/not very/not at all worried/don't use cards

Internet crimes could have happened if the goods or services had been paid for by mail/telephone order rather than over the net.[18]

As for the perspectives of cardholders and the general public, Semmens' (2003) analysis of BCS data found that whilst worry about card fraud had many similarities with the other crimes at a descriptive level, it had a weak association with the other worries. Indeed those who are worried about personal crime are more likely to be worried about several crimes, or even crime generally. In contrast, those who are worried about property crime are less likely to have multiple worries. Worry about card fraud is generally not strongly associated with other worries but does have stronger associations with worry about mugging and attack. Worry about card fraud has the weakest total association with other worries. This suggests that worry about card fraud is quite independent from the other worries and may have different causes and correlates.

The 2002–2003 BCS (Allen et al., 2005) asked card users in England and Wales how worried they were about someone misusing their card or their card details in order to buy items or withdraw cash without their permission:

- Half (48%) of card users indicated a level of worry, with 15% stating that they were very worried and a further third (33%) fairly worried.
- A slightly higher proportion of women card users were worried than men, with 49% saying they were very or fairly worried compared to 46%.
- The proportion worried was lowest in the youngest (from 16 to 25) and oldest age groups (66 or over), compared to middle age groups (from 26 to 65).
- Black and Asian respondents were more likely than White respondents to worry about card fraud (61%, 67%, and 47% respectively).
- Levels of worry were similar regardless of education or social class.
- Those living in noncouncil areas were significantly more likely be very or fairly worried than were those living in council areas.
- Those who had been a victim in the past 12 months were significantly more likely than those users who had not been to be very or fairly worried about being victimized (68% and 47%, respectively). It appears that victimization may well serve to increase levels of anxiety, perhaps by exposing victims to the potential consequences of the crime.

People who used their payment card were asked whether they were worried about potential misuse of their cards or bank details in particular settings. The situation that caused most worry was buying goods over the Internet, with 54% of people who had used their card on the Internet being very or fairly worried about misuse in that context. The proportion of users of each of the other services had relatively similar worry levels, at just under half.

---

[18] Though readers should note that online purchasing has stimulated the growth of remote purchases, way beyond what would have happened if sales could occur only by phone or mail order after viewing products in catalogs or online.

In the 2003–2004 BCS (Wilson et al., 2006), over half (54%) of adults who had used the Internet said they had used a payment card in order to buy goods or services over it. This is a significant increase from 49% in the 2002/03 survey and may be expected to rise much further in future, as new generations appear who become accustomed to Internet purchases. Among Internet users who had *not* bought goods or services over the Internet, the most common reason given for not doing so was concern about security (72%); or worry about entering personal details online (37%). Despite reservations expressed earlier about the validity of identifying crime as the reason for avoiding activities, these seem grounded enough to be plausible. The noncrime issue of preferring to see the actual product before purchasing (22%) was another common concern. Those who did shop online were asked what precautions they took to secure their details on the Internet. The most popular precaution was to look for a secure site to buy from (73% mentioned this). Over a half said they only used well-known sites or companies (53% and 56% respectively) – though (not raised in the survey) the rise in 'pharming' and 'phishing'[19] with simulated websites might nullify this precaution as an effective prevention measure or even stimulate fraud by giving false reassurance. Unfortunately, there are no parallel findings for the United States or other jurisdictions.

According to the UK Financial Services Authority (FSA 2007)'s Financial Risk Outlook 2006, half of active Internet users were 'extremely' or 'very' concerned about the potential fraud risk of making an online transaction. Consumers who conduct their banking online are taking steps to protect themselves against fraud, by installing security software on their PC, but over a quarter do not know when they last updated their software or update it infrequently. Five percent of online bankers have no security software installed on their PC at all. The most common reasons cited are that it is too expensive, that they do not need it or they do not understand what it is. Many banks' terms and conditions reflect the voluntary UK Banking Code, whose current 2005 edition tells customers to use up-to-date antivirus and spyware software and a personal firewall (and some banks send antivirus software as well as other antifraud equipment free to their online banking customers). But the FSA found that nearly all users (95%) surveyed believe that at least some security responsibility should lie with the bank, while 45% believe banks should take sole responsibility (though there is no indication in the questions or answers about how the banks might do that).

Some intriguing data that may repay further critical exploration are contained in the survey of almost 1,400 people 18 or over reported by UK government campaign Get Safe Online (GSOL, 2006). To the question, 'Which of the following do you feel

---

[19] 'Pharming' is a hacker's attack aiming to redirect a website's traffic to another, bogus website. It can be conducted either by changing the host's file on a victim's computer or by exploitation of a vulnerability in DNS server software. DNS servers are computers that resolve Internet names into their real addresses. 'Phishing' is a social engineering virtual attack to obtain user names and passwords that enable access to personal data.

most at risk from in your everyday life?'[20] Twenty-one percent (compared with 17% the previous year) stated that they felt most at risk from Internet crime, compared to 16% from burglary and 11% from mugging. For 27% (compared with an extraordinary 40% in 2005), bank card fraud was the crime they stated they felt most at risk from. Fifty-two percent of Internet users do their banking online, nearly a third (32%) pay their utility bills online and almost a quarter (23%) buy their groceries online. Half the public admitted to gaps in their knowledge about staying safe, and 76% of respondents felt that other people should have responsibility for their online safety. There is a significant portion of the population, though, whose fear of security breaches stops them conducting sensitive transactions online. Twenty-four percent of survey respondents had been deterred from online banking; 21% will not perform any financial management tasks online; 18% refuse to shop online and 17% will not use the Internet at all due to security fears (or so they respond). Though they may not add up to a very significant proportion of the total spend, the latter data are examples of fears that have economic consequences for financial institutions (and, perhaps, for the individuals themselves if they have to pay more for goods by purchasing only offline). However, the former do not measure fear at all, nor harm, but rather perceptions of riskiness. Nevertheless, the notion of fear of Internet crime does make sense, and this is a category that some people themselves use when describing their Internet-avoiding behavior.

Apart from surveys and interview based studies, one approach – the 'willingness to pay' model – might be to examine what products and services people are prepared to pay for in order to try to safeguard themselves or reduce (re)victimization. But quite apart from issues of affordability that hit the poor more heavily than the rich (who anyway can afford to self-insure), how do people make rational decisions based on knowledge rather than on rough guesses or even on disinformation by those seeking to make money from their fears? Direct retelling of actual victimization experiences can occur primarily only at a local level or through occupational networks (and then one must appreciate that many frauds against self and friends/colleagues are unknown to victims, since there are apparently innocent explanations for loss which fraudsters have deceived them into believing). Otherwise the media are an important source, but there are limits to the outreach of the regular warnings in both tabloid and broadsheet financial pages and on UK radio programs, and to the impact of such warnings on behavior. The UK Financial Services Authority and the Office of Fair Trading (and their Australian equivalents) have begun to follow US Federal agencies in communicating risk messages to investors in firms not covered by the Compensation Schemes (because the firms are not officially regulated). But the

---

[20] Unfortunately, these data were highlighted in box texts in the report and in the media coverage which, as so often, was drawn solely from the press release, as "People are more worried about criminals breaking in through their computer than they are about burglars breaking through their doors and windows" and "People fear internet crime more than burglary, mugging and car theft." This is typical of the constant elision between concern, fear, risk, and worry in the popular debate about crime. Analytically, it is far from clear that people would exclude Internet fraud when answering questions about bank card fraud.

extent to which these risk messages are read or taken notice of remains unassessed, at least publicly.

Nils Christie (2000) has drawn our attention to the role of the private sector, especially in North America, as a stimulator for profit of fear of street and household crime and of punitiveness: *inter alia*, these lead individuals and governments to purchase crime prevention technology, private policing and private prisons. In the twenty-first century, 'identity fraud' (often described as 'theft,' though the identity itself is mostly duplication or 'borrowing' rather than a pure zero-sum game) has become a particularly popular theme in the electronic and print media; in spite of guarantees by many card issuers to consumers against suffering losses from fraud when making Internet purchases, it appears to evoke significant levels of fear. This is enhanced by media coverage whenever large quantities of data are hacked or merely lost, as one may see from cases involving millions of people's data from the Veterans Administration (US, in 2006), TK Maxx (US and UK, in 2007), and HM Revenue & Customs (which in late 2007 lost in the normal mail unencrypted CDs containing the financial details of one third of the UK population!): in none of these cases was a significant proportion of the 'stolen' data *actually* used to commit fraud (interviews with the author), but the media/political row and the social anxiety continued notwithstanding. 'Awareness campaigns' are popular with vendors not just of physical security such as shredders – which have enjoyed significant rises in sales following publicity – but also of paid-for services such as account monitoring. There are annual 'Identity Theft' awareness weeks in the United Kingdom 'badged' by the Home Office but largely paid for by the industry, with local media events around the country. In addition to existing 'card fraud protection' bodies, which guaranteed compensation for card fraud losses that banks in the United Kingdom and United States are required to compensate anyway, paid-for services include 'fraud alerts' with credit reference agencies such as Experian and Equifax (plus Callcredit in the United Kingdom and TransUnion in the United States) that may tell you if someone has applied for credit in your name (but not, apparently, if they have used your US Social Security number with a different name); or indeed programs that hide one's IP address when going online.[21] There has indeed been criticism that suggests that like many forms of 'protection,' this constitutes secondary victimization by having people pay again for a service that offers very little more than what they could get for free or at best a partial, one-credit bureau service, compared with newer forms of ID fraud prevention and detection, some of which do limited credit monitoring but which keep an eye on other ID fraud windows by trawling Internet chat rooms and directories and by sifting through online public records for signs

---

[21] One such product, Zone Alarm's Anonymous Surfing, claims that it "protects you and your family from online identity theft by keeping your IP address (and your identity) private. It also protects you from visiting phishing, pharming, or spyware sites by displaying a warning notification of the hidden dangers ahead." Either this is an overstatement or it protects cybercriminals as well as potential victims. Many other products such as Internet Explorer 7 now offer phishing filters as defaults, in response both to consumer anxieties and objective risks: though objective risks by themselves do not create a market.

of Social Security number fraud, stolen credit card account trafficking, and other types of ID theft (http://www.consumerreports.org/cro/money/credit-loan/costly-credit-monitoring-services-offer-limited-fraud-protection-4-07/overview/0704_costly-credit-monitoring-services-offer-limited-fraud-protection_ov.htm?resultPage Index=1&resultIndex=1&searchTerm=credit%20monitoring). Despite these limitations, Javelin Research and Consultancy estimates that some 24 million US consumers have paid $60–180 a year for these 'protection' services. (The number subscribing to equivalent services in the United Kingdom is unknown but also substantial: in addition, there are subscribers to Card Protection Programs which offer one-stop card cancellation services for cardholders plus largely unnecessary insurance against card fraud.) From November 1, 2007, all three major credit bureaus have made this protection available to all consumers in these states within the USA, even if they have not had their identities stolen.

In one-third of the several million cases of identity theft each year in the United States, 'stolen' (or, more accurately, illegally borrowed/duplicated) personal information like Social Security numbers are used to open new accounts in their victim's name. A security freeze gives consumers the choice to lock access to their credit file against anyone trying to open up a new account or to get new credit in their name. When a security freeze is in place at all three major credit bureaus, a would-be identity thief cannot open a new account because the potential creditor or seller of services will not be able to check the credit file. When the rightful consumer is applying for credit, he or she can lift the freeze temporarily using a PIN, so that legitimate applications for credit or services can be processed. For the 11 American states currently without security freeze laws, Experian, Equifax, and TransUnion will provide the freeze at no charge to identity theft victims and charge nonvictims $10 to initiate the freeze and $10 to lift it temporarily or remove it altogether (http://www.consumersunion.org/pub/core_financial_services/005085.html). A critical article in the New York Times (17 November 2007) asks the question why such freezes have taken so long and are so hard to implement: the answer surely lies in the profitability of these protection services, though one should add that the service provision is not cost free to the providers. Legislation mandating free security freezing thus costs the credit bureau owners something (though far less than the fees currently charged for implementing them).

These services are not offered free to British consumers, except occasionally in the aftermath of major private sector data losses or as part of some credit products. For an administration fee of £14.10 ($28) the UK not-for-profit fraud prevention service CIFAS offers a service, currently provided on their behalf by Equifax, to protect the name and address from identity fraud. People may contact Equifax, and request 'Protective Registration.' A CIFAS warning will then be placed against their address marked Category '0' which indicates the individual has been recorded on the CIFAS database at their own request for their protection. CIFAS members when undertaking a search against this address will see 'CIFAS-DO NOT REJECT-REFER FOR VALIDATION,' whatever name they search for. They will then contact Equifax to establish the reason for the entry. As a result of the entry CIFAS members will verify further the identity of applicants, and in some cases request from them further proof of identification, and this may mean the citizens personally experience delays while their credentials are fully checked out. If people want to ensure the identity of a deceased person is not used by a fraudster to obtain credit or other products and services, a CIFAS Protective Registration may be placed by a relative or executor against the deceased person's address. Clearly the fact that people request this service and pay for it implies that they are afraid of fraud and the stress that resolving it generates.

Fear of crime and judgments about its probability and consequences might plausibly be viewed from the perspective of different participants, who may have very different levels of knowledge and experience, and may directly (as with bank financial crime directors) or indirectly (as contributors to Trusted Third Party industry-wide data bodies like CIFAS in the United Kingdom or to the liquidators/trustees of pyramid/securities fraud schemes) share their experiences to pool data as closed user groups (see Levi and Pithouse, forthcoming). In some cases, like CIFAS and the Insurance Fraud Bureau (in the United Kingdom), this fraud data sharing has a primarily preventative function, managing business risks collectively; in others, it serves less of a future crime-proofing function and more as a venue for communicating victim experiences and obtaining a share, however modest, in the payout from the assets of the defaulting firm or individual. There are also differences in offender and victim perspectives. As Semmens (2003: Chapter 7) acutely observes:

> The perpetrator of this kind of crime is simply using information, raw data, in the course of his/her criminal activities. By assuming control of information which does not 'belong' to him/her, s/he takes advantage of the pure instrumental value of the information. In contrast, the victim who loses control of the information attaches both instrumental and intrinsic value to that information and this impacts on the victim's identity. In short, the criminal act is simply the 'theft of identifying information' but the victim suffers 'theft of identity'.

The literature on fear of crime, especially violent crime, tends to focus upon the issue of 'stranger danger' and though violence-against-women analysts stress the analytical misguidedness of this, the general message that crime comes from 'without' remains strong and universal in different national research studies. Cross-national insights into fear of crime are underdeveloped in the literature. The rhetoric of globalization tends to underplay variations (Grabosky, this volume) – a point seldom made in television documentary or news programs that homogenize experiences or even in the criminological literature. However, when examining 'fear and risk of fraud' (and other crimes) comparatively, one should take into account national and regional differences in susceptibility, for example

- to have identities 'stolen' – for example, the far easier availability of identifiers such as Social Security numbers and criminal records in the United States compared with the United Kingdom;
- the clustering of people susceptible to fraud – for example, in 'gated communities' or favored retirement states such as Florida, which can be penetrated:

    (a) by remote telemarketers (Shover et al., 2003); or

(b) by face-to-face local or even national con artists pretending to be deeply religious people offering select chances to people of 'their' group. They, in a sense, succeed by disarming fears of strangers and expectations that fraud is committed by people who are 'not like us.' In faith communities, marketing is often 'viral' and all the more compelling because of this. It seems plausible that the willingness of respected people in our own communities to 'invest' acts as a trigger for others to follow, disarming fears and suspicions.

To some extent, these national and regional differences are becoming reduced via the use of social networking sites such as Facebook, MySpace, and Bebo. Data protection measures vary over time, but some such networking sites have data vulnerabilities that can be exploited by fraudsters and other criminals. As in many other areas, for example risks of violent victimization outside the home, young people may engage in risk-taking behavior and therefore, arguably, 'fail' to fear enough to protect themselves, for example, by putting online photographs and personal identifiers that can be used to build up composite pictures of themselves that make identity cloning easier. (Though they may also risk less because they appreciate that commonly used industry identifiers such as dates of birth and mother's maiden name are inherently weak and will be compromised.) However unsurprisingly, the networking firms themselves (including more business-oriented ones such as 'Linked-in') do not advertise their vulnerabilities, and whether risk knowledge reaches the kind of media that users see or hear *and take note of* remains uncertain.

Business and Fear of Crime

Fear is not a property one can readily impute to inanimate objects, so in strict terms, only business executives and their staff – not businesses themselves – can fear crime or worry about it. Several features of late modernity – in particular the requirements on financial services firms and professionals to report 'significant' frauds to financial services regulators and 'suspicious activities' (SARs) to Financial Intelligence Units (like FinCEN in the United States and the Serious Organized Crime Agency in the United Kingdom) – make total suppression of information about financial crimes practically more difficult and legally riskier than in the past. There is also more collaborative 'benchmarking' of fraud and money-laundering risks, though most such activities remain private and cooperation against fraud may be less common in countries such as the United States, where there is fear of regulatory/prosecutorial action for 'anticompetitive' behavior. Finally, one important difference between financial crimes and more conventional crimes is that the former break the normal *necessary* link of geographic propinquity between victim and offender that is logically necessary for involuntary asportation. Acts of corruption, fraud, product counterfeiting, and even consumer/worker safety violations may take place in different cities or countries from where the impact is felt. Whereas the normal construct of 'stranger danger' is of unacquainted offenders in one's locale, the fraudster could be a transnational offender posing as a local.

It is worth taking into account the economic externalities (costs) arising from risks and risk perceptions, not just in a domestic context but also internationally, an issue brought into sharper focus by events in Iraq and Russia in the early twenty-first century. Thus, 'business resilience' in the face of economic and political risk (including cybercrimes, extortion, and terrorism) has become a significant element in corporate risk management, and a substantial transnational private risk advisory and management sector has grown up to deal with such problems, to which a prelude is concern about, if not fear of, crime as one among many sources of business risk (Demos, 2006; Dorn and Levi, 2007, forthcoming; Gill, 2006).

One might add to this that insofar as retail businesses are located in areas perceived to be dangerous or risky by potential shoppers – an issue altered by e-tailing, which does not require physical proximity between vendors and purchasers – the risk judgments of those actual and potential shoppers also affect the level and time pattern of sales. Even ignoring the customers, however, one cannot make a neat division between fear of crime by businesspeople *in relation to their business activities* and the fear of crime by businesspeople and their employees *in relation to their personal lives*. Fear of being mugged or attacked for nonfinancial motives (including racial attacks) on the way to and from work, as well as – in the case of shopkeepers who live over the shop – fear of burglary, arson, or racial attacks are all relevant. Unfortunately, they are also under-researched.[22]

Many business crime risks and fears are only intermittently related to the area of corporate headquarter residence or to the residences of workers, and the globalization of retail and financial services create difficulties for these traditional constructs of space (Whimster, 1992), and for the physical space focus of the 'hot spots' literature. There is a paucity of survey as well as ethnographic data about business fear of crime, and what there is tends to focus upon the large retail sector and/or on fear of violence. However in principle, the issue of business and insecurity about crime in urban space can be represented in a number of different ways. First, in terms of the threats facing business, principally

- property crimes of different types (theft and fraud by outsiders, theft and fraud by insiders – perhaps collusively with outsiders – and criminal damage);
- violent crime (solely to cause hurt, without pecuniary motives); and
- both property and violent crime (i.e., robbery, which is *experienced* and feared as violent crime but has an economic instrumental purpose).

Second, in terms of the impact of this upon business and the community, for example, affecting business location decisions, including the flight from the inner city and estate blighted areas, with consequent effects on both employment and shopping (as well as crime) opportunities. (Fear of fraud seems unlikely to have such consequences, though experience/fear of corruption/extortion can drive businesses

---

[22] Ideally, one would like to see research on people who have left employment or self-employment, who have relocated or who have decided not to work in particular urban locations because of fear. However, such data are largely absent, except for the read-across from other research on fear and the city.

out of areas or countries.) Third, in terms of the concern of people at different layers of business organization, from blue-collar workers to senior directors: both their risks and their fears may be quite different, related partly to their economic interests and partly to their ability to purchase or otherwise receive security. Indeed, the term 'fear' should be treated with caution when dealing with a chain of command in a bureaucracy: front line workers and security staff working, living and/or traveling through 'rough' areas may have a very different cognitive approach to dangerous places than do their chauffeur driven finance directors/risk managers, commuting into corporate headquarters from homes in upscale areas. Fourth, about the crimes caused *by* business and the effects these can have, for example on consumer fraud, environmental damage, and health and safety at work. And finally, there are conceptual problems for the meaning of this subject area in relation to cyber crime risks arising in the course of rapidly rising e-tailing rather than face-to-face retailing. The importance of the 'new economy' may have been overstated, not least by those selling 'securities' (sic!) in the 'dot.com' bubble before 9/11, but e-tailing does extend further the disintermediation of the world of production from that of retailing and residence, envisaging customer delivery no longer from local or city center shops but rather from distant distribution centers, altering the shape of crime opportunities. Such vulnerabilities may arise at points close to consumers' residences (for example when fraudsters operate 'drop houses' for delivery of goods obtained by fraud or intercept goods before they are delivered to homes), but they may also arise close to points of distribution, when the loads are at their maximum.

The Fraud Problem and Business

Let us shift gear and focus for a moment on fraud as a social problem, and how it is dealt with. Where frauds – whether by or against otherwise legitimate business, or just outright scams against the public – do cause political concern, this tends to be generated by either hi-tech crime and/or by widespread investment and/or pension fund fraud, communicated via a substantial number of politicians; alternatively, in a sphere with parallels to violent crime, it involves some health risk to the public, such as contaminated meat products or dangerous counterfeit goods such as medicines or toys. Failures in supervision of the supply chain via globalized subcontracting – most recently involving China – may be the cause of or pretext for national alarms about product safety, fed by businesspeople and/or workers' representatives advocating protectionism in pursuit of their economic interests. (There is commonality here between countries as diverse as Australia, Russia, the United Kingdom, and the United States.) In other circumstances, fraud very seldom enters the core political agenda. The low fraud and business crime mail-bag content of ordinary politicians and government Ministers could be simply a reproduction of the lack of general awareness about whose business fraud is, since unlike 'normal' crimes, which are dealt with only by the police, frauds could be dealt with by multifarious bodies in the United Kingdom or North America. This confusion as to which agency(ies) people might turn to is backed up by some research conducted by the Office of Fair Trading (2006) in the United Kingdom and by Kane and Wall (2006) for the United States.

If the allocation of responsibility for business crime enforcement seems complex, so too is the range of commercial bodies dealing with 'it.' It is appropriate to flag here the absence (with the possible exception of Intellectual Property) of a strong unified business lobby against all forms of fraud and other crimes which hurt business, though all business organizations campaign for legislative changes and enforcement action at a national and international level to support their economic interests. Since the criminal activities tend to be transnational, international bodies include the International Chamber of Commerce and the International AntiCounterfeiting Coalition, Inc. (IACC), a Washington, D.C.-based nonprofit organization formed in 1978. The IACC is comprised of a cross-section of business and industry – from autos, apparel, luxury goods, and pharmaceuticals, to food, software, and entertainment. The IACC's members' combined annual revenues exceed $650 billion. There are also sectoral trade bodies as well as individual firms that lobby for the protection of their interests.

Perhaps because 'fear' and 'worry' are seen to be properties of individuals rather than businesses,[23] there is an absence of research on which, if any, business sectors are *worried* about fraud, and this is a deficiency, since judgments about crime seriousness are far more abstract and reflective than are *fears* of crime: fear, after all, is an emotion. Nor are there any studies that explore the congruence or incongruence of fear, worry and crime seriousness judgments. This does not make survey findings meaningless – perhaps judgments about crime seriousness should be taken more seriously than measures that can largely reflect current media publicity campaigns? – but it does make them incomplete, by taking for granted the link between (a) thinking something serious, (b) taking personal or organizational measures against it, and (c) wanting something done about it by law enforcement as a priority.

Cyber Crime, Fears, and Risks

Moving away from areas such as violence (for entertainment and/or for financial gain, i.e., robbery) and burglary risks, which *require* – if not face-to-face in the case of burglary – at least some direct physical interaction between offender and victim (person or location), cyber fraud is disintermediated crime and there is a major question about where it and some other forms of commercial crime are to be located for both criminological and practical intervention purposes. For example, does the place where the crime takes place depend on where the offender is, where the victim(s) is (are), where the money is sent, where it ends up (properly laundered, or just hidden), or any combination thereof? These are not questions that arise in ordinary victimization or crime surveys, but they do have implications for fear of crime since the threats are more distant and less susceptible to normal policing

---

[23] Though media often report about the 'concerns of business' in other spheres affecting their interests.

methods.[24] To some extent the practical issues are taken care of by the shifting constructions of liability in criminal law. The Council of Europe Convention on Cybercrime 2001 (which came into force in 2004) aims to provide a common core to national legislation: the political support for it arises from the widespread fears of this highly dramatized area of crime. For example, in 'Internet sting lures 82,000 isle "lairds", *The Observer*, (10 March 1996) warned about a firm selling square-yard plots of remote crofting land to Americans with a fictitious scroll guaranteeing that for $100, purchasers will become 'an authentic Scottish laird.' The article began: 'In cyberspace no-one can hear the victim scream.'

A decade later, most Internet users have become habituated to receiving e-mails aimed at harvesting – 'phishing' and 'pharming' – data on their personal identities and financial transactions. In addition to dedicated identity fraud websites such as (in the United States) http://www.ftc.gov/bcp/edu/microsites/idtheft/, the regular flow of media stories in the West is part of the general advisory role of the media, but it also reflects the alarmist technophobia that is prevalent whenever risks of new technology are exposed (see also Mann and Sutton, 1998; Grabosky and Smith, 1998; Levi, 2001, 2006; Wall, 2008). In media terms, for *any* type of crime, subject to the (variable) need to be or to appear to be socially responsible, a 'good prog[ram]' is one that alarms the public and attacks the competence of large institutions, in this case their competence to hold our data securely.

This technological risk theme has been re-iterated frequently in trade and general media coverage of credit card Internet transactions, and may be one reason why surveys find considerable anxiety about Internet fraud risks among the general public as well as among retailers. My interviews with major credit card payments systems security heads indicate a unanimous view that fear of being defrauded inhibits commerce substantially, though no work has been done on examining the extent to which this fear relates specifically to factors such as hacker interception or fraud *by* merchants, nor has the opportunity cost of these losses to consumers and to business been quantified. E-tailers normally have to pay all the costs when they are defrauded, even though credit card companies usually absorb the cost of fraud for offline retailers. What has happened has been a two-pronged response, with (1) some card issuers offering consumers a fraud risk guarantee – which is a low-cost option since, unknown to many cardholders, they are liable anyway for a maximum of $50 in the United Kingdom and low amounts in many other countries – and (2) e-tailers and others selling goods over the phone being offered access to the true addresses of cardholders so that if they want to supply to addresses other than the home address, they know that they are taking a risk (about which they might be concerned, if not fearful). Business surveys are repeated quite regularly, for example by CyberSource and by Javelin Strategy and and Research (2007), which reported a fall in identity

---

[24] The distinction between telephone and cyberstalking is far less than that between physical stalking, but all types can occur to businesspeople as well as to individuals. Legal jurisdiction over cyberspace is a particular issue with cybercrime, whose legal venue is particularly problematic, as was discovered when the Philippine authorities released the suspected author of the Love Bug virus because their legislation did not cover it.

fraud the previous year. There are also broader e-crime annual reports in the United States by the Computer Security Institute (2007 – the 12th survey), in collaboration with the FBI, that generate substantial publicity but (other than in ritual introductory remarks) ignore serious problems in response rates and sample frames in a repeat cross-sectional study with an unknown number of repeat respondents rather than the panel study that would indicate far more about trends.

At the *individual* level, there are modest amounts of data, which may reflect as well as stimulate media coverage. Thus reporting on the British Crime Survey, Wilson et al. (2006) note that around 3% of the population were victims of check and payment card fraud in 2003–2004; half of the four fifths of respondents who had used a credit or debit card in the last 12 months were worried (including fairly or very worried) about being a victim of card fraud. Fifteen percent of individuals were very worried about being a victim of credit card fraud: this is similar to levels of worry for car crime and violent crime (15% and 16% respectively) but slightly higher than burglary (13%). Individuals were slightly more likely to be worried about card fraud when they were using their cards to buy goods over the Internet or over the phone (in both cases 52% were very or fairly worried about this). Overall the level of worry rose only modestly compared to 2002/03 (when it was 48%), and – perhaps because the fearful were less likely to buy goods online – slightly fewer who had used their cards to buy goods over the Internet were worried (55% in 2002/03 to 52% in 2003/04). However, one might question whether statements about levels of 'worry' properly reflect people's estimations of the impact that crimes are likely to have on them if they occur (i.e., they relate more to perceived probability than to perceived consequences). Since then, the United Kingdom (though not the United States) has introduced cards with microchips that require a PIN, so despite regular media reports on identity thefts involving cards (most dramatically the 47 million UK and North American cardholders whose data held by retailers TK Maxx were compromised in 2006–2007), the next set of data should be interesting, since Chip and PIN does not affect the Internet and other card not present risks, but has led to a significant fall in frauds on lost and stolen cards (APACS, 2007). Here, again we see the tension between data-informed and mediatized fear of crime.

Though media 'panics' about crimes have become routinized in contemporary society, it is plausible that 'identity fraud' and 'identity theft' – whose parameters are obscure – have indeed become 'signal crimes' that are treated as symbolic of the way in which technology has rendered us defenseless to preserve our unique selves. A report by business intelligence/credit reference agency Experian (2007) notes, with an appropriate degree of statistical caution:

> The rate at which new victims are contacting Experian continues to grow. 2,124 victims contacted Experian's Victims of Fraud team for the first time in the second half of 2006. This compares with 1,478 for the same months in 2005, and 926 in 2004, and represents a 69 per cent year-on-year increase in identity fraud activity reported to Experian. While some of the increase in number of victims contacting Experian could be attributed to increased awareness of identity fraud, rather than an absolute increase in victims, it is more likely a combination of both. . . . .This evidence of the growth in identity fraud activity echoes figures from CIFAS as well as from Experian's own fraud prevention business. CIFAS figures show that the number of victims of impersonation rose by 34 per cent between

2004 and 2006, while the number of fraudulent applications detected by Experian's fraud prevention systems for mortgages, loans, credit cards and other finance and leasing was 25 per cent higher in the second half of 2006 than the first.

However, its press notice was understandably sharper in tone, and all of the media simply reported the 'fact' that identity fraud had risen 69%: the headline, for example, on the front page of London's free Metro newspaper and a major news item in most other newspapers and television (12 April 2007). Experian advertises its free check of credit ratings and requests for credit on its CreditExpert product (though people who sign up for the free service have to agree to pay from one month later, which will be charged unless they remember to cancel!).

This is not to say that there is no deconstruction of fraud risk data. In the United Kingdom, there are prominent people such as Ross Anderson, Professor of Computing at Cambridge University who frequently debunk banking industry statements about security and appear on radio and television; and critics – on both ideological and pragmatic grounds – of the UK government's identity card proposals (www.no2id.net/), who regularly discredit the links between crime and the expensive 'solutions' offered. Privacy advocacy in the United States is also powerful compared with the United Kingdom, though eroded significantly since '9/11.' The consumer movement in the United States has also been more active in relation to identity theft, possibly because of a greater volume of such behavior and poorer general privacy in the United States than in the United Kingdom and Europe as a whole.

Setting aside all the hype, there is a serious social point about the interaction between computers, trust and security. As Grabosky and Smith (1998: 47) put it,

> [T]rust and confidence in the systems that support commerce, communications, air traffic control, electric power generation and other modern institutions are at the very core of our society. Thus, even the potential for disruption and harm is cause for concern.

The difficulty with this National Security perspective on cyber crime – which has become even more pronounced since the Love Bug virus and since '9/11' and subsequent use of the Internet by terrorist networks – is that if social harm is so seamless, what may *not* be affected by such risks and what are the limits of state intervention to prevent them from materializing? Furthermore, though this may affect the large corporate sector rather than the small owner-managed businesses to be found in the poorer areas of the city who may be more worried about transparency to the Internal Revenue Service than to intelligence agencies, is the fear of crime outweighed by concern about invasion of privacy on the part of intelligence agencies seeking to combat organized and/or political crime[25]?

---

[25] or seeking the economic preferment of their own national companies by governmental espionage in the late modern form of what General/President Eisenhower once termed the 'military industrial complex.' French businesses have alleged the misuse of electronic interception to win contracts for American companies, though this is hotly denied by the Americans and British. The irony here is that in the views of many Anglo-Americans, the French have been enthusiastic in their use of corruption to assist their own sales, so even if this had happened, it might merely counterbalance the illicit benefits to French multinationals from transnational corruption.

Fear of Fraud and Fear of Loss: A Problematization

Fear of crime – any crime – is a more difficult construct than might appear, and its application to white-collar crimes is at times tenuous. There is for all crimes a danger that the objects of fear may be mistaken – whether from racist socialization, media projections or other sources. Our exaggerated estimates of the risk of 'stranger danger' and our underestimation of 'male family danger' are a case in point. In relation to fraud, it is easy to see how such emotions of fear might arise from the perception that the drugs one was taking for malaria or HIV might be inactive counterfeits, or the car/airplane parts might be unsafe fakes. With some imagination, the prospective collapse of a retirement fund invested heavily in Enron or a bankrupt insurance company might also fit within that framework. These are dangers and/or evils, and at an abstract level may be recognized as such. It is also hard to tell whether such risks are present or not: the physical characteristics of goods or investment products do not enable the inexpert to tell whether or not they do what they claim – this is especially true of longer term investment products, whose benefits may (or may not) materialize in the distant future. Claims of expertise are hard to verify or falsify in advance. Hence the panic that sets in when people think 'their' bank or other vehicle holding their life savings *may* go bust.

zHowever the specific *fraud* component of such fears is harder to identify, as fraud is just one possible cause of economic catastrophe, or – at a more aggregate level – of what economists term systemic risk. Indeed, the 'credit crunch' of 2008–2009 triggered by excessive subprime loans shows us what happens when banks do not trust each other's ability to repay loans: however for the most part, this is bankers' fear of bank insolvency rather than fear of the banks committing fraud. Thus, during September 2007, television screens and newspapers in the United Kingdom (and – more rarely – even in some other developed countries like the United States) were treated to pictures of lengthy queues outside Northern Rock Bank branches in parts of the United Kingdom to withdraw savings, as people showed their fear of losing money due to possible bank insolvency. Their fears were stimulated by the news pictures, and the panic occurred despite the reassuring words of the Chairman of the Northern Rock, the Chairman of the Financial Services Authority and the Governor of the Bank of England: unlike the United States , where financial institution failures have been more commonplace (and deposit insurance more generous and quicker to pay out), it was the first run on an authorized UK bank since that on Overend Gurney in 1866.[26] The fear of burglary or robbery of the cash

---

[26] Overend Gurney & Company collapsed in 1866 owing about $20 million (at historic prices – around $11 billion today). Unlike Northern Rock, it was not a retail but a wholesale bank second in size only to the Bank of England, lending to other banks and finance houses at higher rates of interest: the day after it suspended payments, panic spread across the City of London, with large crowds waiting around its City offices and it had to be liquidated. The financial crisis following the collapse saw the Bank of England base interest rate rise significantly and over 200 companies, including other banks, failed as a result. Overend Gurney's financial adviser was jailed but the bank directors were acquitted on the grounds that they had merely made errors of judgment. The Gurney family was one of the most respected banking dynasties in England and their family bank

withdrawn from those 'hot spots' must have seemed far less salient to depositors – at least at that moment – than the prospective failure of the bank. This was even though deposits up to $70,000 – a third of the United States guarantee limit – were protected by a compensation fund. One regulator told me that one depositor tried to take out almost $2 million in *cash* from his account, somehow expecting that the branch would have that much in its tills – a cashier's check might have been safer and easier to transport, but not as reassuring! The government had to lend the bank $50 billion to stabilize it and in February 2008, it took Northern Rock into public ownership because the deterioration in availability and cost of wholesale market funds made it unviable, and private sector bidders did not offer a worthwhile alternative. At that point, fears of insolvency disappeared and savers flooded back for the high interest rates in a context of an unlimited government guarantee.

This wholesale loan market shortage for international and local banks arising from the United States subprime credit crisis generated immense anxiety in the United Kingdom, irrespective of the allegations that dishonest mortgage brokers conspired with them (though to a lesser extent than in the United States) to falsify their self-certificated incomes. Indeed it is not clear what the effects of such frauds (or beliefs that fraud was involved) were on the fears and anxieties of American or British savers compared with fears about their 'mere' inability to pay mortgages and their economic futures. Rather, labeling the acts 'fraud' may be a way of (unconsciously) enabling people to feel more comfortable with the fact of loss, diverting self-blame and expectations of low regard by others for 'unwise' savings strategies. In the case of Northern Rock, though fraud might have provoked greater anger among the public, the huge potential costs to British taxpayers of the support were almost independent of any issue of criminality. Fraud might even have given greater possibility of loss recovery from banks and lawyers who might have been held negligent.

Likewise, in relation to the much-discussed US Savings and Loans crisis during the 1980s (e.g., Black, 2005), to what extent were anxieties or even perceptions of wrongfulness the result of fraud by executives rather than simply economic loss compensated ultimately by the taxpayers? In the United States , in the aftermath of the collapse of the subprime market in 2007, there were allegations (interviews with officials and, for example, http://www.nytimes.com/2007/09/09/business/09every.html) that in order to obtain commission from the lenders, mortgage brokers (i) lied to unsophisticated and mostly poor people about the interest rates and other conditions of their loans as well as (ii) helped them lie about their incomes in order to get mortgages. Investigations of such allegations led to widespread FBI raids in 2008. However, although those people may be (rightly) fearful about their futures and may objectively be worse off than if they had not bought a home at all, whether this distress constitutes fear of *crime* remains more doubtful. In a sense, if they had

---

in East Anglia was unscathed: they became founding partners in Barclays Bank 30 years later. For a broader discussion of fraud in the Victorian era, see Wilson (2006). In 2008, bankers were reluctant to lend to other bankers not because they feared fraud but because they feared that the counterparty would not be able to repay them when debts fell due.

been more fearful of their brokers, they might not have become (a) victims of poor investments and (b) arguably, both fraud victims and fraud offenders. (The fact that brokers may have advised them on how to lie about their income when filling in their mortgage forms does not make clients innocent of obtaining loans by fraud.)

Unlike the S & L crisis of the 1970s – where the vast multi-billion dollar direct losses (only some clearly attributable to fraud) were confined to the United States – the losses from subprimes were also globalized through the sale to international financial institutions of Collateralized Debt Obligations rolling up large numbers of mortgages into a 'security' (sic!). However here again, fear of economic and status loss is not the same as fear of fraud. If bankers had been more fearful that what they were buying was overpriced, the market for these securitized loans would have been thinner and the economic damage less: though this assumes optimistically that bankers' respect for institutional and investor interests would have been greater than their personal greed for short-term bonuses. The human capacity for rationalization of self-interest in such circumstances is profound, especially if retribution is not anticipated.

Conclusions

It has proven difficult to demonstrate what students of 'fear of crime' can learn from the literature on fear of white-collar crime, and vice versa. This is partly because they are different sorts of activities that are often committed by different sorts of people, though there is an under-researched overlap in those who are offenders or victims of both. White-collar offenders purposively manipulate fear by trying to lower it, in circumstances where distrust exists; while fear of crime arguably is a consequence of street-crime victimization and the way in which information about it is constructed and disseminated. The closest to fear of street crime is fear of identity theft, which merges also into our fears about computers and our own loss of control over our 'selves.'

The parallels that are closest to the more general themes of this book are those involving the social construction of fear. Western nations tend to assume that what is bad for business is bad for society, but whether or not one accepts that general proposition, in both policy and theoretical terms, it is important to tease out the range of interests that are being promoted. Except as part of some corporate policy and image development strategy, businesses are primarily interested in the ways in which crime and concern about it on the part of customers, employees and owners affect trade volumes, profit and the cost of capital. Except where it has a reputational effect on the entire business – as *at some currently unknown level of perceived* frequency, e-commerce fraud and insider trading may – neither businesspeople nor law enforcement are especially concerned about fraud *by* businesspeople (though many frauds are by business against business, so it would be mistaken to see this simply in terms of 'class' or group interests). The public normally have little option other than to trust the products they buy: they may have particular insecurities about being sold things by doorstep or by telephone salespeople, but presumably this is not universal or those activities would be unprofitable. Fear – in such contexts – is unproductive because there are no practical steps that one can take other than to withdraw from the market.[27] (Though in the case of Internet sites, they may take their revenge by blackening the reputation of the vendor; or only use one particular credit card for all their Internet purchases, avoiding – by not using a debit card – the risk of having their bank account emptied.)

Whereas fears of some crimes may narrow down opportunities but can seldom provide total protection from predatory attacks, fear of fraud might lead us to choose arenas of saving and investment that are wholly protected by government or insurance-based compensation schemes. To that extent, it may be a tautology that the absence of (or submergence of) fear is a precondition for fraud. Shapiro's (1990) classic article on 'collaring the crime, not the criminal' argued that the key to white-collar crime was the separation between agent and principal, the implication being that in a modern economy it was impractical fully to negate the risk of fraud. However, subject to maxima fixed by law in compensation schemes and the ability to recover assets in excess of this from the offenders themselves, fraud risks can be mitigated and therefore fear rationally reduced in some areas of life such as financial services/pensions schemes. However it is less plausible that evasive action arising from fear of fraud can succeed in *all* areas of consumption and work in which one can be deceived. In any event, it is clear that fear of fraud is one of several sources of risk of loss that has a social cost in denying people access to higher interest on their capital and to lower prices on consumer goods and services purchased on the Internet. This is the analog of other costs of social participation generated by fear of non-white-collar crimes.

In *Crime Control as Industry: Towards Gulags Western Style*, Christie (2000) elaborates the notion that particular ways of dealing with crime (and fear of crime) are important sources of profit in Western society. Students of fear of crime may find there a bridge between fear of white-collar and fear of other offenses. Businesses such as investment and long-term savings/pensions require imagery of reassurance about both competence and integrity, and much advertising takes place to sustain that branded positive *gestalt* for each firm; hence, too, the government's focus on avoiding systemic risk of general financial meltdown by rescuing or facilitating the rescue of firms such as Bear Sterns and Northern Rock. (The street crime equivalent might be sending out the National Guard or paramilitary police to stop mayhem on the streets.) Certainly one may see that both preceding frauds and in the aftermath of frauds, substantial funds are spent on fraud-risk management, with in most areas of activity, very imperfect knowledge of actual risk levels. In the case of international businesses deciding where to locate, reputation for (low) crime presumably is one of many factors comprising attractiveness, and this affects key staff judgments not

---

[27] The fact that fear is unproductive in practical terms does not of course mean that it is not experienced as an emotion. It is intriguing to think about what 'fight or flight' means in the context of fraud, except perhaps when Mafiosi are making offers one cannot refuse.

only as it relates to the workplace but also residence and schooling: but specific fraud risks are unlikely to feature heavily except where locally recruited staff untrustworthiness is seen to be endemic. Detailed area-based information regarding crime risks is seldom available (though corporate security staff might be asked for briefings), and there is no evidence about how often it is requested or how salient it would be if available. Some crime risks, such as fraud risks, would seldom be local in nature anyway. As for residents, their risks of being defrauded *by* businesses would be unlikely to be material in decisions where to live: as Croall (2001) notes – though one should *caveat* that her research preceded the growth of neighborhood supermarkets in the United Kingdom – most of the food and drugs violations that are prosecuted are committed by small, local shops, and if people knew they were being cheated, most could shop elsewhere unless there were large price differences. Poor people have little choice where to live anyway, and they may be regular targets for consumer fraud. If staff thought that employers were stealing their national insurance/Social Security contributions or, *a fortiori,* their occupational pension funds, this might make a considerable difference to their choice of employer: but if they had this knowledge, the frauds probably would not be allowed to be perpetrated.[28]

Cities, and fear of crime within them, remain relevant to business survival and prosperity, but to the extent that the locus of economic regeneration has shifted to dematerialized factors of production such as global financial services which have little sunk capital, business location – though still tied to cultural capital, reservoirs of expertise, prestige and plausible commutability for staff – is more flexible than it was within as well as between nations. Consequently, the commercial impact of fear of urban crime in general and fraud in particular has shifted. Where goods (rather than electronic services, which include pornographic services) have to be delivered physically, there is some nexus between fear of crime and business in the city, since that is where many consumers will remain. The depth of this effect may depend on the growth of e-business, and the propinquity of other deal makers and clients will continue to favor the continuation of the financial district as a place rather than a pure abstraction, even though deals have increasingly become transnational, as financial institutions merge to enable them to offer one-stop financial shopping to clients (and, doubtless, for other less customer-led reasons). Such mergers accelerated after the financial services crashes of 2008.

For élites, the ability to insulate themselves personally from risk of common crimes is important. However, although much has been written about the central-

---

[28] However, the post-Maxwell pension fund fraud reforms to company pensions in the mid-1990s did not give workers the right of representation as pension fund trustees, reflecting the UK government's fear of upsetting employers. Enron employees – unlike their directors - famously were forbidden to sell Enron shares in the run up to corporate failure. Enron instituted a "lockdown," which prevented employees from selling their shares of Enron stock between October 26, 2001 and November 13, 2001, while the company spiralled into bankruptcy. According to Enron, the lockdown was administratively necessary for the company to proceed with a desired change of the pension plan's trustee and record keeper; however it conveniently reduced the level of stock sales and thus kept the share price higher than it otherwise would have been. Enron employees, 62% of whose pension scheme – or 401(k) plan – consisted of Enron stock, lost as much as $1bn in funds.

ity of trust in late modern as well as in early modern commerce, fraud risks are usually judgments about particular individuals or about ethnicities/national origins (e.g., Nigerians, Russians) with whom one may be dealing professionally, which may be assessed by 'due diligence' conducted by professionals. (In other arenas, of course, elites may be victims of identity fraud, card counterfeiting, etcetera, but their losses from these are relatively immaterial.) Protection from terrorism, extortion, kidnapping for protest or for profit, ecoprotests, and cybercrime, as well as from the more traditional forms of crime, becomes part of the security quilt around urban financial services, and the City of London's Ring of Steel, supported by extensive police video surveillance in the streets (though not in the boardroom), becomes the equivalent of the Gated City, with crime reductive effects at least in areas where the poor and other sources of threat are not already inside. These commercial risks may vary considerably between countries: corruption, extortion, and kidnap and ransom are a far larger problem in many eastern European and Latin American countries than in most industrialized countries (Mayhew et al., 1997; van Kesteren et al., 2001; van Dijk et al., 2007), excepting parts of Italy. Elsewhere, the industrial estate, the shopping mall, and local corner shop have their own diverse problems of security, involving insecurities about transportation of customers and staff to and from the premises as well as about the security of buildings and contents from burglary, criminal damage, fraud, robbery and theft. The effects of fear on business and the collateral effects of this remain underexplored empirically and conceptually. The business context of crime and fear in urban space has been neglected in criminological literature and research, but despite the growth of e-tailing, it remains relevant, especially for areas in which access to home computers is limited not just by poverty but by the abnormally high risks of having computers stolen.

Frustrating though it may be for fraud departments of major corporations, however, their senior executives seem more fixated on their performance targets and consequent bonuses for the coming year than on strategic fraud reduction which may cost them substantial upfront expenditure which may not produce a yield within their period of company stewardship: so on a 'willingness to pay' measure of fear or concern, directors clearly are not fearful enough, most of the time. An exception is the massive multi-billion dollar investment of United Kingdom and other European card issuers in Chip and PIN to reduce losses from 'card present' frauds. Fuelled by regular media reports about e-invasions, public anxieties about 'identity theft' – and losses to banks themselves from 'card not present' (e.g., Internet) transactions – will doubtless lead to further expenditure on authentication of users, but in the United States particularly, identity duplication remains an omnipresent risk. It remains to be seen whether in the case of the variety of forms of fraud, there are sufficient 'capable guardians' (in the language of situational opportunity 'theory') with the organizational power and legitimacy both to reduce risks objectively and to reassure the public that (with apologies to Roosevelt) the only thing they have to fear is fear itself.

Acknowledgments The author is grateful for the Economic and Social Research Council Professorial Fellowship RES-051-27-0208, under whose auspices this research was conducted.

References

Babiak, P. and Hare, R. (2006) *Snakes in Suits: When Psychopaths Go to Work*, New York: Harper Collins.
Baum, K. (2006) *Identity Theft, 2004*, Washington DC: Bureau of Justice Statistics.
Baum, K. (2007) *Identity Theft 2005*, Washington DC: Bureau of Justice Statistics. http://www.ojp.usdoj.gov/bjs/pub/pdf/it05.pdf.
Black, W. (2005) *The Best Way to Rob a Bank is to Own One: How Corporate Executives and Politicians Looted the S&L Industry*, Austin TX: University of Texas Press.
Christie, N. (2000) *Crime Control as Industry: Towards Gulags Western Style*. London: Routledge.
Coates, J. and Herbert, J. (2008) Endogenous steroids and financial risk taking on a London trading floor, *PNAS April 22, 2008.* vol. 105, no. 16, 6167–6172.
Computer Security Institute (2007) *CSI Survey 2007*. http://www.gocsi.com.
Croall, H. (2001) *White-Collar Crime*. 2nd ed., Milton Keynes: Open University Press.
Demos (2006) *The Business of Resilience* http://www.demos.co.uk/publications/thebusiness ofresilience.
Ditton, J., Chadee, D., Farrall, S., Gilchrist, E. and Bannister, J. (2004) From imitation to intimidation: a note on the curious and changing relationship between the media, crime and fear of crime. *British Journal of Criminology* 44(4): 595–610.
Dijk, J. van, Manchin, R., Kesteren, J. van, Nevala, S. and Hideg, G. (2007) *The Burden of Crime in the European Union.* http://www.gallup-europe.be/euics/Xz38/downloads/EUICS%20-%20The%20Burden%20of%20Crime%20in%20the%20EU.pdf.
Dorn, N. and Levi, M. (2007)European Private Security, Corporate Investigation and Military Services: Collective Security, Market Regulation and Structuring the Public Sphere, *Policing and Society*, 17(3): 213–238.
Dorn, N. and Levi, M. (forthcoming). Private-public or public-private? Strategic dialogue on serious crime and terrorism in the EU. *Security Journal.*
Financial Services Authority (2007) *Financial Outlook, 2006*, London: FSA.
Gabriel, U. and Greve, W. (2003)Fear of crime: towards a psychological approach. *British Journal of Criminology*, 43: 600–614.
Gardner, D. (2008) *Risk: the Science of Politics and Fear*, London: Virgin.
Gill, M. (ed.) (2006) *The Handbook of Security*, London: Palgrave Macmillan.
Goodey, J. (1998) Doing research on 'fear of crime, boys, race and masculinities': utilizing a feminist standpoint epistemology. *International Journal of Social Research Methodology*. 1(2): 137–152.
Goodey, J. (2005) *Victims and Victimology: Research, Policy and Practice* London: Pearson Education.
Grabosky, P. and Smith, R. (1998)*Crime in the Digital Age*, London: Transaction.
Ichheiser, G. (1944) Fear of Violence and Fear of Fraud: With Some Remarks on the Social Psychology of Antisemitism. *Sociometry* 7(4): 376–383.
Innes, M. (2004) Signal crimes and signal disorders: notes on deviance as communicative action. *The British Journal of Sociology*, 55(3): 335–355.
Jackson, J. (2004) Experience and expression: social and cultural significance in the fear of crime. *British Journal of Criminology* 44: 946–966.
James, M., Graycar, A. and Mayhew, P. (2003) *A safe and secure environment for older Australians.* Research and public policy series no. 51. Canberra: Australian Institute of Criminology http://www.aic.gov.au/publications/rpp/51.
Javelin Strategy and Research (2007) *Identity Fraud Survey Report 2007*. http://www.javelinstrategy.com/uploads/701.R_2007IdentityFraudSurveyReport_Brochure.pdf.
Kane, J. and Wall, A. (2006) *The National Public Household Survey 2005*, Virginia: National Center for White-Collar Crime.
Jones, T. and Newburn, T. (2006a) Three Strikes and You're Out: Exploring Symbol and Substance in American and British Crime Control Politics. *British Journal of Criminology*, 46(5): 781–802.

Jones, T. and Newburn, T. (2006b) *Policy Transfer and Criminal Justice*, Milton Keynes: Open University Press.

Kesteren, J. van, Mayhew, P. and Nieuwbeerta, P. (2001) *Criminal Victimisation in Seventeen Industrialised Countries: Key Findings from the 2000 International Crime Victims Survey.* http://www.unicri.it/wwd/analysis/icvs/pdf_files/key2000i/index.htm.

Killias, M. (1990) Vulnerability: towards a better understanding of a key variable in the genesis of fear of crime. *Violence Vict.* 5(2):97–108.

LaGrange, R.L. and Ferraro K.F. (1987)The elderly's fear of crime: a critical examination of the research. *Research on Ageing* 9: 372–391.

Levi, M. (2001) 'Between the risk and the reality falls the shadow': Evidence and urban legends in computer fraud, *Crime and the Internet* D. Wall (ed.), London: Routledge. 44–58.

Levi, M. (2006) 'The Media Construction of Financial White-Collar Crimes', *British Journal of Criminology*, Special Issue on Markets, Risk and Crime, 46: 1037–1057.

Levi, M. (2008) 'White-collar, organised and cyber crimes in the media: some contrasts and similarities', *Crime, Law and Social Change*, 10.1007/s10611-008-9111-y.

Levi, M. and A. Pithouse (forthcoming) *White-Collar Crime and its Victims*, Oxford: Clarendon Press.

Levi, M., Burrows, J., Fleming, M. and Hopkins, M. with the assistance of Matthews, K. (2007a) *The Nature, Extent and Economic Impact of Fraud in the UK.* London: Association of Chief Police Officers. http://www.acpo.police.uk/asp/policies/Data/Fraud%20in%20the%20UK.pdf.

Levi, M., Maguire, M. and Brookman, F. (2007b) Violent Crime. *The Oxford Handbook of Criminology* M. Maguire, R. Morgan and R. Reiner (eds.), Fourth Edition, Oxford: Oxford University Press.

Mann, D. and Sutton, M. (1998)'NetCrime: more change in the organisation of thieving', *British Journal of Criminology*, 38, 201–229.

Mayhew, P. and van Dijk, J. (1997) *Criminal Victimization in Eleven Industrialised Countries*, The Hague: WODC, Ministry of Justice.

Pew (2006) *Are "Wired Seniors" Sitting Ducks?* http://www.pewinternet.org/pdfs/PIP_Wired_Senior_2006_Memo.pdf.

Pew (2007) *Spam 2007 Data Memo*, http://www.pewinternet.org/pdfs/PIP_Spam_May_2007.pdf.

Rountree, P. (1998) A Reexamination of the Crime-Fear Linkage. *Journal of Research in Crime and Delinquency*, 35(3): 341–372.

Semmens, N. (2003) *Fear of Plastic Fraud.* unpublished Ph.D. thesis, University of Sheffield, UK.

Skogan, W. (1995) Crime and the Racial Fears of White Americans. *The Annals of the American Academy of Political and Social Science.* 539(1): 59–71.

Titus, R. and Gover, A. (2001)Personal Fraud: The Victims and the Scams. *Repeat Victimization* G. Farrell and K. Pease (eds.), Monsey, NJ: Criminal Justice Press.

Wall, D. (2008) "Cybercrime, Media and Insecurity: The Shaping of Public Perceptions of Cybercrime". *International Review of Law, Computers and Technology*, 22(1–2): 45–63.

Warr, M. (2001) Fear of crime in the United States: Avenues for Research and Policy. *Criminal Justice 2000*, Vol.4 Measurement and Analysis of Crime and Justice: 451–489. http://www.ncjrs.gov/criminal_justice2000/vol_4/04i.pdf.

Whimster, S. (ed.) (1992) *Global Finance and Urban Living: A study of Metropolitan change*, London: Routledge.

Wilson, S. (2006) Law, morality, and regulation: Victorian experiences of financial crime. *British Journal of Criminology*, 46: 1073–1090.

Wilson, D., Patterson, D., Powell, G. and Hembury, R. (2006) *Fraud and technology crimes: Findings from the 2003/04 British Crime Survey, the 2004 Offending, Crime and Justice Survey and administrative sources*, http://www.homeoffice.gov.uk/rds/pdfs06/rdsolr0906.pdf.

The Role of Organizational Structure in the Control of Corporate Crime and Terrorism

Laura Dugan and Carole Gibbs

Abstract In this chapter, we draw direct comparisons between corporate crime and terrorism in order to improve our understanding on how to better control each. We acknowledge obvious differences between the corporate criminal and the terrorist organization, but also raise important similarities between them. Namely, corporations and terrorist organizations both strive to survive in highly competitive environments and have adopted more complex organizational structures over time to achieve this goal. However, it is this organizational complexity that makes it difficult for criminal justice officials to detect and prosecute illicit behavior. After drawing upon the literature in both areas to describe organizational complexity, we offer several (surprisingly similar) recommendations to better control the corporate criminal and the terrorist organization.

Introduction

The purpose of this chapter is to draw direct comparisons between corporate crime and a form of violence that has only begun to be studied by criminologists—terrorism. In an essay that compares terrorism with more traditional topics in criminology the lead author and colleague demonstrate the important contributions criminologists can make toward better understanding terrorism (LaFree and Dugan, 2004). The essay notes that the primary differences between typical street crime and terrorism mirror similar differences between street crime and other specialized forms of crime—gang violence and organized crime. In this chapter, we examine similarities between corporate crime and terrorism, despite obvious differences, in order to improve our understanding on how to control each. More specifically, we argue that by developing our understanding of the nature of corporate and terrorist organizational structures, we can gain valuable insight on the ways to detect

L. Dugan (✉)
Department of Criminology and Criminal Justice, The University of Maryland, College Park, MD, USA
e-mail: ldugan@crim.umd.edu

S.S. Simpson, D. Weisburd (eds.), *The Criminology of White-Collar Crime*,
DOI 10.1007/978-0-387-09502-8_6, © Springer Science+Business Media, LLC 2009

and prosecute both types of illicit activity. We conclude that by jointly examining both types of crime, we are able to strengthen our understanding of each separately.

One might not naturally be tempted to compare corporate crime and terrorism, as the most apparent goals of each organization seem to be completely divergent. Corporations are created for the legitimate purpose of selling goods and services to make a profit (Pearce, 2001). Terrorist organizations, on the other hand, are, by definition, illegal entities. Instead of being created for "legitimate" purposes, terrorist groups push for radical change by violently breaking the law.

Yet, a closer look reveals that corporations and terrorist groups share the same fundamental goal: each strives to survive in a highly competitive environment. In fact, Crenshaw (2001) directly compares terrorist organizations to corporations that are pressured to survive through competition. In her explanation of organizational process theory, Crenshaw (2001) defines survival as the fundamental purpose of any political organization. For a terrorist organization, the key to survival is to recruit and maintain strong membership. With strong membership, the organization can survive despite outside pressures that could easily compromise its well-being. Corporations, on the other hand, are best able to survive when they successfully pursue profit. In fact, public corporations have shareholders, who may be more concerned with profits than the methods used to obtain them (Pearce, 2001).

Thus, the underlying goals of corporations and terrorist organizations are actually similar. As we will demonstrate in this chapter, the parallels between these two unique forms of crime do not end here. First, both corporations and terrorist groups have created complex organizational structures. The complex structures allow both types of organizations to more effectively pursue their respective goals, while also hindering the detection and prosecution of illicit activity. In light of the parallels between these forms of crime, we conclude with some recommendations for improving traditional criminal justice approaches to facilitate the detection, investigation, and prosecution of corporate crime and terrorism despite their structural complexities. We end by describing some proactive strategies that may be used to prevent corporate crime and terrorism.

The Nature and Structure of the Organization

Corporations and terrorist groups are fundamentally different organizations. Perhaps most importantly, corporations are engaged in legal business activity. Corporations (whether owned privately or by shareholders) are also public entities. The corporation and top managers are known, legally identifiable and legally liable "beings" that disclose a substantial amount of information to the public, including mission statements, financial statements, and even illegal activity (e.g., publicly traded companies must disclose significant crimes to shareholders in their annual reports). These disclosures are partly the result of heavy government regulation of corporate activity. In addition to the government, corporations are also accountable to the public.

Terrorist groups, on the other hand, are explicitly illegal organizations that operate clandestinely to avoid direct exposure to officials and the public. Despite their covertness, however, most terrorist organizations are accountable to constituents or "shareholders," referring to those with similar ideological perspectives and who provide the basis for recruitment or financial support (McCauley et al., 2008). In fact, many terrorist organizations rely on media sources to publicize their activities, thus encouraging further constituency support. In recent years, these groups have begun to openly exploit the Internet to raise funds, recruit members, disseminate ideological messages, plan attacks, and publicize the results of these attacks (Weimann, 2006). Regardless of the growing visibility of many terrorist organizations, their violent tactics continue to prevent them from obtaining the same broad-based legitimacy and accountability as corporations.[1]

Despite these operational differences, we argue that similarities can be drawn between corporate and terrorist organizational form. Organizational scholars have long highlighted the role that corporate structure plays to assure corporate goals (i.e., profitability). As such, organizational scholars have delineated various types and measures of corporate structure and documented how those structures have changed over time. In the following section, we apply the types and measures of corporate organizational structure to the structure (and shifts in the structure) of terrorist groups.

Organizational structure refers to the design of the organization, including the lines of authority and communication. Structural complexity is more specifically defined as the "degree of spread and segmentation in an organization's structure" (McKendall and Wagner, 1997, p. 627). Corporate structures are often quite complex, particularly as firms add new functions by expanding volume or growing geographically (Chandler, 1962). They can have at least three dimensions of complexity or differentiation: vertical, horizontal, and spatial. Vertical differentiation refers to layers of hierarchy and supervision. Horizontal complexity increases with the number of interdependent subunits working on pieces of a larger and more complex task. Finally, organizations that have many operating sites in geographically dispersed locations have a high degree of spatial differentiation (McKendall and Wagner, 1997).

The broad range of terrorist group structures can also be characterized by these three dimensions of complexity. Vertical organizations describe hierarchical groups similar to the Red Army Faction, whose operation is delineated by a clear set of leaders and subordinates (Crenshaw, 2001, 1985). Groups like Hamas are horizontally structured by loosely organized cells where some members operate openly through mosques and social services while others operate more clandestinely (Hill and Ward, 2002). Groups like al-Qaeda are paragons of the horizontally and spatially complex models of organization, where a large number of horizontally oriented cells can operate independently of a central planning structure and persist internationally for many years, both gathering support and carrying out attacks (Cronin, 2006).

---

[1] Some terrorist organizations, such as the African National Council, have become legitimate political parties, but only after denouncing terrorism. Other organizations, like Hamas, are not received in the international community as legitimate political parties, despite successful elections, because of their continued terrorist practices (e.g., see Fisher, 2007).

Evidence suggests that the nature of corporate and terrorist group structures have shifted toward more horizontally complex organizations. Up until the 1920s and 1930s, larger companies generally followed a functional form resembling a pyramid with integrated levels of management (Chandler, 1962). In this form, activities are divided into specialized departments with unique functions, but department heads report to a chief coordinator who continuously reconciles the subgoals of each department (Caves, 1980). Over time firms shifted to a more decentralized, independent structure referred to as the corporate multidivisional form (Chandler, 1962). Rather than a unified top management, company operations are divided into divisions (according to product line or region) with different executives. Executives at company headquarters (in Chandler's terms "the general office") maintain some level of oversight and control by making long-term decisions, evaluating performance and distributing resources across multiple divisions. Division leaders, however, are actually responsible for maintaining a product line or service. In fact, division leaders are responsible for the financial results of his or her unit.

The organization is further decentralized within each division, as each division is responsible for a number of departments with a specific function (e.g., manufacturing, selling, engineering, etc.). In addition, each department coordinates a number of field units. For example, the manufacturing department may coordinate production plants.

Structural shifts in terrorist organizations are much less documented because of the clandestine and illicit nature of their movements. Still, when we examine the structures of long-running organizations, we see some parallels to documented corporate organizational structures. Many older terrorist organizations rely upon hierarchical planning and decision making. The African National Congress (ANC), an older South African group that was formed in 1912 and became violent in 1961, has an 87 member executive committee that makes legislative decisions and a 26 member working committee that manages day-to-day affairs (Hill and Ward, 2002).[2] Similarly, the Revolutionary Armed Forces of Colombia (FARC), which began in 1964 and became violent in 1966, follows a rigid hierarchy (Hill and Ward, 2002).

However, other older groups have relied on more diffuse structures. For example, the major decisions of Euskadi Ta Askatasuna (ETA), which was formed in 1959, are believed to be made by a command council that is run by only six persons (Hill and Ward, 2002). Despite this centralization, the majority of members are organized into three or four member independent cells and live open lives without suspicion. Two cells are assigned to each region, with only one serving as the current operating unit for the area. The second cell lays dormant, waiting to be called into action if the current operating unit is detected, arrested, or destroyed (Hill and Ward, 2002). Thus, ETA's structure is characterized by vertical, horizontal, and spatial complexity, demonstrating that older groups can be complex. In fact, one of the United States' oldest modern terrorist organizations relies heavily on a large network of

---

[2] ANC is now actively involved in the South African Government holding 69.7% of the seats in the National Assembly (Central Intelligence Agency, 2007).

small independent operators located throughout the country. Formed in 1864, the Ku Klux Klan (KKK) is comprised of about 97 distinct groups that rarely cooperate with one another and have no recognized central authority (Hill and Ward, 2002).

Although this seeming mix of organizational types over time suggests no pattern of change, many have written about recent fundamental changes in terrorism calling it the New Terrorism—characterized as being more dangerous than the older terrorism (Laqueur, 1999). The more networked structure, comprised of amateurs who join together for transitory groupings to produce mass casualties, is one of the characteristics that qualify the new terrorism (Hoffman, 1998; Laqueur, 1999; Cronin, 2006; Weimann, 2006). While others (e.g., Tucker, 2001; Crenshaw, 1985) argue that earlier terrorist organizations also relied on networked operations, the evident change of al-Qaeda from the centralized organization that attacked New York and Washington, DC in 2001 to a global network of mostly Sunni Islamist extremists (Pillar, 2004) provides anecdotal evidence of this change. In fact, Mockaitis (2007) argues that al-Qaeda has evolved beyond the network and is now a movement of many smaller unaffiliated groups. Those who attack under the name of al-Qaeda have no direct affiliation with the original organization, other than receiving inspiration, guidance, and perhaps some material support readily available on the Internet. Even when turning aside from al-Qaeda, we see that other relatively recent groups, such as the Animal Liberation Front and Hamas, formed in 1978 and 1987, respectively, do indeed rely on a horizontally complex loosely organized cell structures that follow no real centralized leadership (Hill and Ward, 2002).

Thus, corporations and terrorist organizations have similarly complex structures. While evidence suggests terrorist groups have exhibited the full range of complexity over the past century, the more recent shifts toward decentralization, argued by some researchers, suggest that terrorist organizational structure has evolved in ways that are quite similar to shifts found in corporate structure. Terrorist organizations (like companies) seemed to have moved from a hierarchical to a more diffuse multidivisional form. Regardless of the extent of the shift in terrorist structure, it is clear that the measures of corporate structure (i.e., horizontal, vertical, and spatial complexity) can be usefully applied to the structure of terrorist organizations.

The similarities and differences in the nature and structure of corporate and terrorist organizations have implications for crime control and prevention. In the following section, we describe how structural complexity hinders the use of traditional crime controls for each type of crime. Despite the problems with traditional interventions, the nature of corporations may make them more amenable to deterrence strategies. However, we draw on the terrorism literature to urge caution in relying exclusively on the targeting of top management to prevent future crime.

Implications for Traditional Crime Controls

Structural complexity hinders the detection and prosecution of corporate crime and terrorism in a variety of ways. Beginning with companies, structural complexity reduces the ability of criminal justice officials to pinpoint specific individuals responsible for crime. Larger, decentralized organizations have a higher degree of diffused responsibility. For corporations, a greater number of employees or product types make the dispersion of responsibilities necessary, but also make it extremely difficult to pinpoint individuals or groups of individuals responsible for illegal actions because multiple parties are responsible for a final product (Jamieson, 1994).

Similarly, diffuse organizational structure makes terrorism participants less vulnerable to legal detection. For example, after al-Qaeda lost its training and operational infrastructure in Afghanistan, members relied on associated groups for survival making it nearly impossible to target the group as a whole (Gunaratna, 2004). As noted above, al-Qaeda eventually became a more networked organization and is now considered a global jihad movement of independent, yet loosely affiliated groups. While each group may remain vulnerable to authorities, together, they strengthen the movement's chances of survival. Networked organizations are more difficult to apprehend and prosecute since they have only an informal organizational structure and no permanent existence (Tucker, 2001). Thus, as the movement becomes more decentralized, it is more difficult to collect and analyze intelligence. The mission of intelligence has been to monitor known terrorist groups and uncover any individuals who might become a threat to US interests (Pillar, 2004). This mission becomes more difficult as the number of independent actors increases and the number of large centralized organizations decrease. Pillar (2004) emphasizes this point by stating that a "decentralized terrorist threat will not necessarily leave an intelligence trail" (p. 104).

Although it is difficult to use traditional criminal justice methods for both forms of crime, the nature of the organization and the actors within them may create differences in the effectiveness of traditional criminal justice intervention. Despite problems with prosecuting and deterring corporations that have been extensively discussed by regulatory scholars, the nature of the corporate organization may make it more amenable to this traditional form of crime control than terrorist organizations.

As public (and sometimes publicly traded) entities, corporations must remain in good standing with investors and consumers in order to be profitable. Formal sanctions can damage the reputation of companies among these important groups. In fact, losing individual and firm prestige can lead to company reform (Fisse and Braithwaite, 1983). Top managers also have a lot to lose in the event of formal sanctions. These individuals are employed and are likely to live fairly conventional and affluent lifestyles. The threat or application of criminal penalties, such as prison sentences, may make corporate crime "a personal issue" (Benson and Cullen, 1998).[3]

---

[3] We recognize that the existing empirical literature (objective and perceptual), however, contains mixed support for the impact of formal sanctions on corporate offending (Block et al., 1981; Jamieson, 1994; Simpson and Koper, 1992; Braithwaite and Makkai, 1991; Paternoster and Simpson, 1996; Simpson, 2002). However, penalties for corporate crime are often relatively lenient (for Environmental Protection Agency examples see Harrington, 1988; Hunter and Waterman, 1996). In addition, penalties often come in the form of fines that can be passed on to the consumer. Because it is so difficult to penetrate the organizational structure to detect and prosecute corporate crime (discussed below), harsher penalties may also be necessary to create a stronger deterrent threat

In addition, top managers (and lower level employees) may be deterred from crime by the threat of shame and embarrassment if the act is discovered (Paternoster and Simpson, 1996; Simpson, 2002). As Simpson (1998) states, "informal social control exerts more power over human behavior than does formal social control and, in the case of corporate crime, it may be even more relevant in the crime control equation than it is for street criminals" (p. 105).

Consumers and shareholders may introduce market sanctions beyond the criminal justice penalty. For example, evidence suggests that firm stock prices suffer following negative publicity about the firm's environmental record. The EPA's Toxic Release Inventory (TRI) requires firms to publicly report legal emissions over a specified amount. When the first disclosure of TRI was made, researchers found a significant reduction in the market value for some firms. The average firm experienced a −0.3% negative abnormal return (Hamilton, 1995).

Contrary to our suspicions about corporate criminals, terrorists are unlikely to be deterred by harsher sanctions, especially since they are often wholly willing to exchange their lives or their freedom to strike a blow against their enemies (Pedahzru, 2005). In fact, of the eight reasons that Cronin (2006) gives for a terrorist group's decline, only two are directly related to deterrence through harsher sanctions.[4] Military intervention or repression, has at times contributed to a group's decline, as was the case of the Shining Path in Peru and the Kurdistan Workers' Party in Turkey (Cronin, 2006). Yet, other cases suggest that repression has increased violence, as with the Chechen rebels in Russia and the Irish Republican Army in Northern Ireland (Cronin, 2006; LaFree et al., 2007). Further, long-term repressive measures may challenge civil liberties and human rights that can undermine government legitimacy (Cronin, 2006). Thus, relying on severe sanctioning to deter terrorism is, at best, risky.

However, deterrence strategies that increase sanction certainty, such as target hardening, have been shown to deter airline hijacking (Dugan et al., 2005). Yet, even this strategy should be implemented with caution. Enders and Sandler (1993) found that the deterrence gained from installing metal detectors in airports and fortifying US embassies is counterbalanced by an increase in other kind of hostage-based attacks and assassinations, suggesting that the terrorists simply substituted tactics to avoid hard targets.

While different in this respect, one literature can still inform the other. Corporate crime scholars argue that top management largely sets the tone for corporate culture. Reward structures demonstrate this point. If employees are evaluated solely on economic returns they may feel pressure to resort to illegal methods to maintain or increase profits despite larger economic downturns. In fact, Hill et al. (1992) find that companies that rely mostly on financial data to evaluate divisions have higher

---

for *potential* offenders (Benson et al., 1990). Given these qualifications, it is difficult to draw any conclusions regarding the role of formal sanctions from this small body of literature.

[4] Other reasons that terrorist groups might end include unsuccessful generational transition, achievement of the cause, transition to a legitimate political process, and transition out of terrorism to another form of violence (crime or insurgency) (Cronin, 2006).

levels of Environmental Protection Agency and Occupational Safety and Health violations. Similarly, Pearce and Tombs, (1998) argue that the pressure to return to "normal" levels of foreign capital investment was a major cause of the Bhopal chemical plant disaster. Thus, it may seem logical to target top management for prosecution following a corporate crime. In fact, relatively new environmental laws often contain provisions to hold top management legally liable for crimes they did not witness or act as a participant (Cooney et al., 1996).

Yet, the terrorism literature indicates that attention must be paid to the organizational structure to determine the viability of this form of intervention. Under the hierarchical form, the terrorism literature indicates that once the leaders are removed the group tended to dissolve or be crippled (Tucker, 2001). A number of organizations' activity declined substantially or ended after the leader was captured or killed or after military force repressed the group (Cronin, 2006). Yet, in some cases this strategy has proven ineffective. Decentralized structures make the organization more flexible, adaptive, and resilient since each unit acts on its own behalf being only loosely connected to the others (Tucker, 2001). Terrorist organizations have an advantage over governments that tend to be more hierarchical and less adaptive. It also makes terrorist organizations less vulnerable since the organization is unlikely to rely on only a few actors. In addition, these strategies have been known to backfire. For instance, the effectiveness of the first deterrence strategy, leader capturing, depends upon, among other things, a group's organizational structure (Cronin, 2006). In fact, Israel's 1992 deportation of top leaders from Hamas—a complexly structured group—backfired when the more radical mid-level leaders took over using more deadly tactics against the Israelis (Hoffman and Cragin, 2002). Thus, with today's more common complex terrorist organization, removing the leader may prove ineffective. Furthermore, this strategy has also backfired when loyal groups raised their captured or killed leader to the status of martyr, motivating further attacks (Cronin, 2006; United States Institute for Peace, 1999).[5]

Thus, while top management may need to be held accountable for other reasons, changing top management may do little to reduce future offending in structurally diffuse corporations.

We argue that although corporate crime may be more amenable to traditional forms of intervention than terrorism, the issue of structural complexity makes these approaches problematic for both forms of crime. Based on this similarity, we offer three recommendations that could improve detection and prosecution of both crimes despite the complexity of corporate and terrorist structures. Some of these approaches represent leading reforms to address terrorism, but are less developed and resourced when addressing corporate crime. Here, we note the applicability of these interventions to both forms of crime and address the lack of resources given to corporate crime detection, prevention, and sanctioning in the conclusion.

---

[5] Examples of this include the killing of Che Guevera by the Bolivian army, and Sheikh Omar who is imprisoned for life in the United States (Cronin, 2006).

Some Common Alternative Strategies

Interorganizational Task Forces

Ironically, our first recommendation is to centralize existing criminal justice resources to pursue cases of corporate crime and terrorism. While successful offending organizations rely on a greater dispersion to avoid detection by the law, decentralized attempts to detect and pursue corporate and terrorism offenders are inefficient, and often ineffective. The added complexity of the offender requires the centralization of pursuit. In fact, of the five major recommendations by the 9/11 Commission four begins with the word "unifying" (National Commission on Terrorist Attacks Upon the United States, 2004).[6]

Because of the specialized knowledge and time required to build cases against corporate criminals, interorganizational task forces and specialized prosecution units may increase the utility of existing legal tools. District attorneys participating in interorganizational "control networks" tend to prosecute more corporate crimes (controlling for population size, a proxy for business activity). These networks facilitate joint investigations and general cooperation between agencies, possibly creating a web of agencies with unique skills for different portions of the investigation (Benson et al., 1990). Regardless of whether the prosecution occurs at the local, state, or federal level, creating interorganizational teams can reduce the burden of evidence collection and case building on any one unit. Creating special units to prosecute corporate crime may also facilitate detection and prosecution by developing technical knowledge and the skills necessary to penetrate complex organizational structures to build and prosecute complex cases. In addition, bringing in organizational resources for corporate crime investigations and prosecutions sends a signal that they are important cases, potentially defining new career goals for assistant prosecutors (Benson et al., 1990).

September 11 was a wake-up call for our government to better protect us from terrorism. Prior to this catastrophe, the Federal Bureau of Investigation (FBI) was the primary agency for investigating terrorism activity within US territory. However, it was very decentralized with most authority falling at the local office of case origin (National Commission on Terrorist Attacks Upon the United States, 2004). Furthermore, while it had jurisdiction over US terrorism investigations, its budget failed to adequately account for this. Even after the 1993 World Trade Center bombing and the creation of an FBI Counterterrorism Division, the FBI leadership was unwilling to shift any significant resources toward countering terrorism. Additionally,

---

[6] They include "unifying strategic intelligence and operation planning against Islamist terrorists across the foreign–domestic divide with a National Counterterrorism Center; unifying the intelligence community with a new National Intelligence Director; unifying the many participants in the counterterrorism effort and their knowledge in a network-based information-sharing system that transcends traditional government boundaries; unifying and strengthening congressional oversight to improve quality and accountability; and strengthening the FBI and homeland defenders" (National Commission on Terrorist Attacks Upon the United States, 2004: 399–400).

FBI incentives were directed toward closing criminal cases and not lengthy intelligence investigations that rarely produced quantifiable results (National Commission on Terrorist Attacks Upon the United States, 2004). Other Justice agencies whose investigatory purview was relevant to terrorism include the US Marshals Service and the Immigration and Naturalization Services (INS). The INS had expertise on immigration issues, but the FBI held the evidence needed for deportation cases, causing information-sharing conflict.

The primary foreign intelligence agencies, National Security Agency (NSA) and Central Intelligence Agency (CIA), also operated through decentralized structures, carefully avoiding any jurisdictional breech with the FBI. The NSA was especially careful to avoid domestic intelligence (National Commission on Terrorist Attacks Upon the United States, 2004). As an effort to unify intelligence activities in 1986 the Director of Central Intelligence, William Casey, established a Counterterrorism Center with members of the FBI and other intelligence agencies. While the Center was relatively successful in some investigations, it was criticized as inadequate by the CIA's Inspector General (National Commission on Terrorist Attacks Upon the United States, 2004).

Since September 11, efforts have been made to abolish the foreign–domestic divide in intelligence gathering. The CIA is still central, but the FBI's role has expanded greatly. Furthermore, the Bush administration established the Department of Homeland Security (DHS) to institutionalize interagency cooperation by collapsing most of the terrorism-relevant domestic agencies into one department (Carter, 2001).[7] For example, some components include the Office of Intelligence and Analysis, the Federal Law Enforcement Training Center, the Transportation Security Administration, United States Citizenship and Immigration Services, and the Federal Emergency Management Agency. However, the jurisdiction of DHS excludes other important investigatory agencies such as the FBI, the CIA, and the National Security Agencies, thus not fully resolving all relevant communication across nonaffiliated agencies.

While prosecution is not yet centralized, it is becoming more specialized. The US justice system currently prosecutes terrorism cases in the federal courts and is already moving toward specialized prosecution. Thus, the US government has moved from treating perpetrators as common criminals to centralizing all cases with the intention to eventually trying them in military tribunals (Smith et al., 2003). In the wake of the Watergate era, 1973 federal guidelines were explicitly designed to depoliticize investigations, framing the defendants as common criminals. This strategy was substantiated later in the 1980s when three terrorism trials failed to convict on charges of seditious conspiracy (Smith et al., 2003). However, even before the

---

[7] DHS (2007) "leverages resources within federal, state, and local governments, coordinating the transition of multiple agencies and programs into a single, integrated agency focused on protecting the American people and their homeland. More than 87,000 different governmental jurisdictions at the federal, state, and local level have homeland security responsibilities. The comprehensive national strategy seeks to develop a complementary system connecting all levels of government without duplicating effort. Homeland Security is truly a 'national mission'."

attacks of September 11, courts became more willing to politicize their prosecution of foreign terrorists after the successful conviction of the 24 defendants in the two World Trade Center trials that ended in 1997 (Smith et al., 2003). Also, the United States in 1995, Chapter 113B of the Federal Criminal Code and Rules added "Terrorism" as a separate offense and the Antiterrorism and Effective Death Penalty Act was signed into law in 1996. Since September 11, the government has been preparing to use military tribunals to prosecute suspected foreign terrorists beginning with the federal order in November 2001 (Smith et al., 2003).[8] More recently the White House has submitted legislation to congress to authorize the creation of military commissions to try terrorists of war crimes (The White House, 2006).

Encouraging Whistle-Blowers

We also suggest further encouraging whistle-blowing. Empirical research suggests that employees are more active in reporting corporate fraud than other actors (Dyck et al., 2007). The authors turn to Hayek (1945) to explain this finding. Information is diffuse, particularly in companies. Thus, employees have an advantage over criminal justice officials because they have "superior access to information about the fraud" (p. 4). Although criminal justice officials have the incentive to detect and prosecute corporate crime, they do not have this type of access to credit information upon which to act (Dyck et al., 2007). Thus, to some extent whistle-blowers reduce the burden on criminal justice officials to penetrate the organizational structure by providing information from inside the organization. However, because there are many disincentives for whistle-blowing, it may be helpful to provide increased incentives to those willing to come forward (Dyck et al., 2007). Data suggest that providing monetary incentives for detection in frauds against the government does not increase frivolous claims (Dyck et al., 2007). Although controversial, laws such as the Sarbanes Oxley Act that increase protections afforded to whistle-blowers may also facilitate this method of detection (Kleckner and Jackson, 2004).

The nature of how whistle-blowers operate would be fairly different in terrorist organizations because the whistle-blowers themselves are already involved in illegal behavior. Yet, the idea is similar. Crenshaw (2001) recommends that one way to facilitate the demise of a terrorism organization is to offer new nonviolent incentives, increasing the opportunity to exit an organization. Similarly, the government can promote the expression of internal dissent. The Italian government used similar strategies to bring down the Red Brigades by offering leniency to members for information leading to the apprehension of other Red Brigade members (Crenshaw, 2001; Cronin, 2006). This strategy might be most successful when the organization is already facing defeat and its members have a clear incentive to leave (Cronin, 2006). However, other terrorists might be ready to leave before this point

---

[8] Military Order, November 13, 2001, Detention, Treatment, and Trial of Certain Non-Citizens in the War Against Terrorism, §1(a), 66 Fed. Reg. 57.833 (Nov. 16, 2001)

because they are already disheartened by the organization. Unlike the leaders, not all foot soldiers are ideologically committed to the mission of the organization. In fact, Crenshaw (1985) claims that the image of the terrorist who is motivated exclusively by overarching goals of the organization is misleading. She argues that they are also motivated by the need to belong, the desire for social status, and the acquisition of material reward. As the organization stops meeting these needs, it may be possible to tempt the terrorist away. According to Roberts (2007), terrorists do value their own lives and only a small percentage of them desire to participate in suicide operations. Furthermore, evidence suggests that most are unwilling to be imprisoned. Work by Anthony (2003) shows that even suicide terrorists will delay their attack until success is more certain, reducing the chances that they are imprisoned rather than killed.

While these suggestions are specifically recommended to increase the certainty of criminal justice prosecution, other methods are available that can disrupt crime before it happens. Because it is very difficult to penetrate complex organizational structures after a crime has occurred, perpetrators are often never discovered. In addition, reactive deterrence-based strategies may be less optimal for both corporate crime and terrorism because of the potentially high consequences, making proactive strategies preferred (Reiss, 1984). The specific proactive methods differ according to the type of crime, but all share a common theme of focusing on prevention.

Focusing on Prevention

Knowledge and monitoring of the conditions that may lead to crime is required to implement proactive systems of control. Thus, compliance systems put procedures in place that alert officials when a violation might occur (Reiss, 1984). Unlike terrorist organizations, corporations operate legitimately, leading many regulatory agencies to rely on the company to monitor itself. For example, in the environmental arena, firms often have to self-report pollution discharges to the Environmental Protection Agency (EPA). In some cases firms also are required to make construction or technological changes over a period of time to increase their ability to comply with permitted pollution levels (i.e., a compliance schedule). Failure to submit a self-report or to reach a compliance schedule deadline may signal that a serious violation has occurred or may occur in the future. The EPA also sends inspectors to examine record keeping, water or air sampling procedures, and other operations to determine whether firms are on the track to compliance. Problematic behavior detected in self-reports or inspections can trigger a proactive response.[9]

Whether proactive or reactive, EPA and other regulatory responses are often cooperative in nature. Regulatory agencies offer compliance assistance (proactive) and often deal with violations reactively in a cooperative manner by issuing informal sanctions (e.g., warning letters, phone calls). These strategies are not used alone;

---

[9] Other regulatory agencies also use this approach. For example, the Securities and Exchange Commission requires a variety of book keeping procedures for a similar purpose (Reiss, 1984).

formal sanctions can always be issued to noncooperative firms. In fact, most regulatory agencies rely on both punishment based and cooperative forms of control (Reiss, 1984).

Since terrorist organizations are definitionally illegal, regulatory strategies are inappropriate. Yet, this does not mean that proactive prevention is a useless approach to terrorism. In fact, three of the four suggestions to stop terrorism by RAND analysts, Hoffman and Cragin, (2002), indirectly focus on prevention. They suggest that governments delegitimize—not just arrest or kill—the top leaders of terrorist groups. Leaders of terrorist organizations are the representatives of the movement. By discrediting the leaders, the followers lose momentum and may naturally become inactive. Another suggestion by RAND is to focus efforts on disrupting support networks and their trafficking activities. By thwarting support efforts, the terrorist organization is less able to maintain everyday activities necessary to maintain operation. Roberts (2007) argues that most operational enablers have much to lose and are therefore important targets for deterrent strategies. Finally, Hoffman and Cragin (2002) recommend that the government establish a dedicated counterintelligence center to obstruct terrorist reconnaissance. This raises the important recognition that sophisticated terrorism operations require at least a basic level of planning and reconnaissance. During this period, US intelligence may be able to intercept terrorist organizations' own intelligence gathering processes.

A final strategy for prevention might be to cooperate with terrorist organizations to some degree by encouraging the organization to participate in a legitimate political process. While the United States currently opposes any negotiations with a known terrorist organization (The White House, 2001), other nations have successfully reduced violence by engaging the perpetrators. One obvious example is when ANC leader Nelson Mandela was elected as president of South Africa following the end of apartheid in 1990, ending a nearly 40 year campaign of violence. Also, the Good Friday agreement in 1998, which brought a reprieve in Northern Ireland violence, resulted from talks between the Provisional Irish Republican Army and the British and Irish governments (Cronin, 2006). Israel engaged in peace agreement talks with Palestinian Liberation Organization during the 1990s, and the Sri Lankan government negotiated with the Liberation Tigers of Tamil Eelam in 2002 (Cronin, 2006).

However, this strategy also comes with historical warnings. In many cases, including some listed above, once a peace agreement is negotiated on either or both sides are likely to form splinter organizations increasing violence in order to sabotage the peace process (Cronin, 2006). Splinter groups are more likely to emerge when the original organizations are already horizontally complex.

Conclusion

In this chapter, we describe several similarities and differences between corporations and terrorist organizations. Although corporate crime and terrorism seem to be very distinct forms of behavior and are distinct in nature, we demonstrate clear overlap in the organizational structure related to both forms of crime. We believe that this odd comparison is important because knowledge of and response to one form of crime can potentially inform knowledge of and response to the other.

First, although terrorist structures are less well documented, the terminology developed by scholars to describe corporate structure can fittingly describe the structure of terrorist organizations. Second, corporate criminals and terrorism groups benefit from complex organizational structures because the structure makes it more difficult to infiltrate the organization. When corporations are broadly structured with many independently operating units, it is difficult for authorities to pinpoint and prosecute exact sources of crime. Similarly, it is harder for governments to dismantle structurally diffuse terrorist organizations. In attempting to address corporate crime, some environmental laws have begun to hold top managers accountable for actions taken by lower level employees. Yet, the terrorism literature suggests caution in assuming that the removal of top leaders will reduce future crime.

Although corporations may be more amenable than terrorist organizations to traditional controls (formal and informal), the consistent role of organizational complexity in masking corporate crime and terrorism leads us to make similar recommendations for taking additional steps to control both types of crime. While corporations and terrorist groups are different in important ways (e.g., one is legal and one is illegal by definition), our ability to make unified recommendations suggests that scholars of each type of crime may benefit from knowing what strategies are promising/effective in controlling the other.

Ironically, in order to be better positioned to detect misconduct, investigate the perpetrator, and prosecute, we recommend that authorities combine resources and expertise to specialize in each area. Furthermore, budgets should adequately support the mission of these efforts. We have already seen some movement in this direction by the US government with the formation of the Department of Homeland Security, and as the FBI and foreign intelligence agencies begin to share information and combine efforts to pursue terrorists. The specific nature of this centralization may be different for corporate crime, but efforts to pursue corporate criminals may still be informed by current efforts to pursue terrorists. Specifically, the prevention, detection, and prosecution of corporate crime may be improved by some level of centralization and by appropriately increasing resources.

Some interorganizational work groups exist (Benson et al., 1990) and the Department of Justice is responsible for most federal prosecutions, but many enforcement activities are still agency specific. Corporations are currently regulated by a variety of agencies, each with their own dedicated function. The laws enforced by each agency are very specific and thus require some degree of specialization. Thus, combating corporate crime may not require the creation of one overarching department, but instead a centralized exchange of information and resources across agencies. This is especially useful earlier in the investigative process, since firms may violate multiple laws that are regulated by different agencies. The EPA, for example, might be unaware that a firm consistently violates Securities and Exchange Commission requirements. With this information, the EPA could more precisely recognize the nature of the firm and choose a more appropriate enforcement approach (i.e., punishment vs. cooperation). Also, a centralized information exchange would also improve research on corporate violations. Efforts to study corporate crime are consistently hindered by a lack of publicly accessible data (Simpson, 2003), an issue magnified by agency specific data sources.

As was the case with US efforts to control terrorism prior to September 11, current efforts to detect and prosecute corporate crime are constrained by insufficient budgets. Many regulatory agencies are underfunded and under-resourced (Hunter and Waterman, 1996). In fact, the number of EPA investigators is currently below what is required under the 1990 Pollution Prosecution Act (Solomon and Eilperin, 2007).

We recognize that this recommendation requires effort and resources and might be met with resistance. The US government was only willing to radically restructure itself to control terrorism after the disaster on September 11. Despite several high profile cases of corporate misdoings—for example, Enron, and the savings and loan scandal—the high costs of corporate crime fails to generate the level of urgency needed to radically restructure our pursuit. In part this may be due to the amount of political power wielded by large corporations today (Clinard and Yeager, 1980), power that could potentially cripple the political careers of those who pursue specialized investigation and prosecution. The United States experienced dramatic drops in enforcement activity of the Nuclear Regulatory Commission; engineering evaluations of the National Highway and Traffic Safety Commission; cessation orders in the Office of Surface Mining during the Reagan administration in the 1980s (Wood and Waterman, 1991). A recent article published in the Washington Post describes a similar drop in the number of EPA prosecutions and the number of criminal investigators under the Bush administration (Solomon and Eilperin, 2007). These trends help us appreciate the far reaching influence of corporate interests on politicians.

Yet, all one really needs to do is examine the high costs of corporate crime on the US taxpayers to appreciate the urgency of this issue (Reiman, 1997). Corporate crime and terrorism have far reaching and consequential impacts. Thus, we hope our comparison of the two will facilitate a similar level of cooperation and resources to detect and prosecute both forms of crime. National Commission on Terrorist Attacks Upon the United States

References

Anthony, Robert W. 2003. *Deterrence and the 9–11 Terrorists.* IDA Document D-2802 Alexandria, VA: Institute for Defense Analysis.

Benson, Michael L., Francis T. Cullen and William J. Maakestad. 1990. "Local prosecutors and corporate crime." *Crime and Delinquency* 36(3): 356–372.

Benson, Michael L. and Francis T. Cullen. 1998. *Combating Corporate Crime: Local Prosecutors at Work.* Boston, MA: Northeastern University press.

Block, Michael K, Frederick C. Nold, and J. Gregory Sidak. 1981. "The deterrent effect of antitrust enforcement." *Journal of Political Economy* 89(3): 429–445.

Braithwaite, John and Toni Makkai. 1991. "Testing an expected utility model of corporate deterrence." *Law and Society Review* 25(1): 7–40.

Carter, Ashton B. 2001. "The architecture of government in the face of terrorism." *International Security* 26: 5–23.

Caves, Richard E. 1980. "Industrial organization, corporate strategy and structure." *Journal of Economic Literature* 18(1): 64–92.

Central Intelligence Agency 2007. *CIA World Factbook*. https://www.cia.gov/library/publications/the-world-factbook/geos/sf.html

Chandler, Alfred D. 1962. *Strategy and Structure: Chapters in the History of the American Industrial Enterprise*. United States: Massachusetts Institute of Technology.

Clinard, Marshall B. and Peter C. Yeager. 1980. *Corporate Crime*. New York: Free Press.

Cooney, John F., Judson W. Starr, Joseph G. Block, Thomas J. Kelly, Jr., Andrew R. Herrup, Valerie K. Mann, and Gregory Braker. 1996. "Criminal enforcement of environmental laws." *Environmental Crimes Deskbook*. Washington, DC: Environmental Law Institute.

Crenshaw, Martha. 1985. "An organizational approach to the analysis of political terrorism." *Orbis* 29: 465–489.

Crenshaw, Martha. 2001. "Theories of terrorism: instrumental and organizational approaches." in D.C. Rapoport (ed.), *Inside Terrorism Organizations* (pp. 13–29). London: Frank Cass.

Cronin, Audrey Kurth. 2006. "How al-Qaida ends." *International Security* 31: 7–48.

Department of Homeland Security. 2007. Department Subcomponents and Agencies, http://www.dhs.gov/xabout/structure/

Dugan, Laura, Gary Lafree, and Alex Piquero. (2005) "Testing a rational choice model of airline Hijackings." *Criminology* 43: 1031–1066.

Dyck, I.J. Alexander, Adair Morse and Luigi Zingales. 2007. "Who blows the whistle on corporate fraud?" AFA 2007 Chicago Meetings Paper Available at SSRN: http://ssrn.com/abstract=891482

Enders, Walter, and Todd Sandler. 1993. "The effectiveness of antiterrorism policies: a vector-autoregression-intervention analysis." *American Political Science Review* 87: 829–844.

Fisher, Ian. 2007. "Top official of Hamas is rebuffed over talks." *The New York Times* June 24, 2007.

Fisse, Brent and John Braithwaite. 1983. *The Impact of Publicity on Corporate Offenders?* Albany, NY: State University of Albany Press.

Gunaratna, Rohan. 2004 "The post-madrid face of Al Qaeda." *The Washington Quarterly* 27: 91–100.

Hamilton, James T. 1995. "Pollution as news: Media and stock market reactions to the toxics release inventory data." *Journal of Environmental Economics and Management* 28: 98–113.

Harrington, Winston. 1988. "Enforcement leverage when penalties are restricted." *Journal of Public Economics* 37(1): 29–54.

Hayek, Friedrich. 1945. "The use of knowledge in society." *American Economic Review* 34(4): 519–530.

Hill, Charles W.L., Patricia C. Kelley, Bradley R. Agle, Michael A. Hitt, and Robert E. Hoskisson. 1992. "An empirical examination of the causes of corporate wrongdoing in the United States." *Human Relations* 45(10): 1055–1076.

Hill, Sean D. and Richard H. Ward. 2002. *Extremist Groups an International Compilation of Terrorist Organizations, Violent Political groups, and Issue-Oriented Militant Movements*. 2nd Ed. Huntsville, TX: Office of International Criminal Justice and the Institute for the Study of Violent Groups.

Hoffman, Bruce. 1998. *Inside Terrorism*. New York: Columbia University Press.

Hoffman, Bruce and Kim Cragin. 2002. "Four lessons from five countries." *Rand Review*, Summer 2002.

Hunter, Susan and Richard W. Waterman. 1996. *Enforcing the Law: The Case of the Clean Water Acts*. Armonk, NY: M.E. Sharpe.

Jamieson, Katherine M. 1994. *The Organization of Corporate Crime: Dynamics of Antitrust Violation*. London: Sage Publications.

Kleckner, Phil and Craig Jackson. 2004. "Sarbanes-Oxley and Whistle Blower protections." *The CPA Journal* 74(6): 14.

LaFree, Gary and Laura Dugan. 2004. "How does studying terrorism compare to studying crime?" in M. DeFlem (ed.), *Terrorism and Counter-Terrorism: Criminological Perspectives* (pp. 53–74). New York: Elsevier.

LaFree, Gary, Laura Dugan, and Raven Korte. 2007. Is Counter Terrorism Counterproductive? Northern Ireland 1969–1992." unpublished manuscript.

Laqueur, Walter. 1999. *The New Terrorism*. New York: Oxford University Press.

McCauley, Clark, Julie Huang, Laura Dugan, and Gary LaFree. 2008. "Sudden Desistence from Terrorism: The Armenian Secret Army for the Liberation of Armenia and the Justice Commandos of the Armenian Genocide." unpublished manuscript.

McKendall, Marie A. and John A. Wagner III. 1997. "Motive, opportunity, choice, and corporate illegality." *Organization Science: A Journal of the Institute of Management Sciences* 8(6): 624–648.

Mockaitis, Thomas R. 2007. *The "New" Terrorism Myths and Reality*. Westport, CT: Praeger Security International.

National Commission on Terrorism Attacks Upon the United States. 2004. *The 9/11 Commission Report*. New York: W.W. Norton & Company Ltd.

Paternoster, Raymond and Sally S. Simpson. 1996. "Sanction threats and appeals to morality: testing a rational choice model of corporate crime." *Law and Society Review* 30(3): 549–585.

Pearce, Frank and Steven Tombs. 1998. Toxic Capitalism: *Corporate Crime and the Chemical Industry*. Farnborough: Ashgate.

Pearce, Frank. 2001. "Crime and capitalist business corporations." in Neal Shover and John Paul Wright (eds.), *Crimes of Privilege: Readings in White-Collar Crime*. Oxford: Oxford University Press.

Pedahzru, Ami. 2005. *Suicide Terrorism*. Cambridge: Polity Press.

Pillar, Paul R. 2004. "Counterterrorism after Al Qaeda." *The Washington Quarterly* 27: 101–113.

Reiman, Jeffrey. 1997. *The Rich Get Richer and the Poor Get Prison*. Boston, MA: Allyn & Bacon.

Reiss, Albert J. Jr. 1984. "Selecting strategies of social control over organizational life." In Keith Hawkins and John M. Thomas (eds.) *Enforcing Regulation*. Boston: Klawer-Nijhoff Publishers.

Roberts, Brad. 2007. *Deterrence and WMD Terrorism: Calibrating its Potential Contributions to Risk Reduction*. IDA Paper P-4231 Alexandria, VA: Institute for Defense Analysis.

Simpson, Sally S. 2003. "The criminological enterprise and corporate crime." *The Criminologist* 28: 1–5.

Simpson, Sally S. 2002. *Corporate Crime, Law, and Social Control*. Cambridge, UK: Cambridge University Press.

Simpson, Sally S. 1998. "Assessing corporate crime control policies: Criminalization versus cooperation." *Kobe University Law Review* 32: 101–127.

Simpson, Sally S. and Christopher S. Koper. 1992. "Deterring corporate crime." *Criminology* 30(3): 347–375.

Smith, Brent L., Kelly R. Dampshousse, Freedom Jackson, and Amy Sellers. 2003. "The prosecution and punishment of international terrorists in federal courts: 1980–1998." *Criminology and Public Policy* 1: 311–338.

Solomon, John and Juliet Eilperin. 2007. "Bush's EPA is pursuing fewer polluters: probes and prosecutions have declined sharply." *The Washington Post*.

Tucker, David. 2001. "What's new about the new terrorism and how dangerous is it?" *Terrorism and Political Violence* 13: 1–14.

United States Institute of Peace. 1999. *How Terrorism Ends*. Special Report, No. 48, Washington, DC: United States Institute for Peace.

Weimann, Gabriel. 2006. *Terror on the Internet*. Washington, DC: United States Institute for Peace.

The White House. 2006. "President discusses creation of military commissions to try suspected terrorists." *White House News Release*, September 2006.

The White House. 2001. "Address to a joint session of congress and the American people." *White House News Release*, September 2001.

Wood, Dan B. and Richard W. Waterman. 1991. "The dynamics of political control of the Bureaucracy." *American Political Science Review* 85: 801–828.

Globalization and White-Collar Crime

Peter Grabosky

Abstract This chapter discusses how globalization facilitates white-collar crime, and how it can foster more effective mechanisms for the prevention and control of white-collar crime. It uses the framework of routine activity theory to explain transnational white-collar crime, then presents a range of offence types with examples of cross-border offending. The essay then turns to a discussion of regulatory institutions that can comprise a system of transnational white-collar crime control. It illustrates the evolution of global regulatory systems with the examples of transnational corruption control and the international cooperation to combat money laundering. The chapter concludes with the observation that, as is the case of conventional domestic "street crime," the effective prevention and control of white-collar crime in an era of globalization requires the involvement of public, private, and nonprofit institutions.

Introduction

Globalization, like community (and indeed, like white-collar crime itself), is an ambiguous concept. The term globalization is used here to refer to the movement around the world of people, ideas, commodities, finance, and viruses (both biological and technological). There is nothing uniquely modern about globalization and its interface with white-collar crime. Legend has it that Persian monks, acting on behalf of the Roman Emperor Justinian, succeeded in smuggling silkworms out of China, thereby breaking the Chinese monopoly on silk production (Ertl 2006, p. 249). Much later, the technology of textile production, a closely guarded secret in Britain, was compromised and transferred across the Atlantic, giving rise to the American textile industry (Fialka 1997, p. xi). But contemporary manifestations of globalization and crime occur in much greater variety, and at a velocity

P. Grabosky (✉)
ARC Centre of Excellence in Policing and Security, Regulatory Institutions Network,
Research School of Pacific and Asian Studies, Australian National University, Australia

S.S. Simpson, D. Weisburd (eds.), *The Criminology of White-Collar Crime*,
DOI 10.1007/978-0-387-09502-8_7, © Springer Science+Business Media, LLC 2009

that was the stuff of science fiction until recently. Findlay's (1999, p. 1) reference to "time-space compression" has a definite sci-fi ring to it. But it rings true today.

There is nothing inherently evil about globalization, although it certainly has brought angry people into the streets in many countries. On the contrary, the benefits are both numerous and spectacular. A half century ago, anyone interested in a particular indigenous community in the northwest of South Australia would either have to venture there oneself (a long and arduous journey), consult a knowledgeable anthropologist (of which there were very few), or go to a library large enough to have very esoteric holdings. Today, one can simply visit the community's own website (see http://waru.org/) and become a virtual tourist. More broadly, the greater accessibility of information has dramatically improved life in many places around the globe.

At the same time, globalization is hardly an unmitigated good. The relentless domination of American culture is eclipsing local tastes and customs in some of the world's most remote areas. I recall first having heard the term "coca-colonization" more than four decades ago, and the process has only intensified (Ritzer 2004). Without appearing to be paternalistic, one might suggest that the choices that people exercise after exposure to western culture may not always be in their best interest—infant formula may be inferior to breast milk.

There are winners and losers in the global village. In bread-and-butter terms, the migration of jobs to low-wage countries has helped raise the standard of living where new jobs are created, but it has lowered the standard of living for many in those countries where jobs were lost. And globalization has created spectacular opportunities for enrichment, both legitimate and illicit. The fall of the Berlin wall and the end of the Cold War produced significant global impacts. In addition to the centrifugal forces unleashed by the demise of some socialist states such as Yugoslavia (Woodward 1995), the transition to market economies was particularly noteworthy. Although this may prove beneficial in the long run, millions of people unfamiliar with capitalist modes of exchange were presented with commercial opportunities that were too good to be true (Bezemer 2001).

Globalization, like gravity, appears immutable. Our task here is not to rail against it, but rather to explore the relationship of globalization to white-collar crime. By *white-collar crime*, we will generally conform to Sutherland's definition of *crime committed by persons of respectability and high social status in the course of their occupation* (Sutherland 1949). Sutherland's conceptual shortcomings have been dissected by Geis (1992) and others, and need not concern us here. In an effort to avoid intruding upon the subject matter of organized crime, we will limit our focus to the criminal activities of persons in legitimate occupations, or of otherwise legitimate organizations, although the distinction is blurred in cases such as the corrupt bank, BCCI (Passas 1996), the Government of North Korea (Perl 2005), and of lawyers or accountants in league with their criminal clients (see also Passas and Nelken 1993).

Globalization and White-Collar Crime

Neal Shover (1998, 155–156) provides a brief and elegant discussion of white-collar crime from a global perspective. He notes that growth in the world economic system has provided unprecedented opportunities for white-collar crime, and that authorities in poor countries lack the resources and capacity to combat it. The unprecedented mobility of capital allows prospective offenders to seek out jurisdictions where they can do business with impunity. The threat of withdrawal of capital, and the loss of the few advantages that otherwise harmful corporate activity might still bring to a jurisdiction, may persuade local authorities to tolerate victimization. Using Shover's analysis as a foundation, let us look at the relationship between globalization and white-collar crime in more detail.

Routine activity theory (Cohen and Felson 1979) provides a convenient lens through which to view white-collar crime in the era of globalization. White-collar crime, like all crime, occurs at the intersection of three factors: a supply of motivated offenders, the availability of suitable targets or victims, and the absence of capable guardians. Remove any one of these three factors, and you prevent white-collar crime. Unfortunately, this is easier said than done.

The Ubiquity of Motivated Offenders

It is overly simplistic to suggest that fraud, much less the wider universe of white-collar crime, is generally attributable to excessive greed. Offenders are also motivated by the desire for power, revenge, celebrity, intellectual challenge, and what might be described as "the thrill of the deal" (Duffield and Grabosky 2001). In the world of business, the quest for competitive advantage may be the dominant factor. And harm itself may result from ignorance, or negligence, rather than criminal intent.

The same broad range of motivations may be seen in the realm of ordinary street crime. Katz' (1988) classic *Seductions of Crime*, is subtitled *Moral and Sensual Attractions in Doing Evil*. Black (1983) observes that much crime can be regarded as social control mobilized in response to an affront. Similarly, Polk (1994) describes many homicides as "masculine honour contests." Sherman's (1993) defiance theory is no less applicable to perpetrators of domestic violence than it is to the organized culture of resistance that can be provoked by unreasonable enforcement of business regulations (Bardach and Kagan 1982).

The significance of globalization to the supply of motivated offenders rests in the abundance of professional and organizational life today that transcends national frontiers. More goods and services are exchanged across international frontiers today than ever before. Transnational corporations are nothing new; the British East India Company began in the seventeenth century. But today there are more companies spanning more physical space than ever before, and occasions for transnational criminal exploitation have never been greater. Whether people today are less honest than in the past, is not the point. What does matter is that more actors, respectable and venal, are on the move.

The Proliferation of Opportunities

This same abundance has a "flip side." The proliferation and widespread global distribution of professional and organizational life makes for an increase in the number of accessible targets. This trend mimics the abundance of consumer goods and the proliferation of shopping centers in affluent western societies in the 1960s, which created unprecedented opportunities for theft (Felson 2006, 13).

This growth and dispersion is significantly enhanced by digital technology, which spectacularly improves communication capabilities. The cost of sending a fraudulent investment solicitation to a million people 50 years ago would have been prohibitively expensive for all but those with access to the financial press. Today, a sole individual can make such a solicitation, without any editorial intermediation, instantaneously and at negligible cost. A company that marketed unsafe products in five countries a quarter century ago might be doing its risky business in 25 countries today.

Crime follows opportunity, and globalization, accelerated by developments in technology, has created an abundance of opportunities for criminal activities of all sorts. The resourcefulness and versatility of criminal organizations has meant that a good deal of their activity now occurs across national borders. Much of this entails what is generally termed "organized crime," and we will take care not to intrude too much on that terrain. But a brief wander along the border might be instructive. A great deal of organized crime involves the complicity, witting or unwitting, of persons of respectability and high social status.

For some time now, it has become recognized that most organized crime is not monolithic. Rather than hierarchical organizations comprised of family members and commanded by a "Mr. Big," one finds loose, temporary coalitions of specialized "units" which perform specific functions in furtherance of a criminal enterprise. In other words, criminal organizations are not vertically integrated, but rather networked. And some elements of these networks may be otherwise legitimate (Morselli and Giguere 2006).

Not all participants in a criminal network, domestic or transnational, are fully complicit. Knowledge of the criminality of the enterprise may vary. An otherwise legitimate courier service may not be aware that it is transporting consignments of contraband. A fertilizer retailer may not be aware that its product is to be used for the manufacture of explosives. A rental car company may be unaware that a lessee is using their vehicle to transport drugs. Bankers may not inquire too deeply about the provenance of funds entrusted to them. Some professional advisors may even be inclined to turn a blind eye to their clients' indiscretions (Ruggiero 2003). At worst, they may become co-conspirators or accomplices.

Interdependencies

Another implication of globalization is the interdependency that accompanies it. It has long been said that when Wall Street sneezes, the world catches a cold. White-collar crimes can reverberate both domestically and around the globe. The fraudulent substitution of inferior products can jeopardize an entire export market, as was the case when kangaroo meat was discovered by United States Department of Agriculture (USDA) inspectors in a consignment of Australian export beef in San Diego (Grabosky 1989).

Some national economies and political systems are robust enough to withstand grievous insults and still recover. The Savings and Loan scandal in the United States (Black 2005) and the collapse of Enron (Tillman and Indergaard 2005) arose from white-collar illegality of colossal magnitude, but did not significantly detract from the attractiveness of the United States as a place to invest. Smaller countries, however, may be more vulnerable.

But large-scale financial crimes, such as those which lead to the collapse of major financial institutions, can have wide ramifications. They can shake the confidence of global markets. In recent years, the demise of Barings Bank and the Sumitomo copper scandal have had significant reverberations. Barings, a venerable British institution which had helped finance the Napoleonic Wars, collapsed in February 1995 after one of its traders lost US $1.4 billion in disastrous trading in derivatives contracts (Singapore 1995). In the immediate aftermath of the collapse, Japan's Nikkei 225 index fell 3.8%, and the British pound plunged to a record low against the Deutsche mark. Around the same time, an employee of the Sumitomo Corporation was blamed for single-handedly losing US $1.8 billion trading copper. Following the announcement, world copper prices fell to their lowest point in over 2 years (Kharouf 1996). The Asian economic crisis of the late 1990s, arising in no small part from criminal fraud, extortion, bribery, and corruption in a number of nations, had a noticeable (if temporary) adverse impact on the export revenues of their major trading partners (Summers 2001). The extent to which criminal activity contributed to the global financial crisis of 2008 was unclear at the time of writing.

Although the rapidly growing economies of the Asian region present golden opportunities for nearby producers, they also create incentives for fraud. Consider, for example, commercial fishing. While Asian-driven demand has been a boon to the Australian, New Zealand, and Pacific Islands fishing industries, it has produced two unfortunate consequences. Foreign fishers may be attracted to waters of small island states, where they fish illegally, unaware, or in disregard of whatever local regulations may exist, to the disadvantage of the local fishing industry. Aqorau (2000) local fishers, mindful of the high prices that their product may fetch, may be tempted to exceed their quotas, and fraudulently understate their catch. This could result in overfishing and the collapse of the entire industry, as occurred with the New England fishery in the United States (Holmes 1994).

Traditional white-collar crime may be no less harmful. Markets that are seen to be rigged will not attract investors. Small investors may shy away from the stock market because they see it as the playground of insider traders; others may be deterred by their perception of corporate high flyers as looters of shareholders' money. To the extent that a major institution of the economy is seen as tainted, the economy will suffer. Some years ago, the government of Albania collapsed after a significant proportion of its citizenry, unfamiliar with institutions of capitalism and their vulnerability to criminal exploitation, fell victim to a Ponzi scheme and as a result lost their life savings (Bezemer 2001). Incidentally, the flood of economic refugees that this scandal triggered placed great stress on maritime and border protection authorities in nearby Italy (Perlmutter 1998). This avoidance is analogous to neighborhood decline resulting from crime and disorder. In some settings, decline may be gradual, while at other times, such as the aftermath of a civil disturbance, it may be more abrupt (Solomon and Vandell 1982; Skogan 1986).

The Absence of Capable Guardians

In the realm of white-collar crime no less than ordinary crime, the term "capable guardian" refers generally to mechanisms of surveillance—arrangements for the scrutiny of individual or of organizational conduct to ensure that illegalities do not occur. These arrangements may entail the activity of state regulatory agencies, professional advisers, nongovernmental organizations (NGOs), industry associations, or in-house compliance officers.

Over a decade ago, Crook et al. (1992) observed that nation states were shedding functions either upwards (to international governmental organizations such as the Council of Europe), or downwards (to local governments, the private sector or individuals, or to NGOs).

One of the characteristic features of globalization is the pressure to rationalize. Global markets favor small government and reward those nations that place minimal constraints on business. The move toward economic rationalism and deregulation emerged under the Thatcher government in Britain, was quickly taken up under the Reagan regime in the United States, and began to spread around the world to settings as diverse as New Zealand and Eastern Europe. Paradoxically, Levi-Faur (2005) observes that the privatization of previously state-owned enterprises has been accompanied by a proliferation of new forms of regulation, designed to exercise a modicum of guardianship over newly privatized entities.

One sees similar patterns in the area of street crime. Over a decade has passed since observers noted that governments had set about devolving responsibility for conventional crime prevention to ordinary citizens (Garland 1996; O'Malley and Palmer 1996). And the growth of the private security industry has, in many countries, been accompanied by moves for its regulation (Sarre and Prenzler 2000).

Varieties of Transnational White-Collar Crime

Let us now look at some of the basic forms of white-collar crime involving cross-border conduct or impact. These examples are far from exhaustive, but do illustrate the forms that white-collar illegality can take in an era of globalization.

Fraudulent Marketing/Sales

In general, fraud entails obtaining something of value by means of deception (Levi 1987). One form of fraud occurs in the course of commerce, where a vendor offers a product for sale that is defective or nonexistent. The offer of investment opportunities that are patently unrealistic is but one of many such practices. Advances in information and communications technologies permit fraudulent investment solicitations to be made across national borders as easily as domestically. Three individuals in the state of Washington conducted a business that offered a minimum income for investors of US $5,250 per month in return for an advance payment of between US $250 and $1,750. The US Federal Trade Commission found that between US $6 and $11 million had been obtained from between 30,000 and 40,000 consumers in 60 countries (Da Silva 1996; Starek and Rozell 1997, 689–690).

Money Laundering

The term "money laundering" refers to the means by which offenders conceal the origins of ill-gotten gains, thereby transforming "dirty money" into "clean money." This can involve numerous complex financial transactions (Robinson 1994; Reuter and Truman 2004). Today, the international system of funds transfers and credit card clearances allows money to transit numerous jurisdictions at the speed of light. In 2004, a Florida-based company that provided credit card billing services was convicted of conspiracy to launder money for a Belarus company that sold memberships to websites containing child pornography (Ashcroft 2004).

Tax Evasion

Tax evasion is the use of illegal means to avoid paying taxes. It differs from tax avoidance, in that the latter entails the use of *legal* means (such as taking legitimate deductions) to reduce the amount of tax that one is required to pay.

In 2002, the US Internal Revenue Service reported that a significant number of Americans were evading taxes by secretly depositing funds in offshore bank accounts and withdrawing them using major credit cards (Johnston 2002). Braithwaite (2005) relates how multinational corporations defeat tax authorities by effecting intra-company sales by buying at high prices in high tax countries and at low prices in low tax countries.

Bribery

Bribery is the offering of a gift to influence the actions of a public official (Noonan 1984). In the competitive world of international commerce, such payments to foreign officials in order to secure contracts or access to markets have been all too common. AWB Limited, formerly known as the Australian Wheat Board, sold wheat to Iraq under the UN Oil for Food program, which ran from 1996 until the US invasion of Iraq in 2003. In order to maintain its sales, the company paid kickbacks to Saddam Hussein's government, concealed as "inland transportation fees" to a Jordanian trucking firm. The transactions were concealed from the UN (Australia 2006).

Environmental Pollution

Overseas Manufacture

Multinational companies with manufacturing facilities in foreign countries may discharge toxic substances to the great detriment of the host nation and its citizens. The companies in question may seek out jurisdictions with lax regulatory standards or enforcement, or they may inflict harm as a result of negligence or design (Leonard 1988). In December 1984, 40 tons of methyl isocyanate gas leaked from a Union Carbide plant in Bhopal, India. The toxic gas killed more than 3,000 people, and injured tens of thousands of others (Trotter et al. (1989).

Cross-Boundary

Manufacturing operations in one sovereign state may produce pollutants that travel through air or water to another jurisdiction, causing significant damage downstream or downwind (Berge et al. (1999). A cyanide spill from a gold mine operated by an Australian company in Romania contaminated waters downstream in Hungary, Serbia, and Bulgaria (Koenig 2000).

Export

Toxic wastes may be dumped in international or territorial waters. They may also be exported to jurisdictions with relaxed regulatory standards, or may be disposed of illegally in an importing country. These are usually developing countries (Sanchez 1994). In 2005–2006, 27 companies were caught illegally shipping hazardous waste out of the port of Vancouver (CBC 2006).

Safety

Products

The growth in international trade that accompanies globalization has seen the export of unsafe products, ranging from pet food to children's toys. In some cases, the products in question were made in developing countries. China has attracted considerable adverse publicity relating to product safety in recent years (Schmidt 2008). However, the flow of dangerous products may also occur from the developed to the developing world. The Dalkon Shield was an intrauterine contraceptive device that was marketed widely in the United States during the 1970s. Despite complications from its use resulting in numerous deaths and thousands of serious pelvic infections in the United States alone, the US Government arranged for millions of the devices to be distributed in developing countries under the auspices of an aid program (Mintz 1985).

Workplaces

Unprecedented movements of people have facilitated the recruitment of low wage employees for dangerous types of work. In some cases, linguistic disadvantage may prevent such workers from understanding the risks they face, and their illegal status may inhibit them from reporting workplace hazards (Acosta-Leon et al. (2006). A company in Chicago recovered silver from discarded photographic film by bathing it in a cyanide solution. An illegal Polish immigrant working at the company's plant died of cyanide poisoning from fumes inhaled on the job. He was unable to read the warning labels on the cyanide containers, some of which had been intentionally obliterated by his employers (Rosner 2000).

Stockmarket Manipulation

The advent of investor chat rooms and online share trading has greatly enhanced the ability of ordinary citizens to disseminate false rumors and contribute to the apparent momentum in the volume of share trading (Grabosky et al. 2001, Chapter 6). In May 1999, a resident of Melbourne, Australia purchased 65,000 shares in a NASDAQ listed company through a broker in Canada. He then obtained access to a number of email servers and sent more than three million messages to addresses in Australia and the United States, purportedly reporting the results of research that predicted a 900 percent rise in the company's share price. The following day, trading in the company's shares was approximately 10 times the average daily volume and the share price doubled. The accused then instructed his broker to sell his shares, and made a profit of A$17,000. The information in his email messages had been false (Smith et al. 2004, 189–190).

Price Fixing

Price fixing entails an agreement between two or more sellers to coordinate the pricing of their products. This serves to elevate the price of the product, to the advantage of the sellers and to the disadvantage of the prospective purchasers (Geis 1968). This subversion of the market may occur domestically, or among producers from different countries.

Lysine is an amino acid commonly used as an animal feed supplement. Executives from the world's five dominant lysine producers met at trade association meetings around the world in 1994 and 1995 and agreed on the exact quantity of lysine each would produce the following year, and specified the exact price that each would charge. One US company, two Japanese companies, and two Korean companies were convicted, as were a number of executives. (Connor 2003; Hammond 2005).

Industrial Espionage

In the quest for a competitive edge in the contemporary global economy, corporations often seek to obtain information about their foreign competitors. Governments, too, may take an interest in learning foreign trade secrets. Considerable economic intelligence may be obtained by mining open source information. But sometimes, inquisitive institutions in both private and public sectors may engage in illegal conduct in order to obtain proprietary information (Nasheri 2005). In November 2001, two men attempted to board an aircraft in San Francisco with trade secret information stolen from Sun Microsystems and Transmeta Corporation in Silicon Valley. They had established a company in China with assistance from municipal and provincial governments, with whom they intended to share profits (US Department of Justice 2006).

Internet Content Infringements/Trade in Prohibited Products

International trade in contraband has occurred for centuries, as various commodities were prohibited from being imported or exported. Beyond the enhanced opportunities for illicit commerce that arise from increased levels of "conventional" trade, the Internet has greatly facilitated the making of illicit international markets for everything from child pornography to wildlife to drugs (Warchol 2004; St George et al. 2004).

The commercial trade in Nazi memorabilia is prohibited by law in France, but permissible in the United States. In 2000, a French court held that the availability of such material on a Yahoo! website hosted in the United States, but accessible to citizens of France, was a violation of French law (Yahoo! Inc v. LICRA, 169 F. Supp. 2d 1181 (N.D. Cal. 2001)).

Homicide

Corporate negligence (as was alleged in the Bhopal case) may contribute to the death of foreign nationals; so too may the conduct of private security contractors on behalf of either public or private sector clients (Forcese 1999). But the more common form of organizational homicide nowadays is state sponsored terrorism or cross-border political assassinations (O'Brien 1998). In 1985, officers of the Direction Générale de la Sécurité Extérieure (DGSE), the French foreign intelligence service, sought to disable a vessel used by the environmental NGO Greenpeace to protest against French nuclear testing in the Pacific. The agents traveled to New Zealand under false identities, attached explosives to the ship and detonated them. A Greenpeace photographer drowned in the flooding that resulted (Sunday Times Insight Team 1986).

None of the above incidents is intrinsically global. Each would have an entirely domestic analog. But globalization made them more likely, and poses new challenges to their prevention and control.

Responses to White-Collar Crime in the Global Village

One of the more prominent analysts of international criminal justice, Ethan Nadelmann (1990; 1993) discussed how regulatory norms evolve in the international system. Nadelmann's analysis was inspired by the antislavery movement, and by international efforts to control piracy on the high seas. Today, we can see such norms in the international system of illicit drug control (Andreas and Nadelmann 2006). It is no less applicable to the control of transnational white-collar crime in the twenty-first century.

The evolution of regulatory norms occurs over four stages. In the beginning, activity occurs that is regarded in most if not all countries as lawful. Next, the activity becomes recognized as a problem, often because harmful consequences become increasingly apparent. As momentum builds, there is agitation for suppression and criminalization of the behavior in question. Then, national regimes act to criminalize the conduct. The stages of problem definition and pressures to criminalize may involve an array of actors, from individual nation states to international governmental bodies such as the UN and the EU. Often however, it has initially involved the efforts of private individuals and NGOs. Indeed, nation states, singly or in concert, have often championed activity that has subsequently come to be defined as criminal, from slavery to whaling.

Of course, this process does not occur evenly across time and space. For a variety of reasons, some states are recalcitrant. Other states lack the capacity to control behavior elsewhere defined as criminal. So one sees the persistence of criminal havens, and the efforts of state and nonstate actors to raise consciousness and build capacity on the part of more reluctant jurisdictions.

It should be noted that this recalcitrance is not always a function of poverty. Japan still opposes the prohibition of whaling because of culture, tradition, and domestic politics. Other nations may be less enthusiastic about joining a mobilization in furtherance of white-collar crime control because of resentments harbored against the major sponsor or proponent. Time will tell how much political capital the United States may have squandered as a result of its invasion of Iraq.

Whether states are to be regarded as part of the solution or as part of the problem, one of the more significant concomitants of globalization has been a shift in their role. It has been suggested that at the best of times, the state has been a meek enforcer of white-collar crime laws, at best "netting the minnows while letting the sharks swim free" (Grabosky and Braithwaite 1986). But increasingly, observers of globalization have noted that the role of the state has changed from that of command to one of coordination. To use the well-worn metaphor of Osborne and Gaebler (1992), states are "steering rather than rowing."

Indeed, the control of white-collar crime, domestically or internationally, has become a pluralistic endeavor. In their classic work *Responsive Regulation*, Ayres and Braithwaite (1992) identified three basic types of regulatory actors: traditional state regulatory agencies; self-regulatory activities by individual companies or by industry associations; and third-party institutions, including public interest groups. To the ranks of third parties could also be added what Kraakman (1986) and Coffee (2006) refers to as "gatekeepers" and what Shapiro (1987, 205) calls "private social control entrepreneurs for hire." In addition, there are what Cutler et al. (1999) refer to as "coordination services firms" such as the ratings services Moody's and Standard and Poor's.

States vary in their capacity and willingness to exercise regulatory vigilance. But it has long been recognized that a great deal of regulatory activity takes place beyond the ambit of the state. The pluralist conception of regulatory institutions gives some comfort that the control of white-collar crime, whether domestic or transnational, does not depend on putting all one's eggs in the regulatory basket of government. This idea is not new, and a look back to the nineteenth century will demonstrate this. One can appreciate the importance to international trade of trust in the quantity, weight and quality of traded goods. In 1878, a grain shipment inspection house was founded in Rouen, France, to certify product integrity at the time of shipment. It was registered in Geneva as Société Générale de Surveillance in 1919, and today maintains over 1000 offices and laboratories around the world. Nongovernment audit and certification services play an important role in regulating the sale of forest products (Meidinger 1997; Cashore 2002).

It should come as no surprise, therefore, that white-collar crime control is a pluralistic undertaking, involving a degree of state or "suprastate" regulation, self-regulation by potential white-collar offenders (singly or in organizations) and what might be termed "regulatory coproduction" by NGOs and public interest groups.

The degree of state primacy and of coordination that exists in a given regulatory space will vary over time and place, depending on the will and capacity of various players. Some domains, such as international commercial aviation, are the subject of strict regulatory scrutiny at national or international levels. The most impressive roadmap for the control of white-collar crime in an era of globalization is the magisterial work of John Braithwaite and Peter Drahos (2000): *Global Business Regulation*. They analyses 13 separate regulatory systems, from air transport to trade and competition, mapping the interplay of the various actors, public and private, national and supranational.

In any given regulatory setting, there is usually no one perfect regulatory instrument. The effective control of transnational white-collar crime, like white-collar crime control within a single jurisdiction, must be a collective endeavor. Efforts may be spontaneous or coordinated, but they must be pluralistic. Braithwaite and Drahos use the metaphor of a web—no one strand of which is sufficient to bear the weight of a load. Many strands, woven together, may however be adequate to the task.

The same principle applies to the control of conventional street crime. The police now implicitly concede that they cannot be everywhere, all the time. Indeed, in many places these concessions are explicit, accompanied by appeals to the public to engage in surveillance, target hardening, and other strategies for crime prevention. The most progressive police nowadays are "leveraging" security through strategic partnerships with external agencies, and mobilizing citizen coproduction (Cherney et al. 2006).

One of the great benefits of globalization to the control of white-collar crime is the technological empowerment of individuals and institutions. It is now possible for an ordinary individual to communicate at the speed of light with millions of people worldwide, at negligible cost. In terms of raising awareness of the risk and reality of corporate offending, this is without precedent. Other actors in a regulatory system are similarly empowered, if not quite so dramatically. Networks of national regulatory agencies engage in collaborative ventures in a manner that was impossible 50 years ago.

And new regulatory institutions are at work. Among these are market forces (Grabosky 1994). Public demand for dolphin-friendly tuna, as much as fisheries regulators, contributed to a change in the practices of tuna fishers of many nationalities. I recall hearing a representative of the South Australian wine industry describe the purchasing practices of a large British supermarket chain that imported large quantities of South Australian wine. The company's buyers visited the wineries and asked to be shown the pesticide application audit records of the wineries' contract grape growers. If the buyers were not satisfied with the type of chemicals applied, the concentration in which they were applied, and the duration between application and harvest, they would take their business elsewhere. So it is that buyers on the other side of the world now exercise more control over the practice of South Australian grape growers than does any Australian government.

By virtue of its size, the retail behemoth Wal-Mart attracts no dearth of attention. Much of this is from commentators who are critical of low-wage policies and other employment practices (Rosoff et al. 2007, 80–87). But Wal-Mart is a significant regulatory power in its own right. With 60,000 suppliers in 70 countries around the world, it is in a position to exert immense influence over those who wish to do business with it. Wal-Mart has publicly declared the goal of being supplied with 100% renewable energy, generating zero waste, and selling products that are environmentally sustainable. The company has also committed to buying seven million kilos of organic cotton from Turkey and India, and to buying all wild-caught fish from Marine Stewardship Council certified sources (Scott 2007).

This is not to suggest that environmentally and socially preferable purchasing power is *the* solution to white-collar crime. One cannot deny, however, the enormous influence that powerful buyers have over their suppliers. When buyers send signals to the market, they can have a significant effect on the motivation of prospective offenders. The customer's demands can dampen any thought of playing fast and loose with potentially dangerous ingredients. Meeting a demand for organic cotton reduces the opportunity for the misuse of agricultural chemicals. To the extent that buyers monitor the their suppliers compliance with the conditions of purchase, it constitutes a degree of capable guardianship that can exceed what might be delivered by the state.

The same principle applies to conventional crime control. Security has become a selling point, whether it entails houses in gated communities, apartments with 24 hour doorkeepers, vehicles with inbuilt immobilizers, or other commodities fitted with location technology. The insurance industry can exert considerable influence, not only on policy holders, but also on the suppliers of everything from motor vehicles to door locks.

To give some indication of how some transnational regulatory systems come to be, let us look briefly at two domains: corruption and money laundering.

The Emergence of a Global Regulatory System

Transnational Corruption Control

To envisage what a pluralistic regulatory system arrayed against transnational white-collar crime might look like, let us take as an example the control of foreign bribery—that is, the payment of bribes to foreign officials in return for access to a market, or some other consideration. Corruption has existed for as long as human history (Noonan 1984). Globalization has certainly provided occasion for corrupt practices—there are certainly more businesses operating across national frontiers than ever before, and the contemporary business world is nothing if not highly competitive. In nations with highly developed moral sensibilities, the idea of bribing a foreign official is regarded with distaste. This has hardly been a barrier to such practice. In societies of a more pragmatic bent, foreign bribery may be viewed with a blind eye, or even officially condoned.

An outstanding historical map of international efforts to control foreign bribery has been prepared by Posadas (2000). In the competitive world of international business, bribery became all too familiar, so much so that bribery payments were often deductible as business expenses under the tax laws of many nations. Problems arose, however, when disclosures of such practices by disgruntled competitors or inquisitive journalists threatened the stability and the legitimacy of the corrupt official and their regime. Needless to say, this also reflected poorly on the integrity of the offending corporation, and upon that corporation's home country and government. In the 1970s, the Watergate investigations revealed that large corporations controlled "slush funds" for clandestine dispensation to officials in the United States and abroad (Randall 1997).

At the international level, the UN General Assembly had adopted a resolution condemning all corrupt practices, including bribery, in December 1975. In March 1976, the International Chamber of Commerce appointed a commission to study the problem of improper payments in international business transactions. Its 1977 report called for an international treaty, domestic legislation, and business self-regulation.

In August 1976, the Commission on Transnational Corporations of the United Nations Economic and Social Council (ECOSOC) began working on a proposal for an international agreement on the issue. However, the project fell victim to the *immobilisme* that characterized the UN in the late Cold War period.

Meanwhile, developments in the United States in the immediate post-Watergate era began to raise both public consciousness and public indignation, both domestically and internationally. Among the more prominent cases that shed light on the issue were the Lockheed bribery scandals of the 1970s (Posadas 2000). The Lockheed Corporation, a major US defense contractor, paid bribes to the Office of the Prime Minister of Japan and to Prince Bernhard of the Netherlands in an effort to secure contracts for the sale of aircraft.

Public indignation over such practices moved the US Congress to enact the Foreign Corrupt Practices Act, signed into law by President Carter in 1977. This may have begun to address the problem of the public image of the United States and its institutions, but it did not help the competitive advantage of US corporations, who were still competing against foreign counterparts who faced no such restraints.

The end of the Cold War saw renewed efforts at the international level, most prominent of which was the establishment of the NGO, Transparency International (TI). Founded in Germany in 1993, TI developed the Corruption Perceptions Index, a ranking of the world's nations based on the degree of their reputation for corruption as seen by business people and country analysts. It was followed soon after by the Bribe Payers Index, designed to measure the relative propensity of a nation's businesses to proffer bribes to authorities in other countries.

In 1994, the Organization of American States began developing an Inter-American Convention Against Corruption. It was adopted within 2 years and entered into force less than a year later.

Perhaps inspired by progress elsewhere, the United Nations succeeded in delivering a declaration against corruption and bribery in international commercial transactions. More than two decades after initial efforts began, a nonbinding resolution was adopted by the General Assembly in 1996.

An important intergovernmental initiative was the work of the Organization for Economic Cooperation and Development (OECD). The OECD Convention on Combating Bribery of Foreign Public Officials in International Business Transactions came into effect in February 1999, and had been ratified by 36 countries by the end of 2006. Signatories are required to enact legislation that criminalizes the act of bribing a foreign public official, wherever it may occur.

The World Bank, criticized by some as generating pressures in furtherance of white-collar crime (Friedrichs 2007), developed an anticorruption strategy in the 1990s, which focused primarily on its own procurement programs and auditing procedures.

Individual national and subnational jurisdictions have also established institutions for the purpose of corruption control. Among them are the Independent Commissions Against Corruption of the Hong Kong and the Australian state of New South Wales.

A complete mapping of such a regulatory system would include a full inventory of national institutions, and those of subordinate jurisdictions, as well as self-regulatory systems within individual firms. The web of institutions, public and private, that is arrayed against corruption has yet to eliminate international bribery from the human behavioral repertoire, but it has certainly succeeded in enhancing inhibitions, reducing opportunities, and improving surveillance over corrupt practices in international business activity.

Responses to Money Laundering

It has long been recognized that some individuals seeking to conceal their wealth from tax authorities, or from acquisitive spouses, would avail themselves of numbered bank accounts in foreign lands where no questions were asked. The legendary reputation of Swiss banks for client confidentiality made Swiss financial services attractive to many around the world.

In addition to those whose wealth was legitimately acquired, there are those with ill-gotten gains who have reasons to conceal them. The proceeds of crime are also taxable, as Al Capone was to learn. And under some circumstances, the origins of wealth are traceable, thereby providing potential evidence of criminal offences.

The value placed on privacy varies over time and space. In 1929, the US Secretary of State declared, "Gentlemen do not read each others' mail" and ordered the closure of the State Department's cipher office (Kahn 2004). The Second World War saw a renaissance of code breaking, but financial privacy was still regarded as a valued principle. The relationship between banker and client was not unlike that of doctor and patient.

In the late 1960s, as the increase in drug use created substantial illicit wealth, authorities in the United States sought to assist taxation and law enforcement authorities by introducing a degree of transparency into financial transactions. The Bank Secrecy Act was signed into law by President Nixon in 1970.

The global drug trade flourished over the following two decades, and unilateral US action was less than completely effective in the face of the global mobility of finance and the continued existence of financial havens such as Switzerland. The Financial Action Task force was established by the G7 Summit held in Paris in 1989. From its original membership of 16 it has grown to 37, and with a number of satellite groups, it seeks to raise consciousness and build capacity.

The antimoney laundering movement received a substantial stimulus in the aftermath of the September 11, 2001 attacks, when it became apparent that some financial institutions had been the conduit for funds used in furtherance of terrorism. Issues of cost effectiveness aside, western nations redoubled their efforts to monitor money flows from the Muslim world.

One notes that the major impetus for money laundering control has been almost exclusively governmental, and driven almost entirely by the United States. This stands in rather stark contrast to the trajectories of other regulatory systems, especially those arising from wider social movements.

Implications

One of the more significant aspects of white-collar crime posed by globalization relates to the law of jurisdiction. While some countries will assert criminal jurisdiction only over activities that have occurred within their own territorial boundaries, others take a more expansive approach. Most white-collar crime, like most "street" crime, never reaches the courts. This is certainly the case with regard to crimes committed across national borders. The challenge of successful prosecution is made considerably more difficult by the fact that the activity in question may not even be defined as criminal in the jurisdiction where it occurs, even though it might be regarded as a serious offence in the home country of the perpetrator. Even where it is, the victim jurisdiction may not have the resources or the capacity to mobilize the law against the offender.

Each nation state has its own law and policy regarding extradition. Some states, such as Israel and Sweden, will not extradite their own citizens. Others such as Australia will not extradite a person who might face execution in the requesting country. Few if any will extradite juveniles or offenders of any age whose alleged crimes are of a minor nature. In countries with well-established extradition arrangements, such as the United States and the United Kingdom, white-collar offenders are often handed over.

In the early 1990s a young Russian mathematician succeeded in obtaining unauthorized access to the servers of Citibank in the United States. He then enlisted a number of accomplices to establish accounts in financial institutions around the world. The plot was discovered, but Russian authorities were disinclined to cooperate with their US counterparts. The suspect made the mistake of traveling to attend a computer exposition in the United Kingdom, which does have a well-oiled extradition arrangement with the United States. He was handed over to US authorities, tried, convicted and sentenced to imprisonment. More recently, three British bankers were extradited to the United States to face charges in relation to a fraudulent transaction in collaboration with an executive of the Enron Corporation (Hays 2006).

Online gambling is illegal in the United States, but permissible in many other countries. An online gambling service provider who is physically located in a country where online gambling is legal, risks prosecution if he or she has accepted a wager from a US citizen or resident and ever ventures onto US soil (Landes 2007).

The October 28, 2000 edition of *Barron's Online* contained material perceived by an Australian businessman to be personally defamatory. He sued. The publisher contended that the material was published in the United States, where laws of defamation are relatively narrow. The plaintiff contended that the place of publication was Australia, where the laws at the time were relatively broad, and where the alleged harm to his reputation took place. The High Court of Australia ruled in favor of the plaintiff, effectively allowing others to sue for online defamation regardless of where the offensive content originated (Dow Jones & Company Inc. v Gutnick [2002] HCA 56 (10 December 2002)).

In a sense, the problem of cross-border white-collar criminality is analogous to the challenges faced by the United States in the nineteenth century, where offenders could escape with impunity across state lines. This gave rise to growing domestic inter-jurisdictional cooperation, combined with the rise of suprajurisdictional authority (the US federal criminal justice system). Today, one sees an intensification of conventional law enforcement cooperation in places like Europe.

Conclusion

The implications of globalization for criminology and for crime control center on the necessity for concerted effort. Shover (1998) observed that the competitive pressures prevailing in the contemporary world economy facilitate white-collar crime and inhibit white-collar crime control. He sees the solution in cooperative regulation.

Observers of white-collar crime, whether global or local, might do well to think analogously to the issue of conventional crime control. The law is a very imperfect instrument of social control. It is necessary, to be sure, but not sufficient to control crime: The real work of crime prevention is done by informal institutions of social control, family, church, school, and neighborhood. It is only when these institutions weaken or fail that more formal institutions of social control, such as those of the criminal justice system, are mobilized. To this end, the same holds true with white-collar crime, local or global.

Returning to the theoretical framework articulated at the beginning of this essay, we noted that white-collar crime, no less than conventional street crime, could be explained by the conjunction of three factors: a supply of motivated offenders, the availability of suitable targets or victims, and the absence of capable guardians.

A glib solution to the problem of white-collar crime in the era of globalization is simply to retreat behind one's borders and shun transnational relationships. Countries that have tried this (usually for ideological reasons rather than those of white-collar crime control) have not been happy places. Extreme isolationism is antithetical to material well-being. Fewer white-collars means less prosperity.

One can, however, attempt to address the issue of motivation by raising the consciousness of prospective offenders, prospective victims and capable guardians. A century ago, Upton Sinclair's (1906) *The Jungle* called widespread public and governmental attention to issues of food safety. Back in the 1960s, Rachel Carson's (1962) classic *Silent Spring* was the foundation of rising consciousness of the harm occasioned by agricultural chemicals. Ralph Nader's (1965) *Unsafe at Any Speed* called attention to motor vehicle safety. These works themselves provided the impetus for a framework of guardianship. They were reinforced by a tradition of investigative journalism that endures in western industrial societies. This process is the second stage in the evolution of transnational regulatory regimes as discussed by Nadelmann (1990).

Within nations, one has seen conventional crime become the subject of seminal works. Brownmiller's (1975) book *Against Our Will: Men, Women and Rape* was instrumental on elevating the issue of sexual assault on the policy agendas of most English speaking democracies.

Looking to the future, it may be possible to envisage new institutions for the control of transnational white-collar crime. The International Criminal Court exists to prosecute war crimes, crimes against humanity and genocide. It has been suggested that this might serve as a model for the prosecution of other transnational crimes, including white-collar crimes. The reluctance of the United States to submit to the jurisdiction of the International Criminal Court is grounds for pessimism, however. It seems for the time being that responses to white-collar crime, no less than street crime, will reflect national sovereignty and national interest.

Acknowledgments The author gratefully acknowledges the editorial assistance of Christine Nam, the guidance provided by the Editors of this volume, the institutional support of the Regulatory Institutions Network, Australian National University, and the Australian Research Council Centre of Excellence in Policing and Security.

References

Acosta-Leon, A.L., B.P. Grote, S. Salem, N. Daraiseh. (2006). "Risk factors associated with adverse health and safety outcomes in the US Hispanic workforce." *Theoretical Issues in Ergonomics* 7 (3), 299–310.

Andreas, P. and E. Nadelmann. (2006). *Policing the globe*. Oxford University Press, New York.

Aqorau, T. (2000). "Illegal fishing and fisheries law enforcement in small island developing states: The Pacific Islands experience." *The International Journal of Marine and Coastal Law* 15 (1), 37–64.

Ashcroft, J. (2004). Statement of Attorney General John Ashcroft on the REGPAY child pornography indictment. 15 January. U.S. Department of Justice, Washington. http://www.usdoj.gov/opa/pr/2004/January/04_ag_021.htm (visited 26 March 2008).

Australia. (2006). Report of the Inquiry into certain Australian companies in relation to the UN Oil-for-Food Programme. Commonwealth of Australia, Sydney. http://www.ag.gov.au/agd/WWW/unoilforfoodinquiry.nsf/Page/Report (visited 25 January 2007).

Ayres, I. and J. Braithwaite. (1992). *Responsive regulation: Transcending the deregulation debate.* Oxford University Press, New York.

Bardach, E. and R. Kagan. (1982). *Going by the book: The problem of regulatory unreasonableness.* Temple University Press, Philadelphia.

Berge, E., J. Bartnicki, K. Olendrzynski, and S.G. Tsyro. (1999). "Long-term trends in emissions and transboundary transport of acidifying air pollution in Europe." *Journal of Environmental Management* 57 (1), 31–50.

Bezemer, D. (2001). "Post-socialist financial fragility: the case of Albania." *Cambridge Journal of Economics* 25, 1–23.

Black, D. (1983). "Crime as social control." *American Sociological Review* 48 (1), 34–45.

Black, W. (2005). *The best way to rob a bank is to own one*. University of Texas Press, Austin.

Braithwaite, J. (2005). *Markets in vice, markets in virtue*. Federation Press, Sydney.

Braithwaite, J. and P. Drahos. (2000). *Global business regulation*. Cambridge University Press, Cambridge.

Brownmiller, S. (1975). *Against our will: Men, women and rape*. Simon and Schuster, New York.

Carson, R. (1962). *Silent spring*. Houghton Mifflin, Boston.

Cashore, B. (2002). "Legitimacy and the privatization of environmental governance: How Non-State Market-Driven (NSMD) governance systems gain rule-making authority." *Governance* 15 (4), 503–529.

CBC. (2006). Canada cracks down on high-tech trash dumped in China. http://www. ban.org/ban_news/2006/061222_canada_cracks_down.html (visited 26 March 2008).

Cherney, A., J. O'Reilly, and P. Grabosky. (2006). "Networks and meta-regulation: Strategies aimed at governing illicit synthetic drugs." *Policing and Society* 16 (4), 370–385.

Coffee, J.C. Jr. (2006). *Gatekeepers: The professions and corporate governance.* Oxford University Press, New York.

Cohen, L. and M. Felson. (1979). "Social change and crime rate trends: A routine activity approach." *American Sociological Review* 44, 588–608.

Connor, J.M. (2003). "The globalization of corporate crime: Food and agricultural cartels of the 1990s." http://www.agecon.purdue.edu/staff/connor/papers/Paris_March_2003.asp (visited 26 March 2008)

Crook S., J. Pakulski, and M. Waters. (1992). *Postmodernization: Change in advanced society.* Sage Publications, London.

Cutler, C., V. Haufler, and T. Porter. (1999). "The contours and significance of private authority in international affairs," (pp. 333–376). In C. Cutler, V. Haufler, and T. Porter (eds) *Private authority and international affairs.* State University of New York Press, Albany.

Da Silva, W. (1996). "Con artists of the internet," (pp. D1 and 7). *The Age* (Melbourne), 10 December.

Duffield, G. and P. Grabosky. (2001). "The psychology of fraud." *Trends and issues in crime and criminal justice* #200. Australian Institute of Criminology, Canberra.

Ertl, T. (2006). "Silkworms, capital and merchant ships: European silk industry in the medieval world economy." *The Medieval History Journal* 9, 243–270.

Felson, M. (2006). *Crime and nature.* Sage Publications, Thousand Oaks.

Fialka, J. (1997). *War by other means: Economic espionage in America.* W.W. Norton, New York.

Findlay, M. (1999). *The globalisation of crime.* Cambridge University Press, Cambridge.

Forcese, C. (1999). "Deterring militarized commerce: The prospect of liability for privatized human rights abuses." *Ottawa Law Review* 31, 171–211.

Friedrichs, D. (2007). "White collar crime in a postmodern, globalized world," (pp. 163–184). In H. Pontell and G. Geis (eds), *International handbook of white collar and corporate crime.* Springer, New York.

Garland, D. (1996). "The limits of the sovereign state: Strategies of crime control in contemporary society." *British Journal of Criminology* 36, 445–471.

Geis, G. (1968). "The heavy electrical equipment antitrust cases of 1961," (pp. 103–118). In G. Geis (ed), *White collar criminal: The offender in business and the professions.* Atherton, New York.

Geis, G. (1992). "White collar crime: What is it?" (pp. 31–52). In K. Schlegel and D. Weisburd (eds), *White collar crime reconsidered.* Northeastern University Press, Boston.

Grabosky, P. (1989). "The meat substitution scandal," (pp. 60–75). In P. Grabosky and A. Sutton (eds), *Stains on a white collar.* Federation Press, Sydney.

Grabosky, P. (1994). "Green markets: Environmental regulation by the private sector." *Law and Policy* 16 (4), 419–448.

Grabosky, P. and J. Braithwaite. (1986). *Of manners gentle: Enforcement strategies of Australian business regulatory agencies.* Oxford University Press, Melbourne.

Grabosky, P., R. Smith, and G. Dempsey (2001). *Electronic theft: Unlawful acquisition in cyberspace.* Cambridge University Press, Cambridge.

Hammond, S. (2005). "Caught in the act: Inside an international cartel," OECD Competition Committee Working Party No. 3, Public Prosecutors Program http://www. usdoj.gov/atr/public/speeches/212266.htm (visited 26 March 2008).

Hays, K. (2006). "British bankers arrive in Houston to face Enron charges." *Houston Chronicle,* 13 July http://www.chron.com/disp/story.mpl/special/enron/4044456.html (visited 26 March 2008)

Holmes, B. (1994). "Biologists sort the lessons of fisheries collapse." *Science* 264, 1252–1253.

Johnston, D.C. (2002). "IRS says offshore tax evasion is widespread." *New York Times*, March 26, http://www.globalpolicy.org/nations/corrupt/2002/0326evasion.htm (visited 26 March 2008).

Kahn, D. (2004). *The reader of gentlemen's mail: Herbert O. Yardley and the birth of American codebreaking.* Yale University Press, New Haven.

Katz, J. (1988). *Seductions of crime: Moral and sensual attractions in doing evil.* Basic Books, New York.

Kharouf, J. (1996). "The copper trader who fell from grace." *Futures*, August 1.

Koenig, R. (2000). "Wildlife deaths are a grim wake-up call in eastern Europe." *Science* 287 (5459), 1737–1738.

Kraakman, R.H. (1986). "Gatekeepers: The anatomy of a third-party enforcement strategy." *Journal of Law, Economics and Organization* 2, 53–104.

Landes, R. (2007). "Layovers and cargo ships: The prohibition of internet gambling and a proposed system of regulation." *New York University Law Review* 82 (3), 913–943.

Leonard, H.J. (1988). *Pollution and the struggle for the world product: Multinational corporations, environment, and international comparative advantage.* Cambridge University Press, Cambridge.

Levi, M. (1987). *Regulating fraud.* Tavistock Publications, London.

Levi-Faur, D. (2005). "The Global Diffusion of Regulatory Capitalism" *The Annals of the American Academy of Political and Social Science*, 598, 1, 12–32.

Meidinger, E. (1997). "Look who's making the rules: International environmental standard setting by non-governmental organizations." *Human Ecology Forum* 4 (1) http://www.humanecologyreview.org/pastissues/her41/41meidinger2.pdf (visited 26 March 2008).

Mintz, M. (1985). *At any cost: Corporate greed, women, and the Dalkon Shield.* New York: Pantheon.

Morselli, C. and C. Giguere. (2006). "Legitimate strengths in criminal networks." *Crime, Law and Social Change* 45, 185–200.

Nadelmann, E. (1990). "Global prohibition regimes: The Evolution of norms in international society." *International Organization* 44 (4), 479–526.

Nadelmann, E. (1993). *Cops across borders: The internationalization of US criminal law enforcement.* Pennsylvania State University Press, University Park.

Nader, R. (1965). *Unsafe at any speed: The designed-in dangers of the American automobile.* Grossman, New York.

Nasheri, H. (2005). *Economic espionage and industrial spying.* Cambridge University Press, Cambridge.

Noonan, J.T. (1984). *Bribes.* University of California Press, Berkeley.

O'Brien, K. (1998). "The use of assassination as a tool of state policy: South Africa's counter-revolutionary strategy 1979–1992." *Terrorism and Political Violence* 10 (2), 86–105.

O'Malley, P. and D. Palmer. (1996). "Post-Keynesian policing." *Economy and Society* 25 (2), 137–155.

Osborne, D. and T. Gaebler. (1992). *Reinventing government.* Addison-Wesley, Boston.

Passas, N. (1996). "The genesis of the BCCI scandal." *Journal of Law and Society* 23 (1), 57–72.

Passas, N. and D. Nelken. (1993). "The thin line between legitimate and criminal enterprises: subsidizing frauds in the European Community." *Crime, Law and Social Change* 19 (3), 223–44.

Perl, R. (2005). "State crime: The North Korean drug trade," (pp. 117–128). In M. Galeotti (ed), *Global crime today.* Routledge, Abingdon.

Perlmutter, T. (1998). "The politics of proximity: The Italian response to the Albanian crisis." *International Migration Review* 32 (1), 203–222.

Polk, K. (1994). *When men kill: Scenarios of masculine violence.* Cambridge University Press, Cambridge.

Posadas, A. (2000). "Combating corruption under international law." *Duke Journal of Comparative and International Law* 10, 345–414.

Randall, L. (1997). "Multilateralization of the Foreign Corrupt Practices Act." *Minnesota Journal of Global Trade* 6 (2), 657–684.

Reuter, P. and E.M. Truman. (2004). *Chasing dirty money: The fight against money laundering.* Institute for International Economics, Washington.

Ritzer, G. (2004). *The McDonaldization of society* (Revised New Century Edition). Sage Publications, Thousand Oaks.

Robinson, J. (1994). *The laundrymen.* Simon and Schuster, London.

Rosner, D. (2000). "When does a worker's death become murder?" *American Journal of Public Health* 90 (4), 535–540.

Rosoff, S., H. Pontell, and R. Tillman. (2007). *Profit without honor: White collar crime and the looting of America* (4th ed). Pearson Prentice-Hall, Upper Saddle River.

Ruggiero, V. (2003). "Global markets and crime" (pp. 171–182). In M. Beare (ed), *Critical reflections on transnational organized crime.* University of Toronto Press, Toronto.

St George, B.N., J.R. Emmanuel, and K.L. Middleton. (2004). "Overseas-based online pharmacies: A source of supply for illicit drug users." *Medical Journal of Australia* 180, 118–119.

Sanchez, R. (1994). "International trade in hazardous wastes: A global problem with uneven consequences for the third world." *Journal of Environment & Development* 3 (1), 139–152.

Sarre, R. and T. Prenzler. (2000). "The relationship between police and private security: Models and future directions." *International Journal of Comparative and Applied Criminal Justice* 24 (1), 91–113.

Schmidt, C. (2008). "Face to face with toy safety: Understanding an unexpected threat."*Environmental Health Perspectives* 116 (2), A70–A76.

Scott, L. (2007). "Wal-Mart 'greening' could have huge impact." Green Pace Business http://www.walmartstores.com/GlobalWMStoresWeb/navigate.do?catg=610 (visited 16 February 2007).

Shapiro, S. (1987). "Policing trust," (pp. 194–220). In C. Shearing and P. Stenning (eds), *Private policing.* Sage Publications, Beverly Hills.

Sherman, L. (1993). "Defiance, deterrence, and irrelevance: A theory of the criminal sanction." *Journal of Research in Crime and Delinquency* 30 (4), 445–473.

Shover, N. (1998). "White collar crime," (pp. 133–158). In M. Tonry (ed), *The handbook of crime and punishment.* Oxford University Press, Oxford.

Sinclair, U. (1906). *The jungle.* Doubleday, Page and Co., New York.

Singapore, Ministry of Finance. (1995). *Barings futures (Singapore) Pte Ltd: Investigation pursuant to Section 231 of the Companies Act (Chapter 50): The report of the inspectors appointed by the Minister for Finance. Michael Lim Choo San, Nicky Tan Ng Kuang.* Singapore Ministry of Finance, Singapore.

Skogan, W. (1986). "Fear of crime and neighborhood change." *Crime and Justice* 8, 203–229.

Smith, R., P. Grabosky, and G. Urbas (2004). *Cyber criminals on trial.* Cambridge University Press, Cambridge.

Solomon, A. and K. Vandell. (1982). "Alternative perspectives on neighborhood decline." *Journal of the American Planning Association* 48 (1), 81–98.

Starek, R.B. and L.M. Rozell. (1997). "The Federal Trade Commission's commitment to on-line consumer protection." *Journal of Computer and Information Law* 15, 679–702.

Summers, P. (2001). "Forecasting Australia's economic performance during the Asian crisis." *International Journal of Forecasting* 17 (3), 499–515.

Sunday Times Insight Team. (1986). *Rainbow Warrior: The French attempt to sink Greenpeace.* Hutchinson, London.

Sutherland, E.H. (1949). *White Collar Crime.* New York: Dryden Press.

Tillman, R.H. and M. Indergaard. (2005). *Pump and dump: The rancid rules of the new economy.* Rutgers University Press, New Brunswick.

Trotter, R.C., S.G. Day, and A.E. Love. (1989). "Bhopal, India and union carbide: The second tragedy." *Business Ethics* 8 (6), 439–454.

US Department of Justice. (2006). Two men plead guilty to stealing trade secrets from Silicon Valley companies to benefit China. http://www.cybercrime.gov/yePlea.htm (visited 26 March 2008).

Warchol, G. (2004). "The transnational illegal wildlife trade." *Criminal Justice Studies* 17 (1), 57–73.

Woodward S.L. (1995). *Balkan tragedy: Chaos and dissolution after the Cold War.* Brookings Institution, Washington.

Developmental Trajectories of White-Collar Crime

Nicole Leeper Piquero and David Weisburd

Abstract The criminal career paradigm represented a successful shift in criminological thinking, and ensuing research has generated important descriptive information about the key dimensions of active criminals; spurning both theoretical (developmental/life-course criminology) and methodological/statistical advances. Yet, the paradigm has failed to take into account acts of criminality that do not fit into the stereotypical image of street offending, in particular white-collar crime. The current study utilizes group-based trajectory modeling to examine trends of criminal behavior in a sample of convicted white-collar criminals over a more than 10-year follow-up period. Three offender trajectories are identified (low rate, intermittent, and persistent offenders) and suggest the importance of recognizing the variability of offending in a white-collar crime sample, and the overlap between white-collar and common crime criminal careers. This study also suggests the importance of recognizing both static and dynamic factors in the understanding of criminal careers. This research confirms a heterogeneous view of white-collar crime which recognizes that the white-collar crime category includes within it a broad diversity of offenders, and suggests that it is important to recognize that different models of explanation may be needed to provide explanations for different types of offenders.

Introduction

Much work over the last two decades has advanced the study and understanding of the criminal careers of offenders. Building off of the final report of the Panel on Research on Criminal Careers convened by the National Academy of Sciences in the mid-1980s (see Blumstein et al., 1986), a new set of research questions emerged that challenged criminologists to look at the relationship between crime and age in a whole new light.[1] The basic findings of the report launched the criminal career

N.L. Piquero (✉)
Virginia Commonwealth University, Richmond, VA, USA
e-mail: nlpiquero@vcu.edu

[1] Studying the relationship between age and crime is not a new phenomena. By some accounts, it is one of the oldest areas of study within criminology (Piquero et al., 2003).

S.S. Simpson, D. Weisburd (eds.), *The Criminology of White-Collar Crime*,   153
DOI 10.1007/978-0-387-09502-8_8, © Springer Science+Business Media, LLC 2009

paradigm, which focuses research questions on the longitudinal patterning of criminal activity over the life course (Piquero et al., 2007).

By many accounts, the criminal career paradigm represented a successful shift in criminological thinking. Research has identified much information about the key dimensions of active criminals. In general, we have learned that offenders are typically arrested for the first time during their teenage years and that they seldom commit a crime beyond the age of 30, a phenomenon commonly referred to as "aging out" of crime (Birkbeck, 1997; Farington, 1992; Petersilia, 1980; Stattin et al., 1989; Visher and Roth, 1986; Wolfgang et al., 1987). As such, it appears that criminals have relatively short criminal careers, averaging five to eight years (Blumstein et al., 1982), with little to no specialization (Gottfredson and Gottfredson, 1992; Kempf, 1987). Rather than specializing, it appears that most offenders are versatile in the crimes they commit, not favoring one type over another (Farrington et al., 1988; Nevares et al., 1990; Tracy et al., 1990; Wolfgang et al., 1972).

The criminal career paradigm also gave rise to a new theoretical "developmental approach" that generated new explanations of criminal behavior and ultimately led to an invigorating theoretical debate. In order to account for the observed relationship between age and patterns of criminality, developmental criminologists brought new theories that could account for the age–crime curve; that is ways to explain why crime peaks early in the life course (e.g., the teenage years) and then drops off as offenders grow older. One line of theoretical thinking assumes that there are multiple paths to delinquency (see Moffitt, 1993; Patterson et al., 1989) where some individuals show signs of antisocial behavior early in life and persist throughout adulthood versus another group who only undergo a brief period of criminality during their teenage years. Even further, another theoretical approach suggests that transitions from adolescence to adulthood can lead to either continuity in offending or change in behavioral patters (see Sampson and Laub, 1993) but do so without distinction between offenders.

The newly articulated developmental explanations of criminal behavior fueled the theoretical debate regarding the importance of static versus dynamic explanations of criminal behavior (Paternoster and Brame, 1997). Some scholars, such as Gottfredson and Hirschi (1990), argued that criminal propensity or a single causal theory works best to explain the age–crime relationship while other scholars, most notably developmental theorists (e.g., Moffitt, 1993; Sampson and Laub, 1993; Patterson et al., 1989), contend that different causal processes are at work at various points throughout one's life course. Those on the static side of the debate contend that cross-sectional data are sufficient while dynamic theorists argue that in order to study change over the life course longitudinal data are necessary.

Several methodological advancements also evolved from the criminal career paradigm that were designed to analyze existing data in new, more informative ways. The techniques, in large part, were designed to deal with the use of longitudinal data commonly employed in this line of research. Because longitudinal data collects information repeatedly for the same person, fixed individual effects or persistent heterogeneity may be present due to the repeated measurement design. Therefore, the analytic techniques must be able to account for both within- and between-individual change in criminal activities over time. Piquero and his colleagues (2003) note that the three main techniques used to analyze criminal activities over the life course include the following: random and fixed effect modeling, trajectory analysis, and hierarchical linear modeling.

The criminal career paradigm, therefore, appears to have been quite successful on several different fronts. It has reinvigorated the field of criminology by refocusing attention on understanding the development of crime across the life course; it spawned new criminological theories that have undergone a wealth of testing and revisions; and it pushed the development of new analytic techniques that have provided researchers with new ways to investigate developmental patterns of offending. However, for all of its success, the criminal career paradigm has failed to take into account acts of criminality that do not fit into the stereotypical image of street offending (see Weisburd and Waring, 2001 for an exception). As Piquero and Benson (2004) suggest life-course criminology is falling prey to the same mistake pointed out by Sutherland (1940) many years ago; that is acting as though common street crime is the only crime type that exists. By relying upon limited samples, predominately juveniles and street crimes, and failing to recognize and account for white-collar crime and criminals, the conclusions drawn from the criminal career body of research will "inevitably lead to a biased and incomplete understanding of trajectories in crime" (Piquero and Benson, 2004, p. 149). It is also important to note that white-collar crime scholars have often disregarded central debates and developments in criminology more generally, treating the study of white-collar crime as if it represented an area apart from mainstream criminology (Schlegel and Weisburd, 1992). While the criminal career paradigm has been applied to white-collar crime by specific scholars (e.g. see Weisburd et al., 1990; Weisburd and Waring, 2001; Benson, 2002; Benson and Kerley, 2000) it is has overall had little influence on white-collar crime study.

The current study is an effort to utilize new tools developed by developmental criminologists to understand the developmental patterns of crime of white-collar offenders. Specifically, we use group-based trajectory modeling to examine trends of criminal behavior in a sample of convicted white-collar criminals over a more than 10-year follow-up period. Reanalyzing data collected in an earlier study, which used static methods to describe the criminal careers of white-collar offenders (Weisburd and Waring, 2001), our study confirms the earlier study's identification of three main offender groupings, representing low rate, intermittent, and persistent offenders. These findings suggest the importance of recognizing the variability of offending in a white-collar crime sample, and the overlap between white-collar and common crime criminal careers. They also suggest the importance of recognizing both static and dynamic factors in the understanding of criminal careers.

White-Collar Crime, Criminals, and Criminal Careers

Prior to the 1980s very little was known about white-collar offenders. The dearth of quantitative data required that descriptions of white-collar offenders be derived from case studies that usually depicted highly publicized, egregious offenders, and offenses (Benson, 2002). Two data collection efforts in the 1980s, one effort lead by Wheeler et al. (1988) (see also Weisburd et al., 1991) and the other by Brian Forst and William Rhodes (n.d.), changed the portrait of white-collar offenders by providing information that detailed both offender and offense characteristics. The sample from both data collection efforts was based upon individual offenders who were convicted in US federal courts of a white-collar crime. As Piquero and Benson (2004) review, two notable findings emerged: (1) most of those convicted of white-collar crimes came from the middle-class of society; that is, they were average citizens with moderate incomes (see Weisburd et al., 1991; Benson and Kerley, 2000) and (2) a substantial proportion of convicted white-collar offenders had at least one prior arrest (Weisburd et al., 1990; Benson, 2002). These conclusions challenged existing assumptions about the characteristics of white-collar criminals, and suggested that study of white-collar crime was relevant to criminal career research.

Building off of the Wheeler et al. data, Weisburd and Waring (2001) gathered longitudinal data tracking the criminal records of the white-collar offenders for more than 10 years (see below for a more detailed description of data collection). After recognizing that many of these offenders were repeat criminals, they set out to examine how the officially recorded criminal careers of white-collar offenders were similar to or different from those of common crime offenders. Their data allowed them to focus upon five specific dimensions of offending employed in criminal career research (see Blumstein et al., 1986): onset, frequency, specialization, duration, and desistance. In terms of offense frequency, Weisburd and Waring (2001, p. 32) report that approximately one-third of the repeat offenders in the sample had only one additional arrest beyond the criterion white-collar crime with a similar proportion having been arrested between two and four additional times. Twenty percent of the sample was arrested between five and nine times while 13% of the sample had ten or more additional arrests since the original white-collar crime offense. Thus, these data show that there is a much higher frequency of recorded offending for white-collar criminals than has commonly been thought.

More differences than similarities appear to exist between the criminal careers of white-collar offenders and those of common offenders. Weisburd and Waring (2001) found that their white-collar offenders were much older at the time of their first and last arrest with the average age of onset at 35 and the average age of last recorded arrest was 43. Additionally, they found a substantial number of offenders who were arrested much later in life with some (though relatively few) offenders arrested in their late sixties or early seventies. Thus, as is generally the case in common crime samples, there does appear to be a decline in the likelihood of offending as the offenders grow older. As such, they find that like common crime samples, the white-collar offenders also age out of crime, though these offenders appear to desist *much* later in life.

Whatever the age at which the white-collar offenders have their last recorded arrest, the duration of their criminal histories seems to be very long. Weisburd and Waring (2001) found a mean duration of criminal career length of about 14 years. However, while the length of time between age of onset and last arrest is very long, the number of offenses on average, committed in this time period is comparatively small. By examining the mix of offenses reflected in the rap sheets, they found evidence of only moderate specialization, a finding similar to the criminal histories of common offenders.

In order to study the criminal careers of white-collar offenders in more detail, Weisburd and Waring (2001) examined the social histories of their offenders as well as the factors which appear to lead to their involvement. Of first concern was the difference between low-frequency offenders, those with one or two arrests in their criminal histories, and the chronic offenders, those with three or more arrests. They found that low frequency offenders were significantly more likely to: own their own homes, be steadily employed, have marital stability, evidence high educational achievement, and were less likely to be defined as a substance or alcohol abuser. In a qualitative review of the presentence investigation reports from the criterion offense, Weisburd and Waring (2001) identified three main criminal career patterns for white-collar criminals. The first pattern that might be termed "crime as an aberration" included the low-frequency offenders, those whose criminal histories were marked with one or two arrests. For this group of offenders, criminal activities appear to be an aberration in an otherwise conventional social record. Other than the instances of crime, these offenders' lives were virtually indistinguishable from those of other people in similar social and economic circumstances. Overall, this group corresponded to images of respectability and conformity rather than instability and deviance, as is often the image associated with criminals.

Some subtle differences did emerge within the "crime as an aberration" group and two categories of offenders appeared. One group, the "crisis responders," engaged in criminality in response to some type of perceived crisis in their professional or personal lives. Although the nature of the crisis varied considerably, in general these individuals responded by taking advantage of a position of trust that they occupied (see also Cressey, 1980; Zietz, 1981). Most members of this group had been in positions of trust for extended periods without, as far as is known, violating that trust. The criminality of the second group, the "opportunity takers," appeared to be linked strongly to some unusual or special set of opportunities that suddenly materialized for the offender. These appeared to be offenders who led otherwise conventional lives and took advantage of a set of specific opportunities despite their understanding that the behaviors involved were criminal. The crimes are usually defined as part of the normal procedures at their families' businesses or in their business networks. Taking advantage of this opportunity does not appear to be consistent with other aspects of their lives or indicative of a tendency toward instability or deviance. In general, they entered into a situation without a plan to engage in criminal activity; but as they become aware of the opportunity for a particular offense, they took it.

By examining the presentence investigation reports of chronic offenders, Weisburd and Waring (2001) clearly identified both an intermittent and persistent offending group of criminals. The intermittent group, referred to as "opportunity seekers," seemed to seek out opportunities to commit crime or, at times, create a situation amenable to committing a specific type of offense. Many of these offenders exhibited characteristics of conventionality and stability with large gaps in time between their arrests. Therefore, people in this category did not fit traditional stereotypes of criminality, but nonetheless, turned more than once or twice to criminal behavior. More generally, there appears to be a defined pattern of offending which suggests a willingness to seek out specific types of situational opportunities for crime.

The persistent offending group of chronic offenders, termed "stereotypical criminals," evinced prior criminal histories indicating a strong commitment to breaking the law, but also evidenced instability and low self-control in their lives more generally. The white-collar crime prosecutions for these offenders were often only one part of a mixed bag of criminal conduct. While they intermittently exhibited conventional lives, their personal histories more often included difficult childhoods, substance abuse, disruptions of divorce, unsteady unemployment, and educational failure. In this sense, they fit a model in which criminality is just one part of a more complete portrait of the offender which reaches deep into his or her personal history and is reflective of a wide group of behaviors beyond criminality itself.

Current Research

In the current study, we set out to examine whether the use of recently developed dynamic modeling techniques would confirm the patterns of white-collar criminal careers identified by Weisburd and Waring (2001), or whether it would suggest different patterns or relationships within the sample. It is likely that there will be variation within the sample of offenders but it is unknown whether the trajectory analysis will converge on identifying the same number of groups as identified in the extant trajectory literature or will confirm the three groups of offenders as qualitative group construction by Weisburd and Waring (2001) would suggest. Group-based trajectory models allow us to identify distinct offender groups, which vary in their rates of offending, as measured by official arrests. It is best to construe trajectory analysis as a descriptive endeavor that allows for groups/trajectories to emerge from the data. As such, it allows us to determine whether there are meaningful subgroups within the white-collar crime data and, if so, what the offending trajectories of these distinct groups look like.

Mixture, trajectory, or group-based models are useful for modeling unobserved heterogeneity in a population (Jones et al., 2001). Although there are several software packages that allow for the estimation of trajectories, the technique employed here is the group-based procedure or the semiparametic mixed Poisson model (SPM) developed by Nagin and Land (1993) and programmed into the SAS computer package by Jones and colleagues (2001). The SPM is a special kind of random-effects model that assumes the distribution of unobserved persistent heterogeneity is discrete and not continuous, as is assumed by general random-effect models. As such, the SPM can identify distinct trajectories within the population of interest and to ascertain the probability of population members following each trajectory (Nagin, 1999; Piquero et al., 2003). A detailed review and discussion of this line of research is beyond the purview of the current study, a more thorough review can be found by consulting Nagin (2005) and Piquero et al. (2007).

Sample

The current study relies on data originally collected by researchers at Yale Law School working under the leadership of Stanton Wheeler (see Wheeler et al., 1988; Weisburd et al., 1991) and then appended with criminal history data that extended for more than 10 years after the "criterion offense" for the crime that led to selection into the sample (see Weisburd and Waring, 2001). The sample consists of individuals who were convicted in federal courts of white-collar crimes, defined as "economic offenses committed through the use of some combination of fraud, deception, or collusion" (Wheeler et al., 1982, p. 642).

The original sample was drawn primarily from seven federal judicial districts during fiscal years 1976–1978. The districts were chosen in part to provide geographic spread, in part because they were being examined in other studies, and in part because some of them were known to have a substantial amount of white-collar crime prosecution. The districts (and their central cities) are: Central California (Los Angeles), Northern Georgia (Atlanta), Northern Illinois (Chicago), Maryland (Baltimore), Southern New York (Manhattan and the Bronx), Northern Texas (Dallas), and Western Washington (Seattle). A stratified random sample of a maximum of 30 convicted defendants were selected for eight offense types: bribery, bank embezzlement, mail and wire fraud, tax fraud, false claims and statements, credit and lending institutional fraud, postal theft, and postal forgery. The sample was stratified to allow a sufficient number of cases of relatively less common, but theoretically important, white-collar crimes such as bribery, antitrust offenses, and securities frauds.[2] A supplementary sample of securities and antitrust offenders was also collected. This supplementary sample included all offenders convicted of these crimes during the

---

[2] The sample thus includes more securities, antitrust, and bribery cases, and fewer bank embezzlement and mail and wire fraud cases than would be expected from a simple random sample. However, oversampling resulting from stratification was constrained by the fact that rarer offenses often did not meet the sampling threshold. This is illustrated by comparing the distribution of offenses in the sample with that in the national population of cases in 1978 (the first year that the Federal Judicial Center reports separate out felony from other cases). Caution should be used in the case of antitrust offenses, as many corporate offenders are included in the Federal Judicial Center statistics: [S-sample; P-national population] Bribery S-7.7% P-3.1%; Income Tax S-19.2% P-17.9%; Bank Embezzlement S-18.3% P-21.3%; Credit and Lending Institution Fraud S-14.4% P-9.6%; False Claims and Statements S-14.4% P-15.2%; Mail and Wire Fraud S-17.4% P-26.4%; Securities Fraud S-6.1% P-2.8%; Antitrust S-2.5% P-3.5%.

3-year sample period from all United States federal judicial districts.[3] Specific information about offenders was drawn from presentence investigation reports (PSIs).

While the sample was carefully selected to include individuals convicted of a white-collar crime it is not an inclusive list of all possible white-collar offenses and is not without limitations. First, there are a number of federal white-collar offenses such as perjury, bankruptcy fraud, and conspiracy that could have been included in the list of criterion white-collar offenses but were not (see Weisburd and Waring, 2001, p. 16 for reasons of their exclusion). Second, all offenders were under the jurisdiction of the US federal courts. In essence, the sample excludes offenders who were prosecuted in state courts or held accountable under civil or administrative laws. Since regulatory agencies are most likely to monitor and control corporate crimes, the exclusion of these types of cases could bias the sample by under reporting the most elite white-collar crime offenders – those more likely to be caught and sanctioned by regulatory agencies. Finally, the sample only includes individuals who were convicted of their offenses; thereby omitting individuals who avoided detection altogether or those who were not successfully prosecuted.

In order to supplement the original data collection, Weisburd and Waring (2001) collected official measures of criminality, defined as arrests, from Federal Bureau of Investigation "rap sheets" for the original sample until April 1990, the "censoring" date of their study or the date when the tracking of criminal histories ends. They were successful in linking the original data with FBI rap sheets for about 70% of the sample. Our sample, like that analyzed by Weisburd and Waring (2001) includes 968 white collar offenders examined over at least a 10-year follow-up period.

It is important to note at the outset that in the analyses below we track developmental patterns of white-collar crime from a static point identified in the Wheeler et al. (1988) data. The original sample was drawn from offenders convicted of white-collar crimes during fiscal years 1976–1978. As the offenders varied in age from 18 to 68 at this point in time, we could not group the offenders by specific ages and examine developmental trends across the life course. Rather, our analyses examine overall developmental trends evidenced by offenders during the follow-up period. Given Weisburd and Waring's (2001) identification of broad developmental trends that persisted over long periods of time, we think that the general groupings they identified should be visible in our analysis if they are indeed present in the sample. At the same time, our data would be expected, only in very general terms, to reflect age-specific trends such as the aging out of crime. Additionally, it should be noted

---

[3] The inclusion of the national sample of SEC and Antitrust cases ($n = 119$) weights the sample, somewhat toward higher status white-collar criminals. This approach was taken to allow the original researchers to contrast more directly the highest status white-collar criminals with others in the sample. Using only the seven district sample, the rate of reoffending is equal to that of the full sample, approximately 51%. We do not weight overall sample estimates according to the actual population frequencies of the offense categories. Following Weisburd and Waring (2001), we believe that the stratified sample provides a broad and heterogeneous sample of offenders convicted of white-collar crimes in the federal courts. Also, direct adjustments or weighting of frequencies would not take into account the fact that the crimes examined themselves are only a selection of offenses. Other scholars might have recommended including other crime categories.

that we, as is the case in most longitudinal criminal career research, did not have access to exposure time data (i.e., time off the street). Thus, our conclusions must be tempered by the fact that the shape and level of the trajectories could be somewhat different had we information on this front (Piquero et al., 2001).

Results

Below, we present our findings using a group-based trajectory approach applied to the Weisburd and Waring (2001) data. Following Nagin (2005), the Bayesian Information Criterion (BIC) is used to evaluate model fit. The BIC, or log-likelihood evaluated at the maximum likelihood estimate less one-half the number of parameters in the model times the log of the sample size (Schwarz, 1978), tends to favor more parsimonious models than likelihood ratio tests when used for model selection. Following previous research (D'Unger et al., 1998), an iterative procedure is used in identifying meaningful groups. The model search was conducted to determine the number of groups present in the data. The BIC values reported indicated a substantial improvement in the model specification and fit to the data as the number of trajectories increased from one to three. The application of the BIC rule implies that the model with three latent groups should be chosen. It is important to note that the groups are intended as an approximation of a more complex underlying reality, the objective is not to identify the "true" number of groups. Instead, the aim is to identify as simple a model as possible that displays the distinctive features of the population distribution of trajectories Nagin and Tremblay, 2005.

Posterior Probability Assignments

For each offender in the data, and the subsequent latent class or offender group identified, the maximum posterior membership probability was computed. Because the model utilizes the 'maximum probability' procedure, offenders are sorted into the trajectory group (or latent class) to which they have the highest probability of belonging. Based on model coefficient estimates, the probability of observing each offender's longitudinal pattern of offending is computed conditional on their being, respectively, in each of the identified latent groups. As such, each offender is assigned to the group to which they have the highest probability of belonging. The higher the posterior probability, the greater likelihood of accurate assignment.

Table 1 shows the mean assignment probabilities for each group. The average high scores (all above 0.84) indicate that the majority of offenders were classified into the latent trajectory group to which they had the highest probability of belonging. For example, the mean posterior probability for group 1 was 0.856 suggesting that the likelihood of assignment to that particular trajectory group was quite high. As can be seen, it is clear that the offenders who comprise group 1 were correctly assigned to the low-rate trajectory group since there is a very low likelihood that they

Table 1 Average posterior probability of group assignment

	Probability of group 1	Probability of group 2	Probability of group 3
Group 1	**0.856**	0.143	0.000
Group 2	0.084	**0.845**	0.070
Group 3	0.000	0.121	**0.878**

would have been assigned to the other trajectory groups. The probability of assignment for these offenders to group 2 was 0.143 and they had virtually no likelihood of being assigned to group 3. Similarly high probability findings of group membership also emerged for the other two trajectory groups. The mean posterior probability for group 2 was 0.845 with low probabilities of assignment to group 1 (0.084) and group 2 (0.070). The mean posterior probability for group 3 was 0.878 with virtually no probability of assignment to group 1 and a low probability of assignment (0.121) to assignment to group 2. In short, the average posterior probability assignments are all above the 0.7 threshold recommended by Nagin (2005).

Offense Trajectories

The predicted arrest trajectories for each of the three groups identified by the model are plotted in Fig. 1. It is important to note at the outset that the three groups follow very closely the typology identified by Weisburd and Waring (2001) using static methods. We labeled the first group of offenders as "low-rate" since they conform to the expected criminal career patterns (identified by Weisburd and Waring) of "crisis responders" and "opportunity takers." These offenders evidence episodic involvement in crime and in some sense the criminal career label is not appropriate for them despite the fact that they have committed a white-collar crime. Weisburd and Waring identified about two-thirds of the sample as fitting in this group. The trajectory approach places approximately 71% of the sample in this group.

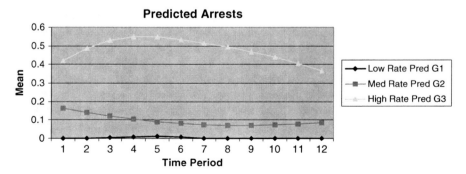

Fig. 1 Three-group predicted trajectories

The second group of offenders, labeled "medium-rate," conforms closely to "opportunity seekers" identified by Weisburd and Waring (2001). In this group, there is clearly a pattern of criminality, though involvement in crime is intermittent and overall the rate of offending in the group across time is relatively low. Interestingly, despite the fact that our grouping of the data does not allow age specific analysis, we find that there is overall evidence of aging out of crime in the sample. In their book, Weisburd and Waring (2001) did not provide a specific estimate of the number of offenders that fell in this group in part because dynamic methods were not available at that time for estimating patterns of offending over time. They suggested however, that these offenders were likely to be found in the lower frequency chronic offender grouping, which comprised about 16% of the sample (see Weisburd and Waring, 2001, p. 71). The trajectory analysis suggests that about 25% of the sample can be placed in this group.

The third group of offenders, labeled "high-rate," conforms closely to the "stereotypical criminals" identified by Weisburd and Waring (2001). These offenders on average evidence persistent criminal behavior across the follow-up period. As with the moderate-rate group, there is also some indication of aging out of crime. Nonetheless, the offending activity of group 3 is fairly high and stable throughout much of the observation period, a pattern of recidivism that is not ordinarily seen in the more general, common crime trajectory research studies (Laub and Sampson, 2003). Importantly, our analyses suggest that Weisburd and Waring (2001) may have overestimated the number of offenders that should fall in this grouping. The trajectory analysis places only 5% of the sample in this group. Weisburd and Waring did not provide a specific estimate for this group, but by implication their contribution to the sample lies between 6% and 16%.[4]

Figures 2, 3 and 4 present the observed and predicted arrest trajectories, respectively, for each of the three groups. As can be seen, the model's predicted arrest trajectories closely mirror the observed arrest trajectories, indicating that each model is providing a good fit to the data. It is important to note the differences in the scale on the y-axis (mean number of arrests) across the three groups. The scale ranges vary according to the nature of offending evinced by the distinct groups. One additional observation that can be drawn from Fig. 2, representing the low-rate offending group, is that if these offenders do offend, they are likely to reoffend between 3 and 7 years after the criterion offense. This may reflect some degree of censoring in our data for almost 50% of the sample that served a prison sentence. But it also suggests again, that there may be an aging out of crime even for offenders that evidence only episodic involvement in criminality.

---

[4] Our estimate is drawn from the fact that Weisburd and Waring suggest that these offenders are found most often in the two highest rate offending categories they describe (see Weisburd and Waring, 2001, p. 175).

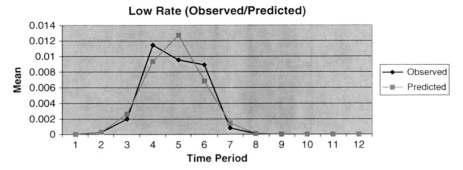

Fig. 2 Arrest Trajectories for Low Rate Group

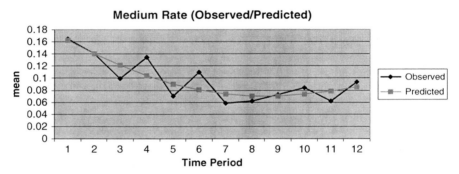

Fig. 3 Arrest Trajectories for Medium Rate Group

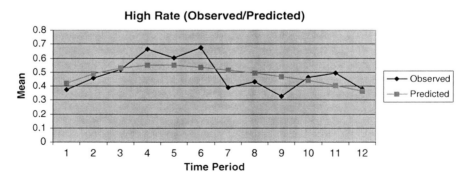

Fig. 4 Arrest Trajectories for High Rate Group

Discussion

Our use of recently developed tools for the examination of criminal careers of white-collar offenders has both confirmed prior studies and enhanced our understanding of developmental trends in white-collar crime. Weisburd and Waring (2001), using static statistical methods identified three main patterns of criminal careers in their sample. Using a dynamic group-based trajectory approach developed for study of criminal careers more generally, our empirical findings are consistent with those of the earlier study. Developmental patterns in white-collar crime appear to be typified either by a very high-rate persistent group of offenders, defined by Weisburd and Waring (2001) as "stereotypical criminals;" an intermittent pattern of criminality, evidenced by "opportunity seekers;" and a very low-rate group of offenders that Weisburd and Waring see as "opportunity takers" and "crises responders."

Our research, therefore, confirms a heterogeneous view of white-collar crime, which recognizes that the white-collar crime category includes within it a broad diversity of offenders. This is an observation made by Weisburd et al. (1991) in their book *Crimes of the Middle Classes*, and which has been confirmed in later studies. This view of white-collar offending of course leads us to abandon the simple binary conception of crime that has often polarized and isolated white-collar crime scholars. The importance of white-collar crime study is not simply its provision of a sharp contrasting group to the common crimes that are the focus of most of criminological work, but also its ability to examine and explore the diversity of offenders in the white-collar crime category.

While our analyses have allowed us to confirm Weisburd and Waring's (2001) observations, they have also led us to reexamine the relative weights of different patterns of offending within their original sample. While the proportion of the sample that are defined as low-rate offenders appears similar for both our and the earlier analyses, divergent findings emerge regarding the two higher rate offending groups. Weisburd and Waring did not have access to a specific methodology that would allow them to typify membership in these groups, but nonetheless they gave greater weight to the stereotypical criminal pattern than is suggested using group-based trajectory methods. Of course, it is important to recognize that the sample itself is not a simple representative sample of white-collar offenders. Accordingly, we cannot draw direct inferences from the proportions of offenders falling in each trajectory to the overall population of white-collar criminals.

Moreover, as developmental scholars have applied trajectory methods they have begun to be more cautious in drawing strong inferences regarding the specific groupings identified by these methods (Nagin, 2005; Laub and Sampson, 2003). Trajectory analysis, as other similar statistical tools, makes choices regarding the division of the sample into groups and such choices in some sense masks the extent to which the underlying data also reflect a continuous distribution of developmental patterns. While we recognize the debate over this question, we think our findings have particular solidity, since they confirm a qualitative examination of the data undertaken in an independent set of analyses. In this context, we think it is important that our approach has yielded a larger trajectory pattern of what Weisburd and

Waring (2001) define as "opportunity takers" and a much smaller group of "stereotypical criminals." Weisburd and Waring may have overestimated the importance of stereotypical criminals in white-collar crime, a position that is in some sense consistent with the traditional focus of white-collar crime scholarship (e.g. see Schlegel and Weisburd, 1992).

Accordingly, our use of recent innovations in research in developmental criminology has helped us confirm and refine our understanding of patterns of white-collar criminality. But we think our findings also have important implications for our understanding of criminal careers more generally. We noted in the introduction of our paper, that criminal career theorists have relied upon two broad paradigms to understand developmental patterns of crime. On one hand, criminologists have identified a persistent underlying trait that predicts criminality throughout the life course (e.g. see Gottfredson and Hirschi, 1990; Nagin and Paternoster, 1991). Whether referring to low self-control (Gottfredson and Hirschi, 1990) or biological or other factors (Moffitt, 1993) this perspective sees criminality as a characteristic that is determined in early development and which is difficult to alter later in life. In contrast, criminologists in recent years have begun to emphasize the importance of situational and developmental factors across the life course (Sampson and Laub, 1993; Nagin and Paternoster, 1991), placing greater importance on such social institutions as marriage, the army or work in fashioning developmental patterns in the lives of offenders.

Scholars have often polarized the debate over these underlying explanations for continuity and change in criminal offending (Paternoster et al., 1997). Nonetheless, in recent theorizing there has been greater recognition of the extent to which both perspectives can play significant roles in our understanding of developmental trends in crime (Laub and Sampson, 2003). In this context, scholars have recognized the fact that some underlying traits such as low self-control are persistent and explain offending throughout the life course (Gottfredson and Hirschi, 1990; Moffitt, 1993). However, this does not preclude the importance of life-course experience and the effects of specific choices such as deciding to marry or being drafted in the army (Sampson and Laub, 1993). In this context, underlying criminal propensity is not a simplistic determinate of future criminality, but rather one part of a complex equation that recognizes the ways in which people develop and change throughout their lives.

We think our research on developmental patterns of offending for white-collar offenders, suggests additional complexity in this nuanced perspective. Our analyses identified groups with very different developmental trends, and accordingly very different underlying explanations for behavior. For example, our low-rate trajectory group, is reflective of offenders who as Weisburd and Waring (2001) note appear in nearly all respects as conventional people. Their social backgrounds and social records give no significant evidence of instability or propensity to offending. This group has also been found to be present among common crime offenders as well (see Nagin et al., 2005), but it is much more prominent in this white-collar crime sample. Therefore, our focus is drawn more to a class of offenders for whom situational factors are predominant in explaining their involvement in crime. Weisburd and Waring (2001) identified this group as "crisis responders" and "opportunity takers" because a very specific situation in the lives of these offenders led to their involvement in crime. As such, the idea of criminal propensity seems hardly relevant for this group.

At the same time, our data also point to a group of offenders for whom criminal propensity is particularly salient. The very high-rate offending group identified in our trajectory analyses, and by Weisburd and Waring (2001), fit very neatly a paradigm that identifies propensities to offending that reach early in the life course. As the following description brought by Weisburd and Wheeler (2001, p. 84) illustrates, the high-rate offenders in this sample do not differ greatly from the common criminals that have informed criminological perspectives that focus on underlying traits developed early in the life course:

> (He) had been arrested ten times between 1966 and 1988. The arrests ranged from white collar related crimes such as fraud, forgery and theft of securities, to aggravated arson, a weapons offense, and, finally, distribution of cocaine. In his brief periods of employment he reportedly had two different hourly jobs and was fired from them both. The defendant's mother was institutionalized when he was young, and he was raised by his father and a housekeeper whom his father eventually married. The defendant was divorced once and was separated at the time of the criterion offense and waiting to marry a woman with whom he was living. While the defendant admitted no addictions, his family revealed a serious drinking problem. The probation officer remarked that the defendant was "an unsettled, poorly adjusted young man of low normal intelligence."

Our analyses accordingly suggest that it is important when charting the course of criminal careers to recognize that different models of explanation may be needed to provide explanations for different types of offenders. Propensity for example, may be the primary underlying factor in understanding patterns of offending for "stereotypical criminals" in the sample, but it appears to have little relevance for the low-rate offenders that form the majority of the sample. Our third offender trajectory group further reinforces the idea of recognizing diversity in the etiological paradigms used to understand criminal careers.

The intermittent criminality group identified in our analyses, suggest that for some offenders both paradigms may operate simultaneously. For this group, termed "opportunity takers" by Weisburd and Waring (2001), there is strong evidence of propensity to crime early on in life; but, there is also evidence that offenders are influenced and strongly affected by events and situations in the life course. As Weisburd and Waring (2001, pp. 78–79) write regarding a defendant whose criterion offense was false claims to a bank:

> (He) contended [in explaining his crime]that he was "in a financial bind and needed money desperately." He noted that "I was about to lose my house and everything. I am sorry for what I have done but at the time, I saw no other way out." To get the loan that he needed he and his wife listed false accounts and then had their credit report changed to list the non-existent assets.

> In contrast to the defendants representation of the situation, the probation officer argued that the "[D]efendant is not prone to criminal behavior but is miserably lacking in scruples and moral values and not above committing criminal acts to perpetuate his life style." Like many of those who fall in this category, he fulfills neither images of respectability and success on

the one hand, nor those of a life which is defined by low self-control, disorganization, and deviance on the other. While the defendant dropped out of high school after performing poorly, he was honorably discharged as a corporal from the marines. After his discharge he completed two years of college as an average student. He was born out of wedlock, did not know his father, and was raised by a great-aunt. Nonetheless, the defendant had a stable marriage of nine years at the time of the criterion offense, although it should be noted that his wife played a key role in the criterion offense by making the first contact with the person who changed their credit report.

This offender held ten different jobs in just ten years, but his employer at the time the PSI report was completed, a home shopping service, considered his performance to be above average. Although his FBI rap sheet shows no arrest prior to the criterion event, the probation officer identified four prior instances of contact with the criminal justice system: speeding and running a red light; use of a fictitious name to secure a drivers license; issuance of bad checks; and illegal use of a credit card.

For this offender, as it is for others who fall in this broad category, it is clear that both criminal propensity and situational factors operate together in determining the nature and timing of criminal offending. Accordingly, he represents well a model of offending that integrates paradigms for understanding developmental patterns of offending. Merging this pattern with the others we have identified, our data emphasize the importance of recognizing that distinct patterns and distinct theoretical understandings may be necessary to understand different types of offenders.

Conclusions

While many advances have been made over the years with regard to understanding the criminal careers of street offenders, little work as been done to understand if the same standards, theories, and methodologies will hold true for a sample of white-collar offenders. Many white-collar criminologists contend that distinct differences exist between white-collar and street offenders, so it only seems logical to examine the criminal careers of white-collar offenders.

The focus of this paper was to examine the offending trajectories of a sample of convicted white-collar offenders. By utilizing recidivism data collected by Weisburd and Waring (2001), which followed up some of the original offenders included in the Yale Study, we were able to empirically investigate whether or not different trajectories of white-collar offenders existed. Weisburd and Waring (2001) qualitatively identified three groups of offenders. Our analyses benefiting from recent methodological innovations in developmental criminology confirm their typology, but also suggest that Weisburd and Waring may have underestimated the importance of a group they define as "opportunity seekers" and overestimated the importance of "stereotypical criminals" in their sample.

Ours is by no means the final word on this issue. In fact, it is just the beginning of what we can only hope will be an active line of research. In turn, we are particularly concerned by two points. First, ours is not an age-cohort study but rather our offenders comprise a mixed-age cohort. Due to the way in which the original data were collected, the criterion for selection into the study was not the individual's year of birth but rather a conviction in a federal court for a white-collar crime. There is no question that confirmation of offender patterns will have to be brought from specific age-cohort studies in white-collar crime as our data and methodology may have masked specific developmental trends. Second, we were unable to control for length of prison stay in the follow-up data. While this is not a problem exclusive to our longitudinal data, it does raise the possibility that the shape of the trajectories that we identified could have been different had exposure time been taken into consideration. While we recognize these concerns, we think our findings are robust, in good part because our analyses follow and confirm the qualitative analyses identified by Weisburd and Waring (2001).

The use of new tools in developmental criminology have allowed us to confirm and draw new insight about criminal careers of white-collar offenders. Our analyses, however, have also allowed us to inform paradigms for understanding criminal careers. The study of a white-collar crime sample, with its broad diversity in patterns of offending, has brought us to recognize the importance of applying different explanatory models to different groups of offenders. Criminal propensity may be relevant for many of those who commit crime, but it provides little explanation for the bulk of people who commit white-collar crime. In turn, in this sample a pattern of intermittent offending is evidenced by large numbers of offenders, suggesting that for many criminals the mix of propensity to crime and situational opportunities and change across the life course interactively influence developmental patterns of criminality. The next step in this line of research will be to pinpoint and examine what factors or correlates account for the distinctiveness of each of the three identified trajectory groups.

References

Birkbeck, C. (1997) A Profile of Offenders Entering New Mexico Prisons, 1991–1994. Albuquereque: New Mexico Criminal and Juvenile Justice Coordinating Council.

Benson, M. L. (2002) Crime and the Life Course. Los Angeles, CA: Roxbury Publishing.

Benson, M. L., and Kerley, K. R.. (2000) Life Course Theory and White-Collar Crime (pp. 121–136). In Contemporary Issues in Crime and Criminal Justice: Essays in Honor of Gilbert Geis, edited by H. N. Pontell and D. Shichor. Upper Saddle, NJ: Prentice Hall.

Blumstein, A., Jacqueline C., and Paul H. (1982) The Duration of Adult Criminal Careers. Final Report Submitted to National Institute of Justice, August 1982. Pittsburgh, PA: School of Urban and Public Affaris, Carnegie Mellon University.

Blumstein, A., Jacqueline C., Jeffrey A. R., and Christy A. V. (1986) Criminal Careers and "Career Criminals." 2 volumes. Panel on Research on Career Criminals, Committee on Research on Law Enforcement and the Administration of Justice, Commission on Behavioral and Social Sciences and Education, National Research Council. Washington, DC: National Academy Press.

Cressey, D. R. (1980) Employee theft: The reasons why. Security World, October: 31–36.

D'Unger, A. V., Kenneth, C. L., and. McCall, P. L (1998) How many latent classes of delinquent/criminal careers? Results from mixed Poisson regression analyses. American Journal of Sociology, 103: 1593–1630.

Farrington, D. P., Howard N. S., and Terrence A. Finnegan (1988) Specialization in juvenile court careers. Criminology, 26: 461–487.

Forst, B., and William R. (n.d.) Sentencing in Eight United States District Courts, 1973–1978. Codebood (Interuniversity Consortium for Political and Social Science Research, Study No. 8622). Ann Arbor, MI: University of Michigan.

Gottfredson, S. D., and Don M. G. (1992) Classification, Prediction and Criminal Justice Policy. Rockville, MD: NCJRS.

Gottfredson, M., and Hirschi, T. (1990) A General Theory of Crime. Stanford, CA: Stanford University Press.

Jones, B. L., Nagin, D. S. and Roeder K. (2001) A SAS procedure based on mixture models for estimating developmental trajectories. Sociological Methods and Research, 29: 374–393.

Kempf, K. L. (1987) Specialization and the criminal career. Criminology, 25(2): 399–420.

Laub, J. H., and Sampson, R. J. (2003) Shared Beginnings, Divergent Lives: Delinquent Boys to Age 70. Cambridge: Harvard University Press.

Moffitt, T. E. (1993) Adolescence-limited and life course persistent antisocial behavior: A developmental taxonomy. Psychological Review, 100: 674–701.

Nagin, D. (1999) Analyzing developmental trajectories: Semi-parametric group-based approach. Psychological Methods, 4: 39–177.

Nagin, D. S. (2005) Group-Based Modeling of Development. Cambridge: Harvard University Press.

Nagin, D. S., Farrington, D. P. and Moffitt, T. E. (1995) Life-course trajectories of different types of offenders. Criminology, 33: 111–139.

Nagin, D. S. and Land, K. C. (1993) Age, criminal careers, and population heterogeneity: Specification and estimation of a nonparametric mixed poisson model. Criminology, 31: 327–362.

Nagin, D. S., and, Paternoster, R.. (1991) On the relationship of past and future participation in delinquency. Criminology, 29: 163–190.

Nagin, D. S., and Tremblay, R. E. (2005) Developmental trajectory groups: Fact or a useful statistical fiction? Criminology, 43: 873–904.

Nevares, D., Wolfgang, M. E. and Tracy, P. E. (1990) Delinquency in Puerto Rico: The 1970 Birth Cohort Study. New York: Greenwood Press.

Paternoster, R., and Brame, R. (1997) Multiple routes to delinquency? A test of developmental and general theories of crime. Criminology, 35(1): 49–84.

Paternoster, R., Dean, C. W., Piquero, A., Mazerolle, P., and Brame, R. (1997) Generality, continuity, an change in offending. Journal of Quantitative Criminology, 13: 231–266.

Patterson, G. R., DeBaryshe, B. and Ramsey, E. (1989) A developmental perspective on antisocial behavior. American Psychologist, 44: 329–335.

Petersilia, J. (1980) Criminal career research: A review of recent evidence (pp. 321–379). In Crime and Justice: An Annual Review of Research, Vol. 2, edited by N. Morris and M. Tonry. Chicago: University of Chicago Press.

Piquero, A. R. (2007) Taking stock of developmental trajectories of criminal activity over the life course. In Longitudinal Research on Crime and Delinquency, edited by A. Liberman. New York: Springer.

Piquero, A. R., Blumstein, A., Brame, R., Haapanen, R. Mulvey, E., and Nagin, D. (2001) Assessing the impact of exposure time and incapacitation on longitudinal trajectories of criminal offending. Journal of Adolescent Research, 16: 54–74.

Piquero, A. R., Farrington, D. P. and Blumstein, A. (2003) The criminal career paradigm (pp. 359–506). Crime and Justice: A Review of Research, Vol. 30. Chicago: University of Chicago Press.

Piquero, A. R., Farrington, D. P., and Blumstein, A. (2007) Key Issues in Criminal Career Research: New Analyses of the Cambridge Study in Delinquent Development. Cambridge: Cambridge University Press.

Piquero, N. L., and Benson, M. L. (2004) White-collar crime and criminal careers: Specifying a trajectory of punctuated situational offending. Journal of Contemporary Criminal Justice, 20(2): 148–165.

Sampson, R. J., and Laub, J. H. (1993) Crime in the Making. Cambridge: Harvard University Press.

Schlegel, K., and Weisburd, D. (1992) White-collar crime: The parallax view (pp. 3–27). In White-Collar Crime Reconsidered, edited by K. Schlegel and D. Weisburd. Boston, MA: Northeastern University Press.

Schwarz, G. (1978) Estimating dimensions of a model. Annals of Statistics, 6: 461–464.

Stattin, H., Magnuson, D., and Reichel, H. (1989) Criminal activity at different ages: A study based on a Swedish longitudinal research population. British Journal of Criminology, 29(4): 368–385.

Sutherland, E. H. (1940) White collar criminality. American Sociological Review, 5: 1–12.

Tracy, P. E., Wolfgang, M. E. and Figlio, R. M. (1990) Delinquency Careers in Two Birth Cohorts. New York: Plenum.

Visher, C. A., and Roth, J. A. (1986) Participation in criminal careers. In Criminal Careers and Career Criminals, edited by A. Blumstein, J. Cohen, J. Roth, and C. Visher. Washington, DC: National Academy Press.

Weisburd, D., and Waring, E. (2001) White-Collar Crime and Criminal Careers. Cambridge: Cambridge University Press.

Weisburd, D., Chayet, E. F. and Waring, E. (1990) White collar crime and criminal careers: Some preliminary findings. Crime and Delinquency, 3: 342–355.

Weisburd, D., Wheeler, S., Waring, E., and Bode, N. (1991) Crimes of the Middle Classes. New Haven: Yale University Press.

Wheeler, S., Weisburd, D., Waring, E., and Bode, N. (1988) White collar crimes and criminals. American Criminal Law Review, 25: 331–357.

Wheeler, S., Weisburd, D. and Bode, N. (1982) Sentencing the white collar offender: Rhetoric and reality. American Sociological Review, 47: 641–659.

Wolfgang, M. E., Figlio, R. M., and Sellin, T. (1972) Delinquency in a Birth Cohort. Chicago: University of Chicago Press.

Wolfgang, M. E., Thornberry, T. P., and Figlio, R. M. (1987) From Boy to Man, from Delinquency to Crime. Chicago: University of Chicago Press.

Zietz, D. (1981) Women Who Embezzle or Defraud: A Study of Convicted Felons. New York: Praeger Publishers.

Part III
Crime Prevention and Control

White-Collar Crime from an Opportunity Perspective

Michael L. Benson, Tamara D. Madensen, and John E. Eck

Abstract It is no longer necessary to argue for the importance of white-collar crime. Its devastating financial and physical effects are obvious. The task now is to develop better ways to control and prevent white-collar crimes. In this paper, we argue that in order to reduce white-collar crime we must first identify the specific opportunity structures associated with the offenses we wish to prevent. That is, we must identify the features of the settings that allow the crime to occur. Three major theories are reviewed here that can help in this task: routine activity theory, crime pattern theory, and situational crime prevention theory. These theories address how crime opportunities are formed by immediate environments and then discovered and evaluated by potential offenders. We demonstrate that they can also be used to uncover how specific forms of white-collar crimes are committed and help structure analyses of the underlying opportunity structures associated with these offenses.

Introduction

It is no longer necessary to argue for the importance of white-collar crime. The devastating effects of what Sutherland (1940) called "crime in relation to business" have been evident for decades, documented in an ever growing multitude of case studies and government reports, as well as by the seemingly tireless efforts of investigative journalists in the electronic and print media.[1] All this attention has not gone unnoticed by the general public. For at least two decades, surveys have found that the public ranks some forms of white-collar crime as similar in seriousness to traditional street crime (Evans et al. 1993; Levi 1987; Braithwaite 1985; Cullen et al. 1982; Schrager and Short 1980). Crimes by corporations that lead to the injury or death of workers or consumers are particularly harshly judged (Schrager and

M.L. Benson (✉)
University of Cincinnati, Cincinnati, OH, USA
e-mail: Michael.benson@uc.edu

[1] For a recent review of the costs of white-collar crime, see Chapter 1 in Cullen et al. (2006). For an exhaustive review and use of news reports about white-collar crimes, see Rosoff et al. (2004).

S.S. Simpson, D. Weisburd (eds.), *The Criminology of White-Collar Crime*,
DOI 10.1007/978-0-387-09502-8_9, © Springer Science+Business Media, LLC 2009

Short 1980). Likewise, governmental officials at all levels of authority have recognized that white-collar crimes demand serious attention. Although it would be wrong to say that white-collar crime is now the top priority of law enforcement officials, it would be just as incorrect to say that it is or has been ignored. Since at least the early 1970s, law enforcement agencies at all levels of government have undertaken initiatives targeting various forms of white-collar crime.[2] Thus, we take it as a given that white-collar crime is widely recognized as an important and serious form of crime.

But what exactly is white-collar crime? As is well known, Sutherland (1949) defined white-collar crime as "a crime committed by a person of respectability and high social status in the course of his occupation." Is this a coherent and useful construct? Opinions on this question differ dramatically. Distinguished scholars, such as Braithwaite (1985) and Geis (1988) argue that we should stick with Sutherland's approach or something pretty much like it. While other commentators, notably Edelhertz (1970), Shapiro (1990), and Felson (2002), argue that we should abandon Sutherland's status-based definition in favor of one that focuses more on the mechanics or modus operandi of the offenses. Even scholars who have no particular expertise in the area of white-collar crime recognize that the definitional problem is complicated and contentious (Hirschi and Gottfredson 1987). We are not going to solve the problem here. However, we suggest that the two approaches can be at least partially reconciled if one recognizes that the offenses committed by the high status people who interested Sutherland depend upon the techniques identified by Edelhertz (1970) and on opportunity structures that are often occupationally related (Felson 2002). Thus, rather than debating the definition of white-collar crime, we think it is more important to focus on the more important task of analyzing how these crimes are committed and how they can be prevented.

The basic assumptions and propositions of this paper can be briefly summarized. First, we assume that all forms of white-collar crime have an opportunity structure. That is, a set of conditions or elements that must be in place in order for the offense to be carried out. This opportunity structure varies from one type of offense to another. However, there may be identifiable groups or classes of white-collar offenses whose opportunity structures are similar. Second, the control and prevention of white-collar crime depends on an understanding of the process by which these types of offenses are committed. Understanding the process through which an offense is committed is not the same as understanding why it is committed. These two questions – how and why – are analytically separable. Although answers to either of these questions may have policy implications in the sense that they may lead to mechanisms to control the prevalence of white-collar crime, we suggest that focusing on how is likely to be more productive than focusing on why.

---

[2] See Benson and Cullen (1998), Skoler (1982), Edelhertz and Rogovin (1982), Katz (1980), Abrams (1980), Cullen et al. (2006).

Crime Versus Criminality

Gottfredson and Hirschi (1990) make an important distinction between crime and criminality. A crime is an event, something that happens in time and space.[3] Criminality, on the other hand, refers to a behavioral disposition, a disposition that is manifested by behaving in ways that are labeled by society as criminal. Whether criminality is expressed as crime depends on situational factors external to the individual, most notably the opportunity structures that a potential offender confronts in daily life. In our view, white-collar crime is a form of crime, not a form of criminality. That is, we are agnostic as to whether the causes of white-collar criminal behavior are different than the causes of other types of criminal behavior. Hence, for the purposes of this paper we leave open the question whether their crimes have special motivations.[4] Rather, we think it is important to recognize that white-collar crimes rely upon techniques that differ from the techniques used in typical street crimes, both property and violent. These differences in techniques and opportunity structures are important in their own right, especially in regards to developing effective control and prevention strategies for white-collar crime. In our view, the same theories and constructs that guide the examination of street crime from an opportunity perspective can be usefully employed for white-collar crime. Indeed, opportunity theorists generally stress the importance of crime specificity for this theoretical framework. Thus, just as the opportunity approach has been applied to street crimes, it can be profitably applied to white-collar crime.

The Opportunity Perspective

It may seem unnecessary to demonstrate that an opportunity must exist before a crime can be committed. To say that a crime has occurred implies that a criminal opportunity existed prior to the commission of the offense. However, for our purposes, it is not the simple presence of opportunity that matters but rather the

---

[3] Actually, the temporal and geographic specificity of white-collar crime can be problematic, as sometimes it is not exactly clear where the offense can be said to have occurred or when. We address these issues below in the section on processes.

[4] We must qualify our agnosticism a bit. There is, of course, a wealth of evidence indicating that a not insignificant proportion of street offenders do suffer from psychological and cognitive difficulties, and there is no evidence that white-collar offenders suffer from gross psychological abnormalities. Nevertheless, the psychology of white-collar offenders is not a subject on which researchers have invested much effort. There is anecdotal and qualitative evidence suggesting that white-collar offenders are unwilling to define their behavior as criminal (Sutherland 1940; Geis 1977; Benson 1985). Case studies suggest that some white-collar offenders have a sense of superiority over their victims (Stotland 1977) and that they are gratified by pulling off complex schemes and need ego challenges (Stotland 1977). One quantitative study found tantalizing personality differences between convicted white-collar offenders and a control group of unconvicted white-collar workers (Collins and Schmidt 1993). However, we are unaware of studies that compare the psychological profiles of white-collar and ordinary street offenders.

specific characteristics of the opportunity. These characteristics define the "opportunity structure" that can be modified to prevent criminal activity in particular settings. Different settings naturally create different opportunities that vary in accessibility and attractiveness to offenders. Thus, we should expect that the opportunity structures of street crimes, such as robberies or thefts from autos, will differ from each other as well as from those afforded by an occupational setting.

For example, cash exchanged at convenience stores provides opportunities for robberies. However, changes in cash handling procedures that limit the amount of cash available (use of time release safes) coupled with increased monitoring of store activity (installing security cameras) alter the opportunity structure for robbery (Hunter and Jeffery 1997). These changes decrease the profitability and increase the risks associated with committing the offense and discourage potential robbers.

Parking facilities provide opportunities for theft from vehicles. Vehicles are left unattended for extended periods of time and these facilities provide access to targets while limiting visibility, thus providing cover for would-be offenders. However, the opportunity structure for theft in these locations can be altered through environmental modifications (e.g., restricting access by creating barriers to entry) and increasing surveillance (e.g., hiring parking attendants, improving lighting). Research has demonstrated that these changes are associated reduced theft from vehicles (Poyner 1991).

To control and prevent white-collar crimes, we must first identify the specific opportunity structure associated with the offense we wish to prevent. That is, we must identify the features of the settings that allow the crime to occur. Three major theories are available to help in this task: routine activity theory, crime pattern theory, and situational crime prevention theory. These theories address how crime opportunities are formed by immediate environments and then discovered and evaluated by potential offenders. Although the theories have been used primarily to analyze and address traditional forms of street crime, they have been recently applied to more atypical problems such as terrorism (Clarke and Newman 2006), child abuse (Wortley and Smallbone 2006), and crowd violence (Madensen and Eck 2006). We will demonstrate that they can also be used to uncover how specific forms of white-collar crimes are committed and help structure analyses of the underlying opportunity structures associated with these offenses.

Routine Activity Theory

The principle assumption of routine activity theory is that three elements must be in place to create the necessary conditions for crime: a target, a motivated offender, and a common place where the offender can gain access to the target (Cohen and Felson 1979; Eck 1994). If these three elements are present, a crime will occur in the absence of an effective controller. Controllers present themselves in the form of guardians for targets (Cohen and Felson 1979), handlers for offenders (Felson 1986), and place managers for places (Eck 1994). For example, a student who carefully monitors his belongings acts as a guardian for his backpack. A mother who watches her child at a playground acts as a handler for her child. A bar owner who monitors the activities of employees and patrons acts as a place manager for her establishment. An intervention by a controller can serve to prevent crime, even when the necessary conditions for crime are present (i.e., a target and offender together in the same place).

Before applying routine activity theory to the study of white-collar crimes, we must revisit the concept of a "common place." Unlike predatory crimes, some white-collar crimes do not require direct physical contact between the target and offender. In telemarketing scams, for example, the telemarketers are never in the physical presence of their victims. Instead, the callers rely on telephone networks to connect them to their targets (Coyne 1991). Similarly, physicians who bill Medicaid for work not performed almost certainly never actually visit any government office. Instead, they rely on the structure of the program and confusion surrounding Medicaid billing procedures to hide their criminal transactions (Jesilow et al. 1993). Despite the fact that offenders are often physically distant from their victims, routine activity theory can be applied to white-collar crimes if the concept of the "common place" is expanded to include the networks that facilitate interaction between offenders and victims (Eck and Clarke 2003). These networks provide offenders a "place" to access their victims or the resources of their victims.

To identify the existing opportunity structure of any particular white-collar crime using routine activity theory, we must examine the three elements that come together to create the conditions necessary for the crime to occur: the offenders, the victims, and the existing occupational or organizational feature(s) that facilitate contact between the victim and offender (i.e., the common place or network that allows the offender to commit the crime). After the elements are identified, we can investigate whether potential controllers for each element are present or absent. If controllers are present their level of effectiveness can be assessed.

Consider a patient who is hospitalized and whose insurance company is over charged by the hospital for services performed. The elements that created the necessary condition for the offense are: (1) the hospital – offender, (2) the insurance company – victim, and (3) the system for submitting insurance claims – network. This type of offense could be prevented if one of the elements received intervention from an effective controller. For the hospital, the handler or intervener could be an employee who threatens to blow the whistle if the inaccurate charges are filed. For the insurance company, the guardian could be a claims reviewer who examines the various charges and compares them to industry standards. The claims systems itself could be managed by the commission that grants hospital accreditation. The commission could establish guidelines and standards for submitting claims or conduct audits to detect over-billing patterns generated by particular facilities. The key point in this case is that the crime can be prevented if hospital officials have reason to believe that any discrepancy between charges and services is likely to be exposed. If in the eyes of hospital officials that is likely to happen, then the risk of filing fraudulent claims would outweigh the potential benefits of the crime.

Crime Pattern Theory

Drawing on the principles of routine activity theory, crime pattern theory (also known as offender search theory) states that offenders become aware of criminal opportunities as they engage in their normal legitimate activities (Brantingham and Brantingham 1991). Offenders tend to find their targets in familiar places. Therefore, criminal opportunities that are close to the "areas" that an offender moves through during their everyday activities are more likely to be taken advantage of by the offender than opportunities in areas less familiar to the offender. This explains why the distribution of crime events is concentrated in time and space, as well as among targets (Brantingham and Brantingham 1991). Offenders identify crime targets as they travel the paths (typically streets for street crimes) that connect the various activity nodes (places such as home, work, and entertainment spots) that the offender moves between (Brantingham and Brantingham 1993). For example, burglaries are more likely to occur at houses located along moderately busy street segments than houses on cul-de-sacs simply because the former is more likely to fall within the action space of more potential offenders (Beavon et al. 1994; White 1990).

Crime pattern theory can be adapted to detect and explain the distribution of white-collar crimes across targets. Although in the case of white-collar offenders, they do not discover their opportunities by walking down familiar streets. Rather, their awareness of white-collar crime opportunities arises out of their employment or occupation. For example, in their study of the criminal careers of white-collar offenders, Weisburd et al. (2001) found that both crisis responders and opportunity takers take advantage of criminal opportunities that arise out of the patterns and activities associated with their occupational positions.

The opportunity structure for any particular white-collar crime is dependent on the "nodes" and "paths" used by the offender. The nodes of a white-collar criminal include the business or organization they work within (or the fictitious business they have created) and any other outside agency, organization, groups of clientele served, or other departments within their own organization that they interact with to accomplish their objectives. The paths used to navigate between these nodes include the procedures and networks used to establish communication or conduct business with others.[5]

Consider the routine activities of a private-practice physician. The professional actions of physicians include such activities as examining patients and billing for services, referring patients to specialists, obtaining hospital privileges, conducting office visits, ordering tests, writing prescriptions, and ordering medical supplies. The agencies, organizations, or individuals they must work with to accomplish these tasks, represent nodes familiar to the physician (see Fig. 1). The methods through which the physician requests the services, orders products, or conducts business

---

[5] The fact that one can use the same modeling structure for social networks as social networks should not be surprising. Both rely on graph theory. Graph theory underlies social network analysis (Wasserman and Faust 1994) and Hillier's Space Syntax to examine street patterns (Hillier 1999).

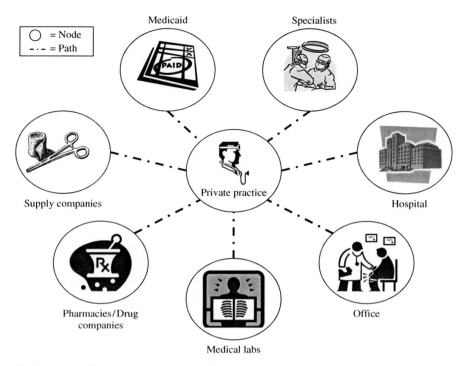

Fig. 1 Nodes and paths of the private-practice physician

with or within each node represent the paths where criminal opportunities may be found. For example, when applying for hospital privileges, doctors may falsify documents demonstrating previous education or experience in order to obtain privileges to practice a particular procedure. Doctors may work with specialists, medical labs, and drug and medical supply companies to develop a system in which fee splitting or kickbacks are provided in exchange for patient referrals, ordering additional tests, treatments or equipment, or prescribing only certain brands of medication, even if these actions are not in the best interest of the patient.

Crime pattern theory would predict that white-collar crimes are more likely to occur along the "paths" used most often and used by more individuals. Therefore, we are likely to find that more physician-related crimes occur within larger networks and by means of more commonly practiced procedures. This explains why physicians are more likely to defraud the Medicaid system than smaller insurance companies; the former provides more opportunities than the latter.

Another concept introduced in crime pattern theory that can help to explain the distribution and opportunity structure of white-collar offenses is the "edge." When dealing with street crimes, edges represent the boundaries of areas designated for specific activities (e.g., residential area adjacent to an entertainment district). The theory predicts that crimes are more likely to occur at edges because these places bring together people who do not know each other, making it difficult to determine who belongs and who does not (Brantingham and Brantingham 1993). Thus, strangers and their behaviors are more likely to go unnoticed and unaddressed in these places.

Edges present themselves to white-collar criminals whenever (1) two nodes intersect using a particular path and (2) verification systems or regulatory oversight is absent or ineffective at identifying criminal activity along that path. When a regulatory system embraces only some nodes and their associated networks, white-collar deviance will form along the paths connecting the regulated nodes to unregulated nodes (see Fig. 2). Edges will appear along paths that are closest to the offenders "home" node and not monitored, or ineffectively monitored, by others.[6] As edges are pushed farther away from the offender, we should find that (1) offending occurs less frequently and (2) the offender may require the cooperation of other nodes in order to reach edges along paths that they do not have direct access to (e.g., in Fig. 2, node 'a' requires the assistance or manipulation of node 'e' to victimize node 'g').

For example, the health care industry's standard detection and control systems create such edges by approving all billing claims that fall within acceptable parameters. This system fails to detect even the most egregious billing patterns and allows physicians to steal "millions of dollars as fast as possible" (Sparrow 1996). Similarly, regulatory agencies charged with the oversight of the savings and loans industry in the 1980s created edges for criminal activity by removing regulations designed to control the interactions between thrifts (effectively withdrawing scrutiny

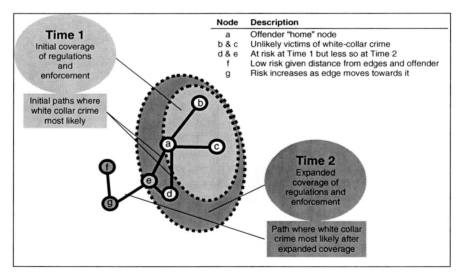

Fig. 2 Edges and white-collar crime

---

[6] Given the special access an offender has to their own node, we should expect frequent offending to take place at this "location" in the absence of internal controls.

from some nodes). This allowed thrifts to engage in "land flips" in which two or more thrifts would continually sell the same piece of land back and forth between them until they drove up the price and found a "sucker" institution to buy the property (Calavita and Pontell 1990).

To summarize, three steps are necessary to identify the existing opportunity structure of any particular white-collar crime using crime pattern theory. First, identify the nodes that the offenders generally work with or against to commit their offense. Second, locate the paths that present the opportunity for criminal activity. Third, determine what opportunities may have formed along those paths.

Situational Crime Prevention Theory

While routine activity theory and crime pattern theory describe how offenders gain access to criminal opportunities, situational crime prevention theory describes why some criminal opportunities are more attractive to offenders than others. Situational crime prevention theory suggests that individuals make decisions on whether or not to engage in criminal activity based on particular characteristics of the opportunities presented to them. This framework draws from the rational choice perspective and assumes that offenders choose to commit crime and that they consider both the costs and benefits of engaging in such activity (Cornish and Clarke 1986). Situational crime prevention theory links these costs and benefits to five dimensions or characteristics of criminal opportunity:

(1) the effort required to carry out the offense;
(2) the risks of detection associated with committing the offense;
(3) the rewards to be gained from the offense;
(4) situational conditions that may encourage criminal action; and
(5) excuses that offenders can use to justify their actions (Cornish and Clarke 2003).

Crimes, including white-collar crimes, are more likely to occur if they are easy to commit, have low risks of detection, provide an attractive reward, are encouraged by the immediate environment, and are easy to justify.

To describe the attractiveness of the existing opportunity structure for any particular white-collar crime using situational crime prevention theory, each of the five dimensions of opportunity must be assessed. For example, physicians billing for services that were either not performed or not medically indicated is a persistent problem for the Medicaid and Medicare programs (Sparrow 1996). From the perspective of physicians, this is an attractive criminal opportunity. The effort required is minimal, simply involving filling out and submitting electronic forms similar to ones submitted routinely for legitimate charges. As long as the charge is reasonable, the risk of detection is low because the claim will only be reviewed electronically to see if it falls within certain predetermined parameters for similar cases (Sparrow 1996). The monetary reward is obvious. A condition that might encourage the offense would be the physician's knowledge that his or her peers have engaged in similar activities. Finally, physicians often feel that they are not adequately reimbursed by Medicare or Medicaid for their services. Hence, they may excuse the offense as simply making up for what they should have received in the first place. These dimensions may vary across relatively similar opportunities (e.g., independent physician fraudulent billing of Medicaid compared to hospital fraudulent billing of Medicaid).

Taken together, the three theories described above can be used to structure efforts to uncover the specific characteristics of any particular crime opportunity and to suggest how these structures may be modified to prevent criminal activity. However, applying the theories to white-collar crimes requires us to consider some additional issues. In particular, we must address the issues of specificity and process. Specificity refers to how we choose our object of analysis. By process, we mean to draw attention to the fact that for most white-collar crime the target of the offense is not a fixed entity, but rather a process that can be subverted in some manner.

Opportunity and Specificity

The opportunity perspective requires us to identify very specific forms of crime. Different forms of crime have different opportunity structures even though they may for other purposes fit under the same conceptual umbrella. For example, rape and aggravated assault are both crimes of violence. Yet, they have different opportunity structures in terms of when and where they occur, who commits them, and who is victimized by them. The opportunity perspective cautions against trying to analyze crimes of violence in general and instead encourage us to focus on particular types of crimes of violence. The same stricture applies to white-collar crime. It is far too broad a category for the opportunity perspective.[7] To apply the approach advocated here to white-collar crime, one must identify specific forms of white-collar crime – the more specific the better. Even such seemingly specific crime categories such as embezzlement may be too broad. Certainly there are substantial differences in the opportunity structures confronted and the techniques used by traditional employee embezzlers, such as those studied by Cressey (1953) and Zeitz (1981) versus the collective embezzlers examined by Calavita and Pontell (1990). Similarly, environmental offenses can be committed in a variety of different ways. Individuals or companies that want to illegally dispose of hazardous wastes, for example, may do it by clandestinely dumping the material late at night (the so-called midnight dumping strategy), or by forging of manifests (so that, hazardous waste is not accurately identified as hazardous), or by bribing public officials, or by mislabeling containers, or by "cocktailing" (mixing hazardous and nonhazardous materials) (Rebovich 1992). These are all different ways of illegally disposing of hazardous wastes. They are all environmental offenses. Yet, from the perspective of the strategy advocated here,

---

[7] For examples of the many different forms or types of white-collar crime see Friedrichs (2004) or Rosoff et al. (2004).

they should be thought of as different offenses and approached individually. Detecting and preventing the bribery of public officials presents different problems and prospects than detecting and preventing midnight dumping.

Processes as Opportunities

Up to this point, we have used the term "opportunity structure" repeatedly. This term carries with it the connotation of something that is solid or fixed in place. For example, an unlocked car sitting in an unsupervised parking lot presents a fixed opportunity for a thief. From the offender's perspective, the target is sitting there waiting for him or her to take advantage of it. However, with respect to white-collar crime, it is important to recognize that their opportunity structures are often, indeed almost always, not like this. The opportunity is in some way related to a legitimate business activity. It arises, that is, out of some sort of process. From our perspective, processes create opportunities.

Take for example a process common in the world of private enterprise: the ordering and shipping of goods. Ideally, the process is supposed work in this manner. A customer needs a product and so places an order for it with a distributor. The distributor gets the order, pulls the product from his or her inventory, and ships it to the customer. The customer receives the stuff and sends the distributor a payment.[8]

Depending how this process is organized it may either create or block opportunities for crime. For example, if not properly supervised, employees of the distributor could create bogus orders and have products shipped to fictitious customers so that they can be resold by the employees or employees might overcharge customers and pocket the difference. On the other hand, an ill-intentioned person might pose as legitimate customer to get products with no intention of ever paying for them. Obviously, there are ways to design processes that would defeat or at least make more difficult these fraudulent schemes. Distributors, for example, may demand payment in advance or require information from potential customers (e.g., address, phone number, letter of credit from a bank, etc.) so as to verify their legitimacy.

We can conceive of white-collar crime as the intersection of at least two processes. The first is a legitimate process that is followed or employed in the business world, and the second is an illegitimate process that is parasitical on the first. Prevention involves making adjustments to the legitimate process that thwart the ability of individuals to act parasitically in relation to the legitimate process. Primarily, prevention involves developing processes that are either difficult to mimic or that raise the likelihood that an illegitimate process will be exposed. Auditing is a classic example of the latter strategy.

For example, inadequate auditing is a primary cause of fraud in the health care system. Consider a physician who sends in a fraudulent claim to Medicaid request-

---

[8] Obviously, there are many variations on this process. The order may be a "standing order" or the distributor may demand payment up front.

ing payment for some service that was not provided to a patient. The claim form contains all of the information normally found on legitimate claims and the fee charged is whatever is standard for the service in question. Normally, claims such as this will be "audited" automatically by a computer program, and because everything looks routine, payment will be authorized. The key weakness in this system is that no one checks to see that the claim form corresponds with what actually happened to a patient. To prevent (or to be realistic about it, reduce) the likelihood of this sort of offense, a different sort of auditing system would have to be developed. Suppose, for instance, that Medicaid randomly sampled some percentage of all claims and subjected them to rigorous personalized audits in which patients were interviewed about the treatment they received from their physicians.[9] From the perspective of fraudulent physicians, such a procedure would raise the risk of detection and presumably deter some of them some of the time.[10]

Whether a change in auditing procedures really would produce a change in the rate of fraudulent claims submissions is, of course, an empirical question. Indeed, for the opportunity perspective it represents a particularly important type of question to investigate. The opportunity perspective assumes that potential offenders react to opportunity structures and that if an opportunity structure changes then offenders should respond in some fashion to the change. If an opportunity structure changes such that a particular type of offense becomes more risky, then we would expect the rate of that particular offense to decline.[11] Finding out if this expectation is correct is an important research question. In the next section, we offer a few observations on the methodologies that should be used to address this and other questions relevant to the opportunity perspective.

Studying Opportunities and Processes: Small-n Versus Large-n Methodologies

As applied to white-collar crime, the opportunity perspective advanced here requires us to look at processes or, to put it more simply, at *how* things happen rather than *who* does them. A research focus on "how" rather than "who" leads to a particular

---

[9] Many health insurance companies do something like this in modified form by sending patients a notification whenever a claim form is filed on their behalf. While this increases the possibility that patients may uncover false claims, it is certainly not a foolproof system. The terminology used in notifications can be difficult for laypersons to understand. In addition, patients may be too ill or cognitively impaired to audit their own health records competently.

[10] We recognize that there are many problems with this "solution." The size of the Medicaid program makes auditing even a small percentage of claims prohibitively expensive. In addition, physicians dislike being audited and would probably resist additional audits. Nevertheless, we hope that the point made by our example is clear.

[11] Our example assumes, of course, that the rise in risk is sufficiently large to be noticed and attended to by potential offenders. We also note that offenders may adapt to the rise in risk associated with a particular type of offense by evolving new methods of offending that reduce the risk back to an acceptable level.

set of research methods. Processes unfold in time, suggesting the need for longitudinal studies that can identify important sequences of actions. In contrast, who questions suggest cross-sectional studies, preferably studies with large samples to find differences among individual offenders. Cross-sectional research has a role when studying opportunity structures – and we will return to this – but these are relatively minor compared to methods that can handle temporal sequences.

Process investigations of how offenders attempt to take advantage of opportunity structures – and how preventive measures block these attempts – require close examination of the details of how crimes unfold. White-collar crime research is not only interested in the sequences of actions taken by offenders. It must also pay attention to the actions of others. Like street crimes where one has to consider the actions of offenders, potential victims, guardians, place managers, and others, there are likely to be multiple agents to be considered. Each actor engages in a sequence of actions that must be identified. Further complicating efforts to study and understand processes is the fact that the actors involved are aware of and respond to each other interactively. As Malcolm Sparrow (1996) puts it, fraud is a dynamic game played between offenders and controllers.

The density of information required has a very practical consequence; except in the most richly financed studies, data sets have to be limited to relatively few cases. Large-n studies seldom produce data of sufficient detail and thickness. So studies of how white-collar crime occurs generally must use case study methods. Case studies can be highly useful for the types of questions that the opportunity perspective poses (George and Bennett 2005). They provide the ability to look closely at processes.

Drawing on recent developments in political science, (Brady and Collier 2004; George and Bennett 2005; Goertz and Starr 2003a) we will briefly examine three points that should be considered in the design of case studies to examine how questions: case selection, theories of necessary conditions, and process tracing.

The case selection procedures used need to be consistent with the theory being examined, and the frequency of white-collar crime being examined. We will discuss theory shortly, so let us look first at frequency. The dependent variable is the occurrence (or absence) of white-collar crime. When the type of white-collar crime is relatively common, selecting cases on the basis of an independent variable is feasible and often desirable. Organizations may be selected based on their use of presumed prevention methods, for example. However, when the type of white-collar crime is rare, then selecting on independent variables (for example, organizations of a particular size in a specified industry) will most likely provide cases without the crime. Selecting on the dependent variable may be best approach: organizations with known occurrences of the crime are chosen and compared to otherwise similar organizations that display no evidence of the crime in question. This is a case–control design (Loftin and McDowall 1988).

Under special conditions, the control in a case–control study can be eliminated. If the theory claims that an independent variable is necessary for a particular outcome (in our case, a white-collar crime), then control units, which by definition lack the outcome variable, provide no useful information to the study (Goertz and Starr 2003b; Most and Starr 2003). Consider Table 1 (derived from Most and

Table 1 The irrelevance of controls when the independent variable is necessary for an outcome

Independent variable	Outcome	
	Present	Absent
Present	(A) Supports theory	(B) Irrelevant
Absent	(C) Contradicts theory	(D) Irrelevant

Starr 2003). We are interested in testing whether a theory claiming that the presence of some condition is necessary for the presence of a particular crime type. We can imagine four types of organizations: (A) those with the condition and with the crime, (B) those with the conditions but without the crime, (C) those without the condition but with the crime, and (D) those without the condition and without the crime. Only cells A and C are useful. If the cases fall into A, this supports the theory. However, if they fall into C the theory is contradicted, because the theory claims that the condition is necessary. Note that the theory does not claim the condition guarantees the outcome. That is, the theory does not claim that the condition is a sufficient cause, only that it is necessary. So, if the crime is not present an organization may or may not have the condition. Therefore, in circumstances where the theory being tested claims some condition is necessary for a particular outcome, only cases with that outcome need to be examined.

Process tracing is a qualitative research method used to explicate a causal mechanism (Brady 2004; George and Bennett 2005). In large-n studies, various forms of correlations can be measured between an independent and dependent variable: the form depending on the scale used to measure the variables and the types of controls being applied. Even in large-n studies correlations are poor evidence for causation unless there is a clear valid mechanism that links the independent variable to the dependent variable (Hedström 2005). It would be like recording the presence of people in the driver seat of many cars, and finding a correlation between their presence and the car moving, but not knowing how presence causes movement. Small-n case studies cannot measure correlations reliably, but it is possible to carefully examine the mechanism to see if there is an unambiguous path from the change in the independent variable, through the mechanism, and to the change in the dependent variable. Continuing with our example, a case study might carefully examine two cars with drivers and tracing the linkage between the depression of the gas peddle through the mechanical system to the movement of the wheels. Process tracing is a natural method for the study of how in white-collar crime.

Although we believe that small-n case studies are likely to be the most productive research method for the time being, there are situations in which cross-sectional large-n studies can play a role in advancing theory. Three criteria must be met.

1. There must be a hypothesis from a process theory of white-collar crime that predicts a particular cross-sectional distribution.
2. This distribution must be distinguishable for other distributions that would falsify the hypothesis.
3. The data set must be able to show this distribution, if the hypothesis is true.

With one exception, if these criteria are absent, then little useful knowledge about how or process type questions can come from a large-n cross-sectional study. The single exception may be studies designed to develop classifications of white-collar crime so that specific opportunity theories of each type can be developed and studied. However, even in such circumstances, it may be preferable to have fewer cases and more details about the processes.

Conclusions and Implications

From the arguments put forward in this paper we can draw five general conclusions, which we summarize here:

1. All forms of white-collar crime have opportunity structures.
2. Opportunity structures vary by type of white-collar crime.
3. Core theories of environmental criminology – routine activity theory, crime pattern theory, and situational crime prevention – apply to white-collar crime and can be used to analyze opportunity structures.
4. Control and prevention of white-collar crime depends on knowing the processes of committing these crimes – how white-collar crimes are committed.
5. The appropriate methods for studying white-collar crime must be able to illuminate processes and case studies are ideally suited to meet this requirement.

Below we comment briefly on the implications that follow from these propositions.

Making opportunity structures central to the study of white-collar crime removes much of the confusion about this topic, and it moves the study of white-collar crime from the periphery of criminology to the center. Rather than an exceptional form of crime we see it as part of the routines of everyday life. By focusing on opportunity structures, the methods for controlling and preventing such crimes become extensions of the very same methods used to control "street crime." In addition, by focusing on how white-collar crimes are committed, and how processes can be altered to prevent these crimes, we see that some research methods, most notably small-n case studies, are more appropriate than others.

White-collar crime scholars, however, will no doubt note that there is no shortage of case studies of white-collar crime. Sutherland himself presented many examples in his study of corporate crime (1949). Since his ground-breaking work, others have followed his lead. One can find excellent case studies of antitrust offenses (Geis 1977; Reuter 1993; Simpson and Piquero 2001), environmental offenses (Block and Bernard 2002), crime in the retail drug industry (Vaughan 1983), accounting frauds (McLean and Elkind 2003), workplace safety violations (Aulette and Michalowski 1993), consumer product safety violations (Mintz 1995; Cullen et al. 2006), securities offenses (Szockyj 1993) and the list could go on.[12] These

---

[12] The texts cited in footnote 7 provide references to many case studies.

case studies often address in some detail how the offense was committed and its opportunity structure, though perhaps not using exactly the terminology employed here. Thus, our call for greater use of the case study methodology may strike some readers as not particularly ground breaking. However, we think that the real value of case studies has not yet been fully realized and that the opportunity perspective advocated here can help show how theoretically useful the case study methodology can be.

White-collar crime studies have often appeared deviant, relative to other criminological studies, because of their extensive use of small-n case studies. Yet, from an opportunity perspective where understanding processes is critical, case studies are the appropriate method. Although opportunity theories have been used primarily to address ordinary street crime, we believe that they provide a set of conceptual tools that can be fruitfully applied to white-collar crime. Significantly in this regard, the opportunity perspective suggests two important ways these case studies can be improved. First, opportunity theories such as routine activity, crime pattern, and situational crime prevention can help organize case studies. They provide a set of clear theoretical frameworks. Systematic application of opportunity frameworks could improve cross-case comparisons. For example, following the logic presented in Table 1, cases could be selected on the basis of the presence of a particular type of white-collar crime and then examined to see whether they have a particular independent variable derived from, say, routine activity theory. Second, opportunity frameworks explicate causal paths that case studies can explore and test. We have, for example, suggested that changes in regulation should create specific changes in the form of white-collar crime, as illustrated in Fig. 2. Case studies can test such propositions. Thus, the opportunity perspective moves white-collar crime research from the creation of interesting stories of theft, duplicity, and mendacity to an organized system that links these stories along common narratives, and further connects them to other forms of crime.

Perhaps most importantly, the opportunity framework provides a systematic approach to the control and prevention of white-collar crime. Opportunity theories give us ways of thinking about crime processes in a more analytical and comparative fashion. When the information gathered through case studies is placed within an opportunity framework, the crime process is described in such a way that potential points of intervention are illuminated. Thus, an opportunity-based approach to white-collar crime may lead to newer and more effective methods of prevention and control.

References

Abrams, N. (1980). Assessing the Federal Government's War on White-Collar Crime. *Temple Law Review* 53, 984–1008.

Aulette, J. R., and Michalowski, R. (1993). Fire in Hamlet: A Case Study of State-Corporate Crime. In G. Geis, R. F. Meier, and L. M. Salinger (Eds.), *White-Collar Crime: Classic and Contemporary Views* (pp. 166–190). New York: The Free Press.

Beavon, D., Brantingham, P., and Brantingham P. (1994). The Influence of Street Networks on the Patterning of Property Offenses. In R. Clarke (Ed.), *Crime Prevention Studies*, Vol. 2 (pp. 115–148). Monsey, NY: Criminal Justice Press.

Benson, M. L. (1985). Denying the Guilty Mind: Accounting for Involvement in a White-Collar Crime. *Criminology* 23, 583–607.

Benson, M. L., and Cullen, F. T. (1998). *Combating Corporate Crime: Local Prosecutors at Work*. Boston, MA: Northeastern University Press.

Block, A. A., and Bernard, T. J. (2002). Crime in the Waste Oil Industry. In D. Shichor, L. Gaines and R. Ball (Eds.), *Readings in White-Collar Crime*, (pp. 263–279). Prospect Heights, IL: Waveland Press.

Braithwaite, J. (1985). White-Collar Crime. *Annual Review of Sociology*. 11, 1–25.

Brady, H. E. (2004). Data-Set Observations versus Causal Process Observations: The 2000 U.S. Presidential Election. In H. E. Brady and D. Collier (Eds.), *Rethinking Social Inquiry: Diverse Tools, Shared Standards*, (pp. 267–272). Lanham, MD: Rowman & Littlefield Publishers.

Brady, H. E., and Collier, E. (Eds.). (2004). *Rethinking Social Inquiry: Diverse Tools, Shared Standards*. Lanham, MD: Rowman & Littlefield Publishers.

Brantingham, P. J., and Brantingham, P. L. (1991). *Environmental Criminology*. Prospect Heights, IL: Waveland Press.

Brantingham, P. L., and Brantingham, P. J. (1993). Nodes, Paths, and Edges: Considerations on the Complexity of Crime and the Physical Environment. *Journal of Environmental Psychology* 13, 3–18.

Calavita, K., and Pontell, H. N. (1990). 'Head's, I Win, Tails, You Lose:' Deregulation, Crime and Crisis in the Savings and Loan Industry. *Crime and Delinquency* 36, 309–341.

Clarke, R. V., and Newman, G. (2006). *Outsmarting the Terrorists*. Westport, CT: Praeger Publishers.

Cohen, L. E., and Felson, M. (1979). Social Change and Crime Rate Trends: A Routine Activity Approach. *American Sociological Review* 44, 588–608.

Collins, J. M., and Schmidt, F. L. (1993). Personality, Integrity and White-Collar Crime: A Construct Validity Study. *Personnel Psychology* 46, 295–311.

Cornish, D., and Clarke, R. V. (1986). Introduction. In D. Cornish and R. V. Clarke (Eds.), *The Reasoning Criminal*, (pp. 1–16). New York: Springer-Verlag.

Cornish, D. B., and Clarke, R. V. (2003). Opportunities, Precipitators, and Criminal Decisions: A Reply to Wortley's Critique of Situational Crime Prevention. *Crime Prevention Studies* 16, 41–96.

Coyne, H. (1991). *Scam: How Con Men Use the Telephone to Steal Your Money*. London, UK: Duckworth.

Cressey, D. R. (1953). *Other People's Money*. Glencoe, IL: The Free Press.

Cullen, F., Link, B., and Polanzi, C. (1982). The Seriousness of Crime Revisited: Have Attitudes Toward White-Collar Crime Changed? *Criminology* 20, 83–102.

Cullen, F., Cavendar, G., Maakestad, W., and Benson, M. L. (2006). *Corporate Crime Under Attack: The Fight to Criminalize Business Violence*. Cincinnati, OH: Anderson Publishing Co.

Eck, J. E. (1994). *Drug Markets and Drug Places: A Case-Control Study of the Spatial Structure of Illicit Drug Dealing*. Unpublished Ph.D. dissertation. Department of Criminology and Criminal Justice. University of Maryland, College Park.

Eck, J. E., and Clarke, R. V. (2003). Classifying Common Police Problems: A Routine Activity Approach. In M. J. Smith and D. B. Cornish (Eds.), *Theory for Practice in Situational Crime Prevention*, Crime Prevention Studies, Vol. 16 (pp. 7–39). Monsey, NY: Criminal Justice Press.

Edelhertz, H. (1970). *The Nature, Impact, and Prosecution of White-Collar Crime*. Washington, DC: U.S. Department of Justice.

Edelhertz, H., and Rogovin, C. (1982). *A National Strategy for Containing White-Collar Crime*. Lexington, MA: Lexington Books.

Evans, T. D., Cullen, F., and Dubeck, P. (1993). Public Perceptions of Corporate Crime. In M. P. Blankenship (Ed.) *Understanding Corporate Criminality*, (pp. 85–114). New York: Garland Press.

Felson, M. (1986). Linking Criminal Choices, Routine Activities, Informal Social Control, and Criminal Outcomes. In D. Cornish and R. V. Clarke (Eds.), *The Reasoning Criminal*, (pp. 119–128). New York: Springer-Verlag.

Felson, M. (2002). *Crime and Everyday Life*. 3rd Edition. Thousand Oaks, CA: Pine Forge Press.

Friedrichs, D. O. (2004). *Trusted Criminals*. 2nd Edition. Belmont, CA: Wadsworth/Thompson Learning.

Geis, G. (1977). The Heavy Electrical Equipment Antitrust Cases of 1961. In G. Geis and R. Meier (Eds.), *White-Collar Crime*, (pp. 117–132). New York: MacMillan.

Geis, G. (1988). From Deuteronomy to Deniability: An Historical Perlustration on White-Collar Crime. *Justice Quarterly* 5, 7–32.

George, A. L., and Bennett, A. (2005). *Case Studies and Theory Development in the Social Sciences*. Cambridge, MA: MIT Press.

Goertz, G., and Starr, H. (2003a). *Necessary Conditions: Theory, Methodology, and Applications*. Lanham, MD: Rowman & Littlefield Publishers.

Goertz, G., and Starr, H. (2003b). Introduction: Necessary Condition Logics, Research Design, and Theory. In G. Goertz and H. Starr (Eds.), *Necessary Conditions: Theory, Methodology, and Applications*, (pp. 1–24). Lanham, MD: Rowman & Littlefield Publishers.

Gottfredson, M., and Hirschi, T. (1990). *The General Theory of Crime*. Stanford, CA: Stanford University Press.

Hedström, P. (2005). *Dissecting the Social: On the Principles of Analytical Sociology*. Cambridge: Cambridge University Press.

Hillier, B. (1999). *Space is the Machine: A Configurational Theory of Architecture*. Cambridge: Cambridge University Press.

Hirschi, T., and Gottfredson, M. (1987). Causes of White-Collar Crime. *Criminology* 25, 949–974.

Hunter, R. D., and Jeffery, C. R. (1997). Preventing Convenience Store Robbery through Environmental Design. In R. V. Clarke (Ed.), *Situational Crime Prevention: Successful Case Studies*, (pp. 191–199). Monsey, NY: Criminal Justice Press.

Jesilow, P., Pontell, H. N., and Geis, G. (1993). *Prescription for Profit: How Doctors Defraud Medicaid*. Berkley, CA: University of California Press.

Katz, J. (1980). The Social Movement Against White-Collar Crime. *Criminology Review* 2, 161–184.

Levi, M. (1987). *Regulating Fraud*. London: Tavistock.

Loftin, C., and McDowall, D. (1988). The Analysis of Case-Control Studies in Criminology. *Journal of Quantitative Criminology* 4(1), 85–98.

Madensen, T. D., and Eck, J. E. (2006). *Student Party Riots*. Problem-Oriented Guides for Police Series. Washington, DC: Office of Community Oriented Policing Services, U.S. Department of Justice.

McLean, B., and Elkind, P. (2003). *The Smartest Guys in the Room: The Amazing Rise and Scandalous Fall of Enron*. New York: Penguin.

Mintz, M. (1995). Corporate Greed, Women, and the Dalkon Shield. In G. Geis, R. F. Meier, and L. M. Salinger (Eds.), *White-Collar Crime: Classic and Contemporary Views*, (pp. 191–199). New York: The Free Press.

Most, B. A., and Starr, H. (2003). Basic Logic and Research Design: Conceptualization, Case Selection, and the Form of Relationships. In G. Goertz and H. Starr (Eds.), *Necessary Conditions: Theory, Methodology, and Applications*, (pp. 24–46). Lanham, MD: Rowman & Littlefield Publishers.

Poyner, B. (1991). Situational Crime Prevention in Two Parking Facilities. *Security Journal* 2, 96–101.

Rebovich, D. J. (1992). *Dangerous Ground: The World of Hazardous Waste Crime*. New Brunswick, NJ: Transaction Press.

Reuter, P. (1993). The Cartage Industry in New York. *Crime and Justice* 18, 149–201.

Rosoff, S. M., Pontell, H. N., and Tillman, R. H. (2004). *Profit Without Honor: White-Collar Crime and the Looting of America*. Upper Saddle River, NJ: Prentice Hall.

Schrager, L. S., and Short, J. (1980). How Serious a Crime: Perceptions of Organizational and Common Crimes. In G. Geis and E. Stotland (Eds.), *White-Collar Crime: Theory and Research*, (pp. 14–31). Beverly Hills, CA: Sage Publications.

Shapiro, S. P. (1990). Collaring the Crime, Not the Criminal: Reconsidering 'White-Collar Crime.' *American Sociological Review* 55, 346–365.

Simpson, S. S., and Piquero, N. L. (2001). The Archer Daniels Midland Antitrust Case of 1996. In Pontell, H. N. and Shichor, D. (Eds.), *Contemporary Issues in Crime and Criminal Justice: Essays in Honor of Gilbert Geis*, (pp. 175–194). Upper Saddle River, NJ: Prentice-Hall.

Skoler, D. L. (1982). White-Collar Crime and the Criminal Justice System: Problems and Challenges. In H. Edelhertz and C. Rogovin (Eds.), *A National Strategy for Containing White-Collar Crime*, (pp. 153–173). Lexington, MA: Lexington Books.

Sparrow, M. K. (1996). *License to Steal: Why Fraud Plagues America's Health Care System*. Boulder, CO: Westview Press.

Stotland, E. (1977). White-Collar Criminals. *Journal of Sociology* 33, 179–196.

Sutherland. E. H. (1940). White-Collar Criminality. *American Sociological Review* 5, 1–12.

Sutherland. E. H. (1949). *White-Collar Crime*. New York: Holt, Rinehart, and Winston.

Szockyj, E. (1993). *The Law and Insider Trading: In Search of a Level Playing Field*. Buffalo, NY: William S. Hein & Co., Inc.

Vaughan, D. (1983). *Controlling Unlawful Organizational Behavior*. Chicago: University of Chicago Press.

Wasserman, S., and Faust, K. (1994). *Social Network Analysis: Methods and Applications*. New York: Cambridge University Press.

Weisburd, D., and Waring, E. with Chayet, E. F. (2001). *White-Collar Crime and Criminal Careers*. Cambridge: Cambridge University Press.

White, G. (1990). Neighborhood Permeability and Burglary Rates. *Justice Quarterly* 7, 57–67.

Wortley, R., and Smallbone, S. (2006). Applying Situational Principles to Sexual Offenses Against Children. In R. Wortley and S. Smallbone (Eds.), *Situational Prevention of Child Sexual Abuse*, (pp. 7–36). New York: Criminal Justice Press.

Zeitz, C. (1981). *Women Who Embezzle or Defraud*. New York: Praeger.

Self-Regulatory Approaches to White-Collar Crime: The Importance of Legitimacy and Procedural Justice

Tom R. Tyler

Abstract Securing employee adherence to workplace rules and company policies is a key antecedent of successful functioning within organizations. It is important for companies to be able to effectively motivate rule following behavior among employees, i.e. to be able to limit white-collar crime. This chapter compares the utility of two approaches to securing such behavior. Those strategies are as follows: (1) the sanction-based command-and-control model and (2) self-regulation approaches that are linked to activating employee's ethical judgments. Research findings suggest that, while command-and-control strategies influence employee behavior, self-regulatory strategies have a stronger influence. Studies also explore the basis of these ethical judgments, and find that the primary factor shaping them is the procedural justice that employees experience in their workplace. These results suggest that the roots of employee policy adherence and rule following behavior lie in the procedural justice of the organization. Overall, this analysis highlights the important role ethical judgments play in motivating both rule following and policy adherence among employees in work settings and provides practical suggestions for shaping those judgments.

Can businesses effectively regulate the behavior of white-collar employees, and if so, what strategies should they use to best achieve that goal? Recent corporate scandals have evoked a heightened concern among members of the public, government officials, and business leaders about both whether businesses can regulate the conduct of their employees, as well as about how to effectively secure employee adherence with corporate rules and policies. White-collar crime is suddenly on the public agenda.

What is white-collar crime and how does it differ from other types of crime? There are two principal distinctions. The first is who commits the crime. White-collar criminals are typically better educated, employed, middle class and, at least historically, white and male. They are central members of society, not marginal

T.R. Tyler (✉)
Department of Psychology, New York University, New York, NY, USA
e-mail: tom.tyler@nyu.edu

S.S. Simpson, D. Weisburd (eds.), *The Criminology of White-Collar Crime*,
DOI 10.1007/978-0-387-09502-8_10, © Springer Science+Business Media, LLC 2009

individuals. Second, the crimes they commit tend to be nonviolent and to focus on money. The crimes involved are not emotionally driven, such as assault or rape, nor are they crimes involving physical harm. Instead, they are efforts by individuals to achieve economic gains outside the rules.

Rule adherence among white-collar employees is important in a wide variety of work settings, and potentially involves organizational policies that cover, among other things, accurate accounting, conflicts of interest, product or service quality, environmental safety, sexual harassment, race, gender and/or sexual orientation discrimination, and just plain stealing of company supplies and equipment and of paid time worked via long-lunch hours or phony sick days. In these and many other ways gaining adherence to organizational policies that control everyday employee behavior is critical for successful organizational functioning (Bell et al., 2002; Laufer and Robertson, 1997).

Unfortunately, there has long been extensive evidence that in many of these areas noncompliance within organizations is widespread (e.g., Frederick, 1995; Healy and Iles, 2002; Mintz, 2001; Rice, 1992; Simon and Eitzen, 1990; Spence, 2001; Vardi and Weitz, 2004). Such issues of compliance and noncompliance have been dramatically thrust into the public eye recently through highly visible incidents of corporate misconduct. The prevalence and damaging consequences of such noncompliance underscores the importance of identifying an effective model of employee rule adherence. Businesses would benefit from such a model since it would allow them to shape employee conduct in desirable ways. Further, from a policy perspective, government agencies are more likely to feel that the active regulation of businesses is important if they believe that businesses lack an effective model for self-regulation.

Of course, it is also important to recognize that a wide variety of issues are involved in recent corporate scandals. In particular, in some cases the issue is linked to misbehavior among corporate leaders, i.e. CEOs. The focus of this chapter is not on the leaders of corporations, but on employees within them. In particular, this chapter does not consider the case in which leaders are creating an unethical climate within their companies so that they can break rules for personal profit. Rather, this chapter begins with the assumption that the situation can be one in which the leaders of a company are motivated to encourage their employees to follow rules, and are seeking to understand how best to do so. Hence, it is important to recognize that I am only addressing one aspect of white-collar crime. One one level, I am considering crime by white-collar workers, rather than "CEO level crime."

However, from the perspective of the law and legal institutions, this analysis assumes that legal authorities are interested in motivating employees to follow the law and are trying to understand the strategies that companies should be encouraged to follow to achieve this objective. In this case, the arguments outlined may well apply to corporate leaders as well as employees. Legal authorities need to create a strategy, which will motivate corporate leaders to follow the law, and the arguments outlined here apply directly to that task. They also need to be able to lessen white-collar crime among employees in general.

Introduction

My goal is to compare the utility of two approaches to employee regulation: the *command-and-control model* and the *self-regulatory model*. The command-and-control model represents a traditional approach to encouraging rule following, insofar as it operates by drawing upon employees' instrumental concerns and utility maximization goals. Specifically, the command-and-control model links employees' motivation to follow rules to the manipulation of sanctions in the workplace. It is based on the view that people follow rules as a function of the costs and benefits they associate with doing so.

The command-and-control model reflects a strategy of *external regulation*, because employee behavior is controlled by managers through their ability to implement sanctions and to punish undesired behavior. In contrast, the self-regulatory model is based upon the activation of *internal motivations*. This distinction develops from prior social psychological research, in particular the work of Kelman (1958), which distinguishes between compliance based upon external contingencies and self-regulation linked to identification and internalization. This distinction is extended to organizational arenas by Kelman and Hamilton (1989) and to work settings by O'Reilly and Chatman (1986).

The *self-regulatory model* represents an alternative approach to employee rule following. The model emphasizes the role that employees' ethical values play in motivating rule following, and in particular those ethical values that are related to—and developed in the course of interactions with—their work organization. That is, I focus on those ethical judgments that are linked to employees' specific experiences at their work organizations. This can be contrasted to a focus on individual differences in ethical judgments, i.e., to those aspects of people's personalities that shape their judgments of particular ethical matters. My focus on organizationally based ethical judgments is rooted in an interest in determining the characteristics of work environments—as opposed to individuals—that may shape employee rule following. This emphasis has the potential to be of particular utility to leaders and managers in their attempts to design workplaces that foster rule following among employees.

Two specific ethical judgments that are linked to organizational conditions are considered here: (1) the perceived legitimacy of organizational rules and authorities and (2) the congruence of those rules with an employee's moral values. The self-regulatory model argues that the concerns embodied in these two ethical judgments have the potential to motivate employees to feel a personal responsibility for bringing their behavior into line with corporate rules and policies. It is based on the assumption that people are motivated to align their behavior with the rules of organizations or groups they belong to when they view those groups as being legitimate and consistent with their own sense of right and wrong.

The first goal of this comparison is to compare the relative efficacy of the two distinct strategies outlined. While the use of sanctions represents a traditional management strategy to securing employee compliance to organizational rules and policies, I consider recent studies that directly examine whether activating employee's ethical values is an effective management strategy for securing their compliance. The use of such a self-regulatory model has been long advocated within discussions of legal regulation of business (Selznick, 1969), and has been advanced with particular frequently in recent years (Aalders and Wilthagen, 1997; Darley et al., 2003; Gunningham and Rees, 1997; King and Lenox, 2000; Rechtschaffen, 1998; Suchman, 1995; Tyler, 2001; Tyler and Darley, 2001). The studies examined consider whether employees' ethical values can in reality—as hypothesized by self-regulatory models—provide a viable basis for encouraging employee policy adherence.

The second goal of this chapter is to examine the antecedents of employee ethical values. To the extent that the self-regulatory model represents and describes an important influence on employee policy adherence it becomes important to understand the factors that shape whether or not employees come to hold ethical values that encourage such adherence. Drawing upon the literature on procedural justice, it is hypothesized that employees' ethical values will be activated and will be more salient in decision making when employees evaluate their organization as being governed with fair procedures. This prediction is linked to one of the core hypotheses of the group engagement model (Tyler and Blader, 2000, 2004): that procedural justice judgments are central to shaping employee cooperative behavior. This procedural justice hypothesis has been supported by prior studies of rule following in legal (Tyler, 2006a) and managerial (Tyler and Blader, 2000, 2005) settings. It has received widespread, but not universal support (Kuperan and Sutinen, 1998). If supported by research, this model provides a theoretical perspective within which managers can develop a strategy for activating employees' ethical values in work settings and thus secure employee compliance with work rules and policies.

What Are the Behaviors We Are Interested in Motivating White-Collar Employees to Engage in?

There are several frameworks within which to conceptualize the ways in which employees may follow or break organizational rules, and this study will examine each of them. Two aspects of policy-related behavior are considered here: policy adherence and rule breaking. On the one hand, organizations want employees to *adhere to organizational policies*. Organizational rules and policies stipulate desired employee behavior, and the organization benefits when those policies are followed. For example, organizational rules often specify behaviors about how work should be carried out, when people arrive at work, etc. Such rules facilitate coordination between employees and ensure the smooth functioning of the organization. This aspect of rule following involves conformity to organizational policies, since it involves employee actions that bring their behavior into line with organizational rules.

I further distinguish between two forms of policy adherence behavior: conformity with organizational policies and voluntary deference to organizational policies. The roots of this distinction lie in the literature on obeying the law, which distinguishes between compliance with the law and voluntary, willing acceptance of the law (see Kelman, 1958; Tyler, 2006a; Tyler and Huo, 2002). The same distinction is important in work settings (O'Reilly and Chatman, 1986).

The distinction between these two forms of behavior lies in the circumstances under which employees indicate that they follow rules. With compliance people indicate how often they follow rules across all settings. With voluntary, willing, acceptance they indicate whether they follow the rules even when they do not have to, when no one is around, and when their behavior is not being monitored. In other words, they choose to follow the rules even when failing to do so will be undetected. Hence voluntary deference refers to rule following in that subset of situations in which issues of detection are largely or completely irrelevant.

On the flip side of conformity or deference to organizational policies lies deviant behavior by employees, or *behaviors that are damaging and prohibited by organizational rules*. For example, employees may use office supplies for personal use or use sick leave when not sick. More seriously, employees may steal or break organizational rules by lying and cheating. I refer to this deviant behavior as *rule breaking* because it involves the decision to ignore or violate organizational rules.

Naturally, companies want to reduce the degree of rule breaking that occurs among employees. For instance, a widely damaging form of inappropriate employee behavior is theft of business supplies and equipment. It is estimated that 30–50% of all business failures are linked to losses from employee theft, a problem that is ten times more costly than street crime in terms of loss to society, and whose costs are often estimated to be in the hundreds of billions of dollars in the United States alone (Greenberg, 1997). Again, the magnitude of these losses, and the suggestion that up to 75% of employees engage in theft in their workplace, indicates the challenge posed by trying to manage this problem.

In making the various distinctions among behaviors outlined above, my primary concern is with distinctly examining voluntary rule following. Even when organizations are successful in lowering the rate of rule breaking via compliance, the results are costly. It is far preferable, as will be outlined, to motivate voluntary rule adherence (Tyler, 2007).

Models of Motivation and Policy Adherence

Command-and-control. The command-and-control perspective focuses on controlling people's behavior via the threat of punishments or sanctions for misbehavior. To the degree that employees are motivated instrumentally—and are thus primarily interested in the resources and outcomes they receive from their organizations— some external authority, either the company or the government, needs to take an active role in enforcing rules regarding their conduct. In other words, to the extent that employees are extrinsically motivated, extrinsic forces are needed to regulate their behavior. In organizational settings, such extrinsic forces typically take the form of incentives (to encourage desired behavior) and sanctions (to discourage undesirable behavior). Incentives and sanctions in many ways represent two sides of the same extrinsic motivational coin—each is an organizational mechanism used to control employee behavior via employees' concerns over the resources and benefits the organization provides them. There is already discussion in the organizational literature about problems with incentives (Kohn, 1999), as well as a parallel discussion regarding the potential inadequacies and pitfalls of punishments as motivational tools (Frey, 1977).

Many of the features of the modern workplace are the result of the use of the command and control model. For example, the extensive use of surveillance techniques—such as the use of cameras, the monitoring of telephone calls and computer usage, etc.—is an artifact of the implementation of command-and-control techniques. Random drug testing, searching employees' cars and lockers, and the use of time clocks and other performance tracking devices similarly reflect the view that compliance develops from a credible fear of detection and ensuing sanctions.

This instrumental strategy addresses the issue of employee motivation from the perspective of traditional economic theory—i.e., by assuming that employees are rational actors who are concerned primarily about maximizing their own outcomes in work settings (Blair and Stout, 2001). Studies generally support the suggestion that instrumental strategies do, as expected, shape people's behavior (Nagin, 1998; Nagin and Paternoster, 1991; Paternoster, 1987, 1989), with some studies supporting this argument in work settings (Huselid, 1995; Jenkins et al., 1998).

However, the use of instrumental strategies—and the control-and-command strategy in particular—requires the availability of resources. For sanctions and deterrence systems to work, organizations must be able (and willing) to devote significant resources to the surveillance needed to make detection of rule breaking sufficiently likely that people are deterred. The cost of such surveillance should not be underestimated, since employees are inherently motivated to conceal their rule breaking behavior, and effective surveillance systems are essential for sanctioning systems to shape behavior. Incentive strategies do not have surveillance problems, but require the availability of resources for incentives, as well as system to define and evaluate performance.

In addition to their financial costs to the organization, there are likewise social costs associated with control-and-command systems. These systems have the potential to communicate a message of mistrust in employees, conveying a sense that the organization is an adversarial force to the employee. Significant repercussions on employee commitment and identification with the organization may thus result. Furthermore, interpersonal dynamics may often be affected, as employees that maintain surveillance systems are pit against those being scrutinized.

Perhaps most importantly, it is also not clear how effective command-and-control strategies are. For example, in legal settings sanction-based deterrence strategies are consistently found to have, at best, a minor influence on rule-breaking behavior (MacCoun, 1993; Tyler, 2006a). In his review of the deterrence effect of drug laws, for example, MacCoun finds that only about 5% of the variance in drug use is explained by deterrence factors. Tyler and Blader (2000) estimate based upon their workplace-based study that around 10% of the variance in employee behavior is shaped by incentives in the work environment. These results suggest that, while they are somewhat effective, such systems may only have a limited impact on employee behavior.

More generally, in recent years the limits of the command-and-control model have been noted (Katyal, 1997; Malloy, 2002; Markell, 2000; Sutinen and Kuperan, 1999). However, this increasing skepticism has occurred within the arena of legal regulation (Tyler and Huo, 2002), and less so in discussions of work organizations. Thus, the managerial relevance of these critiques remains an open issue.

Of course, command-and-control strategies do not only exist within organizations. Organizations also function within a framework of government imposed legal prohibitions and administrative requirements, also based on incentive and sanction systems (Breyer and Stewart, 1985; Gunningham and Grabosky, 1998; Pearce, 2001). Even at this more macro-level, the utility of those systems has been increasingly questioned. For instance, they have been referred to as "ossified" systems that make "compliance difficult and impractical" (Spence, 2001, p. 917). In this domain as well, one oft-noted difficulty is the problem of monitoring behavior (Langevoort, 2002). Within the legal literature on government regulation, such skepticism about command-and-control strategies has lead to the flourishing of market-based models of regulation emphasizing economic incentive systems (Stewart, 2003).

Self-regulation. An alternative model of employee policy adherence is one in which the motivation to follow organizational rules resides in the employee themselves, and not in extrinsic incentives or sanctions stipulated by the organization. According to such a model, employees can be intrinsically motivated to follow organizational rules; that is, they will do so out of their own desire, and not out of the contingencies established by the organization for their behavior. The self-regulatory model tested in these studies specifically examines the role of employees' ethical values in shaping intrinsic motivation to follow rules. The success of this approach depends upon the power of employee's ethical values to motivate their rule and policy following behavior in the workplace.

Calls for greater attention to the teaching of ethics in the business school curricula and for more attention to ethical issues in work cultures flow from the belief that employees' ethical values can be changed within work settings. In other words, is depends upon the view that that values can be taught (Bowie, 1999; Schminke, 1998; Trevino and Weaver, 2003). This belief, when combined with the assumption that ethical values can have an important role in shaping behavior, thus argues for the importance of corporate cultures that shape ethical values in ways that promote employee policy adherence. That is, to the extent that ethical values affect employee rule following, the challenge is to create organizational cultures that harness the motivational power of employees' ethical values.

Several types of evidence suggest that ethical values may shape employee behavior. Research suggests that ethical concerns motivate self-regulatory behavior in organizational settings (Aalders and Wilthagen, 1997; Gunningham and

Rees, 1997; King and Lenox, 2000; Rechtschaffen, 1998; Sinclair, 1997). This includes studies focused on legitimacy (Human and Provan, 2000; Suchman, 1995; Tyler, 2005, 2006a; Tyler and Blader, 2000, 2005; Tyler et al., 2007a; Zimmerman and Zeitz, 2002), on morality (Paternoster and Simpson, 1996; Tyler, 2006a; Tyler and Blader, 2000, 2005), and on the general role of fairness in shaping social behavior (Rabin, 1993; Tyler and Blader, 2000; Vandenbergh, 2003). Ethical values shape behavior when people believe that the rules of their organization are legitimate, and hence ought to be obeyed, and/or that the values defining the organization are more congruent with their own moral values, leading people to feel that they ought to support the organization.

At the organizational level, there is evidence of the importance of ethical values in studies showing that companies are reluctant to use their market power by lowering employee wages during recessions because they believe such an action will be viewed by employees as unethical (Bewley, 1999), that companies often forgo opportunities to press their market advantages when dealing with their customers due to ethical concerns (Kahneman et al., 1986), and that ethical issues shape wage determination (Rees, 1993) as well as other aspects of the employment relationship (Jolls, 2002). These studies argue that companies are motivated to respond to ethical issues because they believe that ethical judgments shape people's reactions and behavior (Estreicher, 2002), an argument supported by studies suggesting that companies regarded as ethical by employees, customers, and other constituencies are more profitable (Huselid, 1995; Margolis and Walsh, 2001).

I focus on the influence of two particular types of ethical values. The first is the belief by employees that their organization's rules and authorities are *legitimate*. Legitimacy refers to the view by employees that they are responsible for obeying organizational rules—e.g., that the organization is entitled to have its rules and policies obeyed (Tyler, 2006a, b). Early discussions of legitimacy, such as the work of Weber, focus on the perceived legitimacy of government and law (Tyler, 1999), but it is clear that legitimacy is also an important concept in the context of work organizations (Selznick, 1969; Suchman, 1995). In work settings, legitimacy refers to the judgment that "the actions of an entity are desirable, proper, or appropriate within some socially constructed system of norms, values, beliefs, and definitions" (Suchman, 1995, p. 574). If people feel that their organization has legitimacy, they are motivated to defer to its rules and policies. This work connects with other work within the broader literature on corporate regulation, which recognizes the importance of legitimacy. For example, Simpson (2002) and Smith et al. (in press) argue for the limits of regulation based solely on sanctions and for the benefits of values such as legitimacy.

The second ethical value is the belief by employees that corporate policies are congruent with their own personal *moral values*. If an employee believes that such value congruence exists, then their own moral values motivate them to follow corporate rules because they see those rules as being consistent with—and developed from—a set of moral values with which they agree. Thus, they may follow rules in their effort to do what they feel is morally right. For example, in legal settings an important motivation that encourages people to bring their behavior into line with the law is their belief that many behaviors that are illegal are also immoral (Carlsmith et al., 2000; Robinson and Darley, 1995, 1997; Tyler, 2006a, b). Similar moral values are found to shape cooperation within experimental games (Kerr, 1995; Kerr et al., 1997; Kerr and Kaufman-Gilliland, 1994). If people feel that their organization acts in ways consistent with their own moral values, they are more strongly motivated to support their organization.

Conversely, in situations in which employee behaviors are contrary to official policy but viewed by people as not being immoral—such as drug use, some sexual practices, and the illegal use of copyrighted software—it is more difficult to bring people's behavior into conformity with the law. Employee theft may be another behavior that violates corporate policy but that is not viewed by employees as immoral when it is done to restore equity in the employee/employer relationship. Similarly, employees in work organizations evaluate the morality of company policies and practices and react to those policies and practices in moral terms (Paternoster and Simpson, 1996). Adherence to those policies is more likely when they are viewed as morally appropriate.

Ethical Values and Workplace Rule Adherence

The findings of recent research support the argument that employee's ethical values shape their behavior and in particular influence their rule-following behavior. Those employees who believe that management is legitimate and/or that company rules and policies are consistent with their moral values are less likely to break policies and violate rules.

One example of research on this topic is provided by Tyler and Blader (2005). Two studies are reported by Tyler and Blader, one of a sample of corporate bankers and another of a large and diverse sample of American employees.[1] Analysis of both samples indicates that employee rule following and policy adherence was strongly influenced by employee's ethical values. This included distinct influences of legitimacy and moral value congruence. Interestingly, when the broad sample is divided into categories reflecting the dimensions separating white-collar and blue-collar employees, similar findings emerge in both groups. Hence, while the focus of this chapter is on white-collar crime, the arguments made apply to workers in general.[2]

These findings suggest that companies benefit by fostering ethical values in their employees that support rule following. Those ethical values are a major motivation leading to employee compliance with company policies and rules. They also lead to lower levels of rule breaking behavior on the part of employees. These results

---

[1] The study conducted by Tyler and Blader (2005) relies on self-report of rule following, validated by independent observations by supervisors. Other studies (see Tyler et al., 2007) similarly validate the impact of legitimacy on behavior using police reports of rule breaking.

[2] In fact, the findings extend beyond the arena of private sector employees. Tyler (2007) demonstrate that agents of social control are also influenced in their job-related behaviors by similar organizational factors.

suggest that one promising way to bring the behavior of corporate employees into line with corporate codes of conduct is to tap into their ethical values. To gain acceptance for corporate rules and policies, companies should activate employee values. These values are central to the self-regulatory strategy for achieving employee compliance.

Of course, the activation of employee values is not the only way to influence rule-related behavior. Organizational sanctions for rule breaking may likewise motivate employees to follow organizational policies, as suggested by the command-and-control model. However, in the two studies reported here, the utility of that approach appears to be smaller in magnitude. These findings suggest that companies have a great deal to gain by going beyond instrumental strategies of social control and also focusing attention on the activation of employee values that are consistent with a self-regulatory strategy. Overall, the studies indicate the viability of such a strategy and, furthermore, the potential superiority of that strategy over the more traditional command-and-control approach.

The empirical support outlined suggests the utility of the self-regulatory strategy. Such an approach also has benefits over a command-and-control strategy. For instance, it prevents organizations from expending resources on creating and maintaining credible systems of surveillance to enforce rules. These problems are typical of any efforts to regulate conduct using incentive or sanction-based strategies. Exacerbating this problem, such strategies actually encourage people to hide their behavior and thus make it necessary to have especially comprehensive and costly surveillance systems.

Besides their actual costs, these strategies have the additional problem that they undermine employee's commitment to their company and enjoyment of their jobs. Employees whose focus is on avoiding sanctions have their intrinsic motivation and commitment to their company undermined (Frey, 1997). They then contribute less to their workplaces. Hence, there is a downside to sanctions and the surveillance associated with them. They hurt company productivity by undermining the ethical values that encourage commitment to work (Tyler and Blader, 2000).

This is not to say that command-and-control systems cannot work. They can, especially if organizations devote sufficient resources to their implementation. For example, some companies engage in extensive monitoring, even putting cameras in restrooms and monitoring telephone and e-mail communication. They may also try to create conditions under which behavior is easily monitored by, for example, requiring employees to time punch in and out of their workplace, to sign out equipment or tools, or to work in publicly accessible spaces. Clearly, such efforts consume organizational resources. Even if they work, these strategies are costly and inefficient.

The findings of the studies considered point to the potential value of using the self-regulatory approach to employee motivation. By activating employee' own ethical values, companies can gain willing cooperation and buy in from their employees. Such willing cooperation is much more efficient and effective, since people become self-regulatory. They take on the responsibility to follow rules and do it without reference to the likelihood of being caught and punished for wrongdoing.

In recent decades, the recognition that self-regulation has value has been a widespread one within the law. Self-regulation is widely touted as a means of avoiding the problems that occur when government seeks to regulate business, and to lessen the costs of government agencies with a regulatory role (Rechtschaffen, 1998; King and Lenox, 2000; Gunningham and Rees, 1997; Aalders and Wilthagen, 1997). These same arguments can be applied within companies. Companies benefit when they can develop self-regulatory strategies that encourage their employees to take increased responsibility for rule following.

Earlier studies in the area of everyday law-related behavior highlight the important role of ethical values in encouraging citizen compliance with the law (Tyler, 2006a). It has been shown that people are more likely to comply with laws when they feel that legal authorities are legitimate and ought to be obeyed. The findings noted support this argument and extend it to a different arena – employees and their relationship to the corporations in which they work. Recent corporate scandals have highlighted the importance of an effort to better understand how to motivate employee compliance with corporate codes of conduct.

The influence of ethical judgments in these studies is especially striking since the work arena is one in which the influence of ethical values has traditionally been downplayed in favor of alternative instrumental or "rational" approaches. They suggest that a model of motivation that only considers rational motivations is incomplete and does not take account of the important role that social motivations can play in shaping employee rule-following behavior.

The current findings also extend previous work by considering not only the social value of legitimacy but also that of value congruence (i.e., the match between the person's moral values and those of the organization). In other words, people who experience justice when dealing with their work organization first think that its rules are legitimate and ought to be obeyed. They also feel that the values of their work organization are more congruent with their own, so that their own motivation to behave morally leads to support for their work organization. Overall, these findings support the argument that developing an appropriately ethical organizational culture is central to the effectiveness and viability of corporations.

It is especially striking that voluntary deference is linked to ethical motivations. Organizations recognize that they depend heavily on the good will of employees who are motivated to go beyond their job descriptions and to defer to rules even when surveillance is weak. Such voluntary behavior is central to organizational effectiveness and is strongly motivated by legitimacy and moral congruence.

Workplace Policies and Practices and Employee Ethical Values

The *self-regulatory model* operates via the activation of employees' ethical values and feelings of responsibility toward their company. The group engagement model (Tyler and Blader, 2000, 2003) hypothesizes that factors such as employees' ethical values are shaped by employee perceptions of how fairly they are treated by management. As has been noted, the potentially important role of fairness in motivating positive work attitudes and behavior has been recognized by economists as well as by social and organizational psychologists. This approach is based upon a psychological model suggesting that an organizational environment characterized by fair procedures will activate strong employee organizational identification, thus leading them to engage in desirable workplace behaviors and to hold positive attitudes toward their work organizations.

Various aspects of an organization's policies, human resource practices, and culture may potentially influence employee rule following and employee's ethical values regarding their work organizations. One set of management theories argues that the primary organizational factor shaping employees' reactions to their work organizations is the distribution of outcomes in the work environment. According to these theories, employee attitudes and behavior are responsive to judgments about the favorability of the outcomes (i.e., resources) provided to them by corporate rules and policies, as well as to the incentives and sanctions associated with their workplace behavior. These arguments flow from an instrumental model that views workers as motivated to maximize the outcomes they receive from their work organizations.

Psychological models of equity and distributive justice also suggest that employees are instrumentally motivated and focus on outcomes, but argue that they focus on issues of distributive fairness (Adams, 1965). They suggest that employees are sensitive to whether or not they feel that they are receiving a fair level of wages and benefits. These models are based on the premise that workers recognize that no one can have all that they want, and subsequently shift the basis of how they react toward their work organization to their judgments of whether they are receiving their fair share of workplace resources (Walster et al., 1978).

An alternative set of management theories argues that employee reactions to their work organizations may be based on their judgments about the fairness of the *procedures* used in their workplace. Factors affecting these fairness judgments may include, for example, whether the procedures allow employees to have input into decision making processes, whether they require that objective information be used in decision making, whether efforts are made to reduce biased treatment, etc. (Lind and Tyler, 1988; Tyler and Lind, 1992). Widespread evidence from all types of organizations attests to the importance of procedural fairness judgments in shaping the behavior of employees in work settings (Colquitt et al., 2001; Cropanzano et al., 2001; Greenberg and Cropanzano, 2001; Lind and Tyler, 1988; Tyler et al., 1997). Typical of this research is a study by Kim and Mauborgne, who demonstrate that procedural justice evaluations influence the willingness of subsidiaries to accept corporate strategic policy decisions in multinational work organizations (Kim and Mauborgne, 1993). Other studies link the fairness of workplace procedures to employee's willingness to voluntarily help their work groups, to their intention to stay with their company, and to the quality of their job performance (Tyler and Blader, 2000).

The procedural justice argument is based upon the belief that people's procedural justice judgments are distinct from their instrumental concerns. That is, the reactions of employees to their judgments about the fairness of their organization's procedures are not related to goals they may have regarding the outcomes that they receive from their organization. Instead, they react to procedures because they make inferences about their relational connections and social identities based on the fairness of those procedures (Lind and Tyler, 1988). These social identity judgments, about issues such as their standing in the organization, the status of the organization, and their level of identification with the organization, in turn influence their workplace attitudes and behaviors (Tyler and Blader, 2000, 2001, 2005). When organizational procedures are regarded as fair, employees feel that they can safely identify with the work organization and thus become engaged in it (Tyler and Blader, 2005). This approach is based on the idea that people are influenced by the nature of the organizational environment in which they work, so that the "fit" between the practices of the organization and a person's impression of themselves (including their ethical values) is important (Chatman, 1989, 1991).

The findings of procedural justice research lead us to hypothesize that procedural justice judgments will impact: (1) employee's views about the legitimacy of corporate rules, policies, and authorities, (2) employee perceptions that their organization's values are consistent with their own, and (3) employee's rule-related behavior. In other words, fair organizational procedures and processes are hypothesized to foster a sense that corporate authorities are legitimate and that the organization itself possesses moral values similar to those of the individual. This activates employee's own internal motivations, and they more voluntarily follow company rules and policies, i.e., they become self-regulatory. This argument has received direct support in several recent studies of rule-related behavior (Gottfredson et al., 2007; Tyler, 2007, Tyler et al., 2007).

This approach can be contrasted to one in which employee's ethical values are found to be shaped by their instrumental concerns. That is, the two instrumental judgments discussed earlier—i.e., the favorability or fairness of outcomes received from the organization—may shape the extent to which corporate authorities are viewed as legitimate and the organization itself possess moral values similar to those of the individual. This would be the prediction of instrumental models which emphasize the concern employees have over the outcomes they receive.

We can consider the antecedents of employee ethical values by investigating the relative influence of employees' outcome judgments (such as outcome favorability and outcome fairness) and procedural justice judgments. The issue is which of these judgments most strongly shape employee perceptions that (1) organizational rules and authorities are legitimate, and (2) that their personal moral values are consistent with those of the organization. To the extent that employee ethical values are linked to their rule following behavior, this investigation of the organizational antecedents of those judgments is critical for encouraging employee adherence to organizational policies.

The findings of studies conducted in work settings suggest that one way that work organizations can motivate their employees is by exercising authority in ways that will be judged by those employees as fair. Tyler and Blader (2000), for example, find that procedural justice judgments are the central antecedent of rule following and policy adherence. Those employees who feel that they work in a fair work environment are especially willing to take the responsibility to follow company policies upon themselves, with the obvious advantage the company does not then have to compel such behavior. Studies show that procedural justice judgments have the potential to shape rule-related behavior, and that that influence is primarily explained by the impact that procedural justice has on ethical values. These findings support the arguments of the group engagement model, which suggests that cooperation is linked to procedural justice judgments.

These findings directly support the argument that fair behavior on the part of management motivates desirable behavior by employees. Hence, it is important for companies to be concerned about acting in ways that employees will judge to be fair. By acting fairly, companies motivate employees to both follow company policies and refrain from engaging in actions that undermine the company, actions ranging from theft to sabotage. These actions are costly to the company, undermining efficiency and effectiveness, and make clear why companies should be motivated to understand and respond to employee's feelings about what is fair.

Many organizations already recognize this strategy, and act fairly toward their employees. The findings outlined here indicate that these intuitions are correct, and support the wisdom of managing through fairness. Further, they support a particular view about what type of fairness to be concerned about. Both employees and researchers distinguish two forms of fairness: distributive and procedural (Tyler et al., 1997). Distributive fairness is concerned with the fairness of a person's outcomes, while procedural justice is concerned about the fairness of the way that decisions are made. In particular, however, these studies indicate that it is primarily a *procedurally* just workplace that encourages ethical values and rule-following behavior.

Of course, companies are hierarchical, with rules and policies flowing down from top levels of management. If upper management does not itself support the value of rule following and conformity to ethical codes of conduct, as appears to have been the case in the recent Enron scandal, then the motivation to create a supportive corporate culture may not exist among managers. In that case knowing how to create an ethical culture will be unimportant since upper management will not be motivated to act toward the objective. Further, employees are likely to become aware that company policies do not follow their own moral values, and they will become less committed to following company rules and policies.

In a situation of this type the effectiveness of regulation falls on the ethical values of semiautonomous groups, such as external lawyers or accountants, whose ethical values may have been activated by their own organizations, and/or to government regulators, who again may be motivated by their own ethical concerns. Or it is shaped by the law and legal institutions, through the policies they adopt for dealing with businesses and the people within them.

These findings have optimistic implications for the ability of organizational authorities to encourage rule following behavior among their employees. Authorities are seldom in the position to expend excessive organizational resources on monitoring and punishing employee misbehavior. The procedural justice perspective suggests that people will comply with, and more strikingly, voluntarily defer to rules when they feel that the rules and authorities within their organization are following fair procedures when they exercise their authority and make managerial decisions. This strategy similarly promotes the view amongst employees that organizational authorities are legitimate and that the moral values of the organization correspond with their own personal moral values. What makes such a finding optimistic from an organizational point of view is that the creation and implementation of procedures that all individuals perceive as fair is not restricted in the same way that allocations of resources are. Procedural fairness is not finite, particularly since it is based on ethical criterion.

Interestingly, the procedural justice perspective is consistent with emerging trends in law and the legal regulation of business. As command-and-control-based strategies of regulation have increasingly been questioned, government regulatory agencies have developed a variety of strategies for enlisting businesses and other "stakeholders" in the formulation and implementation of regulatory policy. These include negotiation to reach consensus on administrative regulations (Coglianese, 1997), cooperative arrangements for delivering social services (Stewart, 2003), and joint efforts to manage wildlife and wildlands (Karkkainen, 2002; Lin, 1996). These policies decentralize power to "enable citizens and other actors to utilize their local knowledge to fit solutions to their individual circumstances (Dorf and Sabel, 1998, p. 267)." All of these efforts involve procedures for decision-making that embody the procedural justice values of voice, participation, neutrality, and acknowledging the rights, needs and concerns of people involved in the decision. This does not mean that they involve wide employee participation, but rather that they reflect the values inherent in procedural justice perspectives on management.

What Is a Fair Procedure?

From a management perspective, procedural justice judgments are most useful to managers if employees distinguish them from outcome judgments, and rely on distinct procedural justice assessments when evaluating the actions of management. Based upon research in work settings, I argue that employees' views about the fairness of corporate procedures are, in fact, heavily influenced by distinct judgments about procedural fairness that are not linked to the favorability or fairness of the outcomes that results from those procedures (Tyler and Blader, 2000). These include, for example, whether the procedures allow employees to have input into evaluations; whether they require that objective information be used; whether they try to control the influence of bias; etc (Lind and Tyler, 1988; Tyler and Lind, 1992). Recent research draws upon the four component model of procedural justice and tests the importance of four potential procedural justice criteria (see Blader and Tyler, 2003a, b).

Understanding the nature of employee's procedural justice judgments is central to efforts to design a corporate culture that encourages supportive employee values and that enhances employee rule-following behavior. The argument advanced here is that the potential impact of these procedural issues lies in the ability of corporations to design systems of management that are sensitive to employee procedural concerns, even when companies cannot or do not provide workers with the outcomes they desire.

The four component model of procedural justice identifies four procedural components, or evaluations, each of which contributes to overall procedural justice judgments. Those components are defined by: (1) two distinct aspects of organizational processes, and (2) two sources of information about procedures. I will discuss the influence of each of these four components on employee definitions of procedural justice.

One of the aspects of organizational processes considered in the model refers to the organization's decision-making procedures. Specifically, the model considers employees' evaluations of the *quality of decision making* in their organization. Consideration of these evaluations links to the elements of legal procedures and emphasizes issues of decision-maker neutrality, the objectivity and factuality of decision making, and the consistency of rule application (Lind and Tyler, 1988; Tyler and Lind, 1992).

There is a distinct, but potentially equally important issue involving *the quality of people's treatment by organizational authorities*. Issues linked to the quality of interpersonal treatment constitute the second aspect of organizational processes. Quality of treatment involves treatment with politeness and dignity, concern for people's rights, and other aspects of procedures that are not directly linked to the decisions being made through the procedure.

Each of these two aspects of procedures (quality of decision making, quality of treatment) can potentially be linked to two sources of procedure. One source of information involves *the rules of the organization*. The formal rules and structures of the organization, as well as statements of organizational values, communicate information about organizational procedures. For example, organizations vary in terms of whether they have formal grievance procedures that allow people to voice complaints. They also differ in their statements of corporate values ("corporate vision statements"). For example, one common formal organizational statement that concerns relationships among employees is to: "Treat each other with respect, dignity, and common courtesy" and "express disagreements openly and respectfully." These are both statements about the type of procedures that the corporation views as reflecting its values.

The other source of information is *an employee's experience with their supervisor or supervisors*. While they are constrained by formal institutions and procedures, organizational authorities typically have considerable discretion concerning the manner in which they implement decision-making procedures and how they make decisions regarding issues that have no formal procedures associated with them. Further, they have a great deal of flexibility about how they treat those with whom they deal. The same decision-making procedure can be implemented in a way that emphasizes the dignity of those involved, or employees can be treated rudely or dismissively. A similar situation is found with the law. There are formal laws and rules constraining the conduct of police officers and judges. However, those authorities typically have considerable latitude in the manner in which they exercise their authority within the framework of those rules.

The four component model argues that each of the four components defined by these two dimensions has an important role in the definition of the fairness of procedures. While the four component model provides a guideline for the types of evaluations that compose overall evaluations of an organization's procedural justice, the essential argument advanced here is that the nature of those evaluations is noninstrumental and nonmaterial. Neither of the aspects of organizational processes emphasized in this model of the antecedents of procedural justice (quality of decision making, quality of treatment) is directly linked to evaluations of the favorability or fairness of the outcomes people receive.

The four component model highlights a set of procedural criterion that are distinct from judgments about the favorability or fairness of employee's outcomes. This is, of course, typical of procedures in anytime of organization. We can, for example, distinguish the adversary trial procedure from the verdict of the trial, and can contrast that procedure to other ways of making decisions, such as the inquisitorial trial procedure.

In studies of work settings four criteria of procedural justice are typically measured: organizational level quality of decision making, organizational level quality of treatment, supervisor level quality of decision making, and supervisor level quality of treatment. Procedural criterion linked to supervisors, rather than organizational rules, are viewed more positively. That is, employees viewed their supervisors as using fair procedures when implementing organizational policies that they generally viewed as being unfair.

Conclusion

The argument advanced here is for a broader view of the employee and of the antecedents of rule-following behavior among employees. We want to articulate and show the importance of a broader and more realistic picture of the motivation of employees in work settings. This model looks at the influence of both instrumental and value-based motivations in shaping rule-following behaviors such as white-collar crime. The results presented suggest that the consideration of both models together better explains such behavior than is possible via either model taken alone.

The view presented here includes not only the motivations traditionally studied, motivations that are linked to sanctions, but also includes ethical motivations for following group rules. These ethical motivations are linked to concerns about acting in ethical and fair ways in work settings. The case for this broader model rests on the finding that corporate actors are motivated in their rule following by their ethical values concerning legitimacy and morality, their judgments about the procedural fairness of their workplace, and by their assessments of process aspects of procedures. These findings suggest that we would be better able to understand rule following behavior in work organizations, as well as other settings, if we adopted a broader model of human motivation that added an account of ethical motivations to our models of employee behavior.

The results outlined suggest that one promising approach to stopping employee misbehavior, and thus the recent wave of corporate scandals (i.e., white-collar crimes) that have dominated the business press, is to emphasize the ability of appropriate work cultures to motivate employees to act based upon their feelings of responsibility and obligation to both company codes of conduct and to their own personal feelings of morality. Encouraging such motivations leads to an enhanced likelihood that companies will be able to bring their own behavior into line with their internal principles, as well as formal laws and government regulations, even in the absence of government and corporate regulation.

And, of course, I would argue, these same suggestions speak more broadly to strategies for dealing with all types of crime. Although street crime and those involved in violent criminal offenses differ in many ways from white-collar criminals, the same issues outlined here are central to dealing with all times of crime (Tyler, 2003, 2006c, 2007). Rehabilitation involves reestablishing connections to the values that support the legitimacy of the law, and to the ties to significant others that are central to restorative justice (Tyler et al., 2007). Both of these efforts lead to long-term adherence to the law.

Further, this model of authority applies in arenas beyond the criminal. The command-and-control model or management is central to work organizations. That model seeks to gain both rule adherence and workplace productivity through the use of incentives and sanctions (Tyler et al., 2007, *The psychology of cooperation: Beyond material self-interest.* Unpublished manuscript). And, again, research suggests that these behaviors can more effectively be motivated by linking to values.

References

Aalders, M. and Wilthagen, T. (1997). Moving beyond command and control: Reflexivity in the regulation of occupational safety and health and the environment. *Law and Policy¡u¿,¡/u¿* 19, 415–443.

Adams, J.S. (1965). Inequity in social exchange. In, L. Berkowitz (Ed.), *Advances in Experimental Social Psychology*, 2, 267–299. N.Y.: Academic Press.

Bell, M.P., McLaughlin, M.E., and Sequeira, J.M. (2002). Discrimination, harassment, and the glass ceiling: Women executives as change agents. *Journal of Business Ethics*, 37, 65–76.

Bewley, T. (1999). *Why wages don't fall during a recession*. Cambridge, Mass.: Harvard. 1999.

Blader, S. and Tyler, T.R., (2003a). The four component model of procedural justice. *Human Resource Management Review*, 13, 107–126.

Blader, S. and Tyler, T.R. (2003b). Testing the four component model of procedural justice. *Personality and Social Psychology Bulletin*, 29, 747–758.

Blair, M. and Stout, L. (2001). Trust, trustworthiness, and the behavioral foundations of corporate law. *University of Pennsylvania Law Review*, 149, 1735–1810.

Bowie, N.E. (1999). *Business ethics: A Kantian perspective*. Malden, MA: Blackwell.

Breyer, S.G. and Stewart, R.B. (1985). *Administrative law and regulatory policy* (2nd ed.). Boston: Little.

Carlsmith, K.M., Darley, J.M., and Robinson, P.H. (2000). Why do we punish? Deterrence and just deserts as motives for punishment. *Journal of Personality and Social Psychology*, 83, 284–299.

Chatman, J.A. (1989). Improving interactional organizational research: A model of person-organization fit. *Academy of Management Review*, 14, 333–349.

Chatman, J.A. (1991). Matching people and organizations: Selection and socialization in public accounting firms. *Administrative Science Quarterly*, 36, 459–484.

Coglianese, C. (1997). Assessing consensus: The promise and performance of negotiated rulemaking. *Duke Law Journal*, 46, 1255–1349.

Colquitt, J.A., Conlon, D.E., Wesson, M.J., Porter, C.O. and Yee Ng, K. (2001). Justice at the millennium. *Journal of Applied Psychology*, 86, 425–445.

Cropanzano, R., Byrne, Z.S., Bobocel, D.R. and Rupp, D.E. (2001). Moral virtues, fairness heuristics, social entities, and other denizens of organizational justice. *Journal of vocational psychology*, 58, 164–209.

Darley, J.M., Tyler, T.R., and Bilz, K. (2003). Enacting justice: The interplay of individual and institutional perspectives. In M.A.Hogg and J. Cooper (Eds.), *The Sage Handbook of Social Psychology*. London: Sage.

Dorf, M.C. and Sabel, C.F. (1998). A constitution of democratic experimentalism. *Columbia Law Review*, 98, 267–371.

Estreicher, S. (2002). *Human behavior and the economic paradigm at work*. New York University Law Review, 77, 1–5.

Frederick, William C. (1995). *Values, nature, and culture in the American Corporation*. New York: Oxford University Press.

Frey, B.S. (1997). *Not just for the money*. Cheltenham, England: Edward Elgar.

Gottfredson, D.C., Kearley, B.W., Najaka, S.S., and Rocha, C.M. (2007). How drug treatment courts work: An analysis of mediators. *Journal of Research on Crime and Delinquency*, 44, 3–35.

Greenberg, J. (1997). The STEAL motive: Managing the social determinants of employee theft. In R. Giacalone and J. Greenberg (Eds), *Antisocial behavior in organizations*. Thousand Oaks, CA: Sage.

Greenberg, J. and Cropanzano, R. (2001). (Eds.), *Advances in organizational justice*. Stanford: Stanford University Press.

Gunningham, N. and Grabosky, P. (1998). *Smart regulation: Designing environmental policy*. Oxford: Oxford University Press.

Gunningham, N. and Rees, J. (1997). Industry self-regulation. *Law and Policy*, 19, 363–414.

Healy, M. and Iles, J. (2002). The establishment and enforcement of codes. *Journal of Business Ethics*, 39, 117–124.

Human, S.E. and Provan, K.G. (2000). Legitimacy building in the evolution of small firm multilateral networks: A comparative study of success and demise. *Administrative Science Quarterly*, 45, 327–365.

Huselid, M.A. (1995). The impact of human resource management practices on turnover, productivity, and corporate financial performance. *Academy of Management Journal*, 38, 635–672.

Jenkins, G.D., Mitra, A. Gupta, N., and Shaw, J.D. (1998). Are financial incentives related to performance? *Journal of Applied Psychology*, 83, 777–787.

Jolls, C. (2002). Fairness, minimul wage law, and employee benefits. *New York University Law Review*, 77, 47–70.

Kahneman, D., Knetsch J. and Thaler, R. (1986). Fairness and the assumptions of economics. *Journal of Business*, 59, 5285–5300.

Karkkainen, B.C. (2002). Collaborative ecosystem governance. *Virginia Environmental Law Journal*, 21, 190–243.

Katyal, N. (1997). Deterrence's difficulty. *Michigan Law Review*, 95, 2385–2476.

Kelman, H.C. (1958). Compliance, identification, and internalization. *Journal of Conflict Resolution*, 2, 51–60.

Kelman, H.C. and Hamilton, V.L. (1989). *Crimes of obedience*. New Haven: Yale.

Kim, W.C. and Mauborgne, R.A. (1993). Procedural justice, attitudes, and subsidiary top management compliance with multinationals' corporate strategic decisions. *Academy of Management Journal*, 36, 502–526.

King, A. and Lenox, M. (2000). Industry self-regulation without sanctions. *Academy of Management Journal*, 43, 698–716.

Kohn, A. (1999). *Punished by Rewards*. New York: Houghton Mifflin Company.

Kuperan, K. and Sutinen, J.G. (1998). Blue water crime: Deterrence, legitimacy, and compliance in fisheries. *Law and Society Review*, 32, 309–337.

Langevoort, D.C. (2002). Monitoring: The behavioral economics of corporate compliance with law. *Columbia Business Law Review*, 2002, 71–118.

Kerr, N.L. (1995). Norms in social dilemmas. In D. Schroeder (Ed.), *Social dilemmas* (pp. 31–48). Westport, CT: Praeger.

Kerr, N.L. and Kaufman-Gilliland, C.M. (1994). Communication, commitment, and cooperation in social dilemmas. *Journal of Personality and Social Psychology*, 66, 513–529.

Kerr, N.L., Garst, J., Lewandowski, D.A., and Harris, S.E. (1997). That still, small voice: Commitment to cooperate as an internalized versus a social norm. *Personality and Social Psychology Bulletin*, 23, 1300–1311.

Laufer, W.S. and Robertson, D.C. (1997). Corporate ethics initiatives as social control. *Journal of Business Ethics*, 16, 1029–1048.

Lin, A.C. (1996). Participants' experiences with habitat conservation plans and suggestions for streamlining the process. *Ecology Law Quarterly*, 23, 369–437.

Lind, E.A. and Tyler, T.R. (1988). *The social psychology of procedural justice*. New York: Plenum.

MacCoun, R.J. (1993). Drugs and the law: A psychological analysis of drug prohibition. *Psychological Bulletin*, 113, 497–512.

Margolis, J.D. and Walsh, J.P. (2001). *People and profits?: The search for a link between a company's social and financial performance*. Mahwah, N.J.: Erlbaum.

Markell, D.L. (2000). The role of deterrence-based enforcement in a "reinvented" state/Federal relationship. *Harvard Environmental Law Review*, 24, 1–114.

Mintz, J. (2001). Scrutinizing environmental enforcement. *Journal of Land Use and Environmental Law*, 17, 127–148.

Nagin, D. (1998). Criminal deterrence at the outset of the twenty-first century. In M. Tonry (Ed.), *Crime and justice: A review of research* (vol. 23, pp. 1–42). Chicago: University of Chicago Press.

Nagin, D. and Paternoster, R. (1991). The preventive effects of the perceived risk of arrest. *Criminology*, 29, 561–585.

O'Reilly, C.A., Chatman, J.A. (1986). Organizational commitment and psychological attachment. *Journal of Applied Psychology*, 71, 492–499.

Paternoster, R. (1987). The deterrent effect of the perceived certainty and severity of punishment. *Justice Quarterly*, 4, 173–217.

Paternoster, R. (1989). Decisions to participate in and desist from four types of common delinquency. *Law and Society Review*, 23, 7–40.

Paternoster, R., and Simpson, S. (1996). Sanction threats and appeals to morality: Testing a rational choice model of corporate crime. *Law and Society Review*, 30, 549–584.

Pearce, J.L. (2001). *Organization and management in the embrace of government*. Mahwah, NJ: Erlbaum.

Rabin, M. (1993). Incorporating fairness into game theory and economics, 83, *American Economic Review*, 1281–1302.

Rechtschaffen, C. (1998). Deterrence vs. cooperation and the evolving theory of environmental enforcement. *Southern California Law Review*, 71, 1181–1272.

Rees, A. (1993). The role of fairness in wage determination. *Journal of Labor Economics*, 11, 243–253.

Rice, E.M. (1992). The corporate tax gap: Evidence on tax compliance by small corporations. In J. Slemrod (Ed.), *Why people pay taxes*. Ann Arbor, MI: University of Michigan Press.

Robinson, P.H. and Darley, J.M. (1995). *Justice, liability, and blame*. Boulder, CO: Westview.

Robinson, P.H. and Darley, J.M. (1997). The utility of desert. *Northwestern University Law Review*, 91, 453–499.

Schminke, M. (1998). *Managerial ethics: Moral management of people and processes.* Mahwah, NJ: Erlbaum.

Selznick, P. (1969). *Law, society, and industrial justice.* New York: Russell-Sage Foundation.

Simon, D.R. and Eitzen, D.S. (1990). *Elite deviance* (3rd ed.). Boston, MA: Allyn and Bacon.

Simpson, S.S. (2002). *Corporate crime, law, and social control.* Cambridge: Cambridge University Press.

Smith, N.C., Simpson, S.S., and Huang, C.Y. (2007). *Why managers fail to do the right thing: An empirical study of unethical and illegal conduct.* Business Ethics Quarterly. 17, 633–667.

Spence, D.B. (2001). The shadow of the rational polluter: Rethinking the role of rational actor models in environmental law. *California Law Review*, 89, 917–998.

Stewart, R.B. (February 10, 2003). *Administrative law in the 21st century.* Presentation at the New York University Law School.

Suchman, M. (1995). Managing legitimacy: Strategic and institutional approaches. *Academy of Management Review*, 20, 571–610.

Sutinen, Jon G. and Kuperan, K. (1999). A socio-economic theory of regulatory compliance. *International Journal of Social Economics*, 26, 174–193.

Trevino, L.K. and Weaver, G.R. (2003). *Managing ethics in business organizations.* Palo Alto, CA: Stanford University Press.

Tyler, T.R., (1999). Why people cooperate with organizations: An identity-based perspective. *Research in Organizational Behavior*, 21, 201–246.

Tyler, T.R. (2001). Trust and law-abidingness: A proactive model of social regulation. *Boston University Law Review*, 81, 361–406.

Tyler, T.R. (2003). Procedural justice, legitimacy, and the effective rule of law. In M. Tonry (Ed.), *Crime and justice—A review of research* (vol. 30, pp. 431–505). Chicago: University of Chicago Press.

Tyler, T.R. (2005). Promoting employee policy adherence and rule following in work settings: The value of self-regulatory approaches. *Brooklyn Law Review*, 70, 1287–1312.

Tyler, T.R. (2006a). *Why people obey the law: Procedural justice, legitimacy, and compliance* Princeton, NJ: Princeton University Press.

Tyler, T.R. (2006b). Legitimacy and legitimation. *Annual Review of Psychology*, 57, 375–400.

Tyler, T.R (2006c). Restorative justice and procedural justice. *Journal of Social Issues*, 62, 305–323.

Tyler, T.R. (2007). *Psychology and the design of legal institutions.* Nijmegen, The Netherlands: Wolf Legal Publishers.

Tyler, T.R. and Blader, S.L. (2000). *Cooperation in groups: Procedural justice, social identity, and behavioral engagement.* Philadelphia, PA: Psychology Press.

Tyler, T.R. and Blader, S.L. (2003). The group engagement model: Procedural justice, social identity, and cooperative behavior. *Personality and Social Psychology Review*, 7, 349–361.

Tyler, T.R. and Blader, S.L. (2005). Can businesses effectively regulate employee conduct? The antecedents of rule following in work settings. *Academy of Management Journal*, 48, 1143–1158.

Tyler, T.R., Boeckmann, R.J., Smith, H.J., and Huo, Y.J. (1997). *Social justice in a diverse society.* Boulder, CO: Westview.

Tyler, T.R., Callahan, P., and Frost, J. (2007a). Armed, and dangerous(?): Can self-regulatory approaches shape rule adherence among agents of social control. *Law and Society Review*, 41, 457–492.

Tyler, T.R. and Huo, Y.J. (2002). *Trust in the law.* New York: Russell-Sage Foundation.

Tyler, T.R. and Lind, E.A. (1992). A relational model of authority in groups. *Advances in Experimental Social Psychology*, 25, 115–191).

Tyler, T.R., Sherman, L., Strong, H., Barnes, G., and Woods, D. (2007). Reintegrative shaming, procedural justice, and recidivism: The engagement of offenders' psychological mechanisms in the Canberra RISE drinking and driving experiment. *Law and Society Review*, 41, 553–586.

Vandenbergh, M.P. (2003). Beyond elegance: A test of social norms in corporate environmental compliance. *Stanford Environmental Law Journal*, 22, 55–143.

Vardi, Y. and Weitz, E. (2004). *Misbehavior in organizations.* Mahwah, NJ: Erlbaum.
Walster, E., Walster G.W., and Berscheid, E. (1978). *Equity: Theory and research.* Boston, MA: Allyn and Bacon.
Zimmerman, M.A. and Zeitz, G.J. (2002). Beyond survival: Achieving new venture growth by building legitimacy. *Academy of Management Review*, 27, 414–443.

Index

The letters 'f', 'n' and 't' following the locators refer to figures, notes, and tables respectively.

Breinigsville, PA USA
28 March 2010
235020BV00003B/49/P